MIND GAMES

INSIDE THE
SERIAL KILLER
PHENOMENON

PAUL HARRISON

MIND GAMES

INSIDE THE
SERIAL KILLER
PHENOMENON

PAUL HARRISON

Urbane
PUBLICATIONS

urbanepublications.com

First published in Great Britain in 2018 by Urbane Publications Ltd
Suite 3, Brown Europe House, 33/34 Gleaming Wood Drive,
Chatham, Kent ME5 8RZ
Copyright © Paul Harrison, 2018

A CIP catalogue record for this book is available
from the British Library.

ISBN 978-1-912666-01-0
MOBI 978-1-912666-03-4
EPUB 978-1-912666-02-7

Design and Typeset by Michelle Morgan

Cover by Ben Thomas

Printed and bound by
CPI Group (UK) Ltd, Croydon, CR0 4YY

Urbane
PUBLICATIONS

urbanepublications.com

CONTENTS

'A thousand mistakes of every description would be avoided if people did not base their conclusions upon premises furnished by others, take as established fact what is only possibility, or as a constantly recurring incident what has only been observed once.'

Dr. Johann (Hans) Baptist Gustav Gross (1847–1925)

For victims of crime, everywhere. I will always give you a voice!

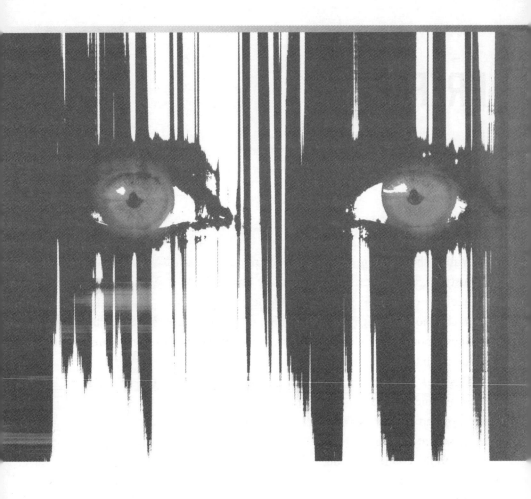

PREFACE

How many books claim to get inside the mind of serial killers? Too many fail to do just that. This book is different, because it's not all about the grisly crimes those people have committed, it's more about them as people, their innermost thoughts from childhood through to incarceration, or in some cases, death. It's about their feelings, emotions, recollections and memories. It truly is about getting inside their heads and into their mindset.

This work isn't a gushing testimony about how wonderful global policing or the academic and scientific studies of serial killers is. None of those fields are supremely flawless, and let's get this straight from the outset - there exists an abundance of misrepresentation relating to the serial killer phenomenon from all sides. Despite claims to the contrary, we don't really understand them or their actions. In fact, after decades of working in this field and studying, researching and interacting with killers and those operating in the forensic aspect of this field, there exists a huge amount of inaccurate data on the subject, including the very origin of the term 'serial killer'.

I would suggest that few people reading this book will have heard of the German, Ernst August Ferdinand Gennat (1880 - 1939). He was, for a time, the Director of the Berlin Criminal Police. It was Gennat who first mentioned the term 'serienmörder' (translated into 'serial murderer') when referring to murderer Peter Kurten, in an article he penned titled 'Die Düsseldorfer Sexualverbrechen' in 1930.

The phrase 'serial killings' was used by concentration camp survivor and biblical scholar, Robert Eisler, in his 1951 book 'Man Into Wolf', during which he referred to serial killings portrayed in the Punch and Judy plays for children.

Thereafter, in 1961, German critic, Siegfried Kracauer (1889 - 1966) used the same phrase when writing a review of the classic German thriller titled 'M'. He referred to the character Hans Beckert (a pervert who preyed on vulnerable young girls in Berlin), played by actor Peter Lorre, as a serial murderer. The term was also used much later by author John Brophy in his 1966 book 'The Meaning of Murder' (Ronald Whiting & Wheaton).

The phrase is also mentioned by the Washington DC newspaper, Evening Star, in a 1967 review of the same Brophy book:

"There is a mass murderer - or what he (Brophy) calls the 'serial killer'- who may be actuated by greed, such as insurance, or retention of growth of power, like the Medicis of Renaissance Italy, or Landru, the 'bluebeard' of the World War I period, who murdered numerous wives after taking their money."

Thus, we have countless printed sources predating the term 'serial killer' - as associated to the late great FBI profiler, Robert Ressler - by five decades. To be fair to Ressler, one of the founders of the legendary FBI Behavioral Science Unit, he never claimed to be the sole creator of the term. That blame can be put down to writers across all fields, including scientific and academic, many of whom have incorrectly bestowed that honour on him. It's fair to say that it was Ressler who adapted its use into everyday crime writing language when, during a visit to Bramshill Police College, Hampshire, England in 1974, he made use of it as a description of killers who kill multiple times. It says something of the phenomenon that today there are few people across the world who do not understand its meaning or the FBI criteria for earning the title.

The first recorded use of profiling in more modern times was that of psychiatrist Walter Langer and some associates who were commissioned by the Official Secret Service, during WWII, to construct a psychodynamic profile of Adolf Hitler. The group carefully studied the German leader, resulting in them being able to correctly identify various predictors, including:

- As the war turns against him, his private emotions will intensify and there will follow more frequent outbursts.
- His public appearances will become less and less, as he is unable to confront a critical audience and he will become paranoid.
- An assassination attempt on him is likely, potentially by the German

aristocracy, the Wehrmacht officers or Oberkommando der Wehrmacht, because of his superhuman self-confidence in his military judgment.

- There will be no surrender, capitulation, or peace negotiations. The course he will follow will almost certainly be the road to ideological immortality, resulting in the greatest vengeance on a world he despises.
- He would likely commit suicide rather than face humiliation at losing the war, essentially having all power and control removed from him.

Langer and his associates proved that profiling does work if the correct methods of analysis are used including every available detail and fact being checked for accuracy.

A myth that for decades has been perpetuated, relates to how the formation of the FBI Behavioral Science Unit and the use of profiling came into being. As can be seen, it wasn't an FBI invention at all. That said, the story goes that in the 1950s, and more specifically in the world of Police investigations, the New York crimes of the 'Mad Bomber' (George Metesky), who, during a 16-year reign of terror planted bombs in movie theatres, train stations, subway stops and public buildings, caused panic throughout the city. No one was killed by any of the explosions, more by good luck than judgment, though Metesky later claimed it was the 'hand of God' that prevented loss of human life. However, much architectural devastation was caused via the explosions. At the time the Police, despite their best efforts, were at a loss about the identity of the mad bomber, and were mercilessly taunted by the offender, with missives and communications sent to them and signed with the initials 'F.P.'.

In December 1956, Police Captain Howard Finney took the unprecedented step of approaching criminologist and psychologist, James Brussel, to carry out an assessment of the crimes, based mainly on crime scene photographs. Brussel had a theory that he could identify an unknown offender by their criminal behaviour. This, he determined, was a result of his work with deviants, who, he claimed, had their own logic. By entering their mindset, walking in their shoes, he claimed he could somehow decode patterns of behaviour and understand the personality of the offender.

Two full cases of evidence were handed to him for his professional assessment, from which he created an offender profile that ultimately led to an arrest and conviction of the bomber. If that all sounds rather too good to be true, you'd be right. The profile Brussel created, rather than providing a clear vision of the offender, was altogether murkier and extremely generic in its description.

The block capital handwriting in the missives held further clues to the offender's mindset he claimed. The letter 'W' was different, misshaped to look like two joined letter U's; and to his trained eye, looked not dissimilar to a pair of female breasts. The guess work didn't stop there as he went on to suggest the writer was a Slav. Two cases of evidence were deposited at his office for assessment from which he created a profile that ultimately led to an arrest. This is the profile he later claimed was the official one (it is very much different to the official profile submitted to the Police):

"Male. Knowledge of metalworking, pipefitting, and electricity who had suffered some grave injustice by Con Ed (Con Edison, being the company who he often maligned in communications with Police and the media) which had rendered him chronically ill. In addition, he suffered from paranoia with insidious development of his disorder. He would have a chronic disorder and suffered from persistent delusions which were unalterable, systematized and logically constructed. He was pathologically self-centered. Had a symmetric 'athletic' body type due to his paranoia, was middle-aged, due to onset of mental illness and duration of bombings. He had achieved a good level of education, not college but most if not all of high school. Unmarried and possibly a virgin, who lived alone or with a female, mother-like relative. Slavic Roman Catholic and he lived in Connecticut and was fond of wearing a buttoned, double-breasted suit."

He then alleges that he told the case detectives:

"One more thing. I closed my eyes because I didn't want to see their reaction. I saw the Bomber; impeccably neat, absolutely proper. A man who would avoid the newer style of clothing until long custom had made them more conservative. I saw him clearly - much more clearly than the facts really warranted. I knew I was letting my imagination get the better of me, but I couldn't help it. 'When you catch him - and I have no doubt you will, he'll be wearing a double-breasted suit, and it will be buttoned'."

A month later, George Metesky was arrested and charged with the 'mad bomber' crimes. On arrest at his home, which he shared with his two older sisters, he was dressed in his nightclothes, a pair of pyjamas. He asked detectives if he could go and get changed before being taken to the Police station; they agreed. A few minutes later, he returned and was wearing a double-breasted suit, just as Brussel had suggested.

In his memoir 'Casebook of a Crime Psychiatrist' (Mayflower Press 1970) Brussel alludes to his profile being altogether more refined and focused. He becomes a legend with his unique set of skills which are almost mystical. He fails to mention the copious anomalies in the generalised profile he produced not only in this case, but in many others too.

One person who was convinced by the grandiose claims of Brussel was FBI agent Howard Teten. A serving Police officer in the USA, he seized the opportunity to develop the potential advantages of psychological profiling of criminal behaviour. When he joined the FBI in July 1969 he was to become the forefather of all things relating to the science of criminal behavioural and the formation of the legendary FBI Behavioural Science Unit in 1974. Teten was the mastermind behind it all and he can be forgiven for mistakenly believing the overinflated claims of psychologist Brussel.

The reality of this tale, and it is very much a tall tale, is very different to what genuinely happened. The story was sensationalised and produced by Brussel himself and he alone embellished the truth to portray himself in a better light in his own book. In the official profile not once did he mention Slavic descent to detectives; he advised them to look for someone born and educated in Germany. His claim that the bomber was someone between the age of forty and fifty was close; Metesky was over fifty. The official profile claimed he would live alone at home with his mother. He did not. He lived instead with his two older sisters - close but not accurate. The mad bomber was eventually caught not by the profile produced by Brussel, but as a result of a woman going through the personnel files of Con Edison employees past and present. The author of the taunting communications received by the Police clearly had issues with the company and felt he had been treated badly by them. It didn't take much working out that the killer may have been a disgruntled ex-employee, and so it made sense to conduct a thorough search of the personnel files for persons matching that criterion. Ultimately, it was a woman called Alice Kelly who initially identified George Metesky as a person of interest, and so passed his details to the Police. Based on her evidence alone, the Police were able to identify him as the person they had been looking for.

Mind Games is about conversations with and the psyche of serial killers, I've taken a very special and unique journey in my life, and I've undoubtedly encountered the worst of the world's most violent and extreme offenders. When I set out on this exploration of killers who repeatedly snuffed out human lives, they were more commonly referred to as multiple murderers. So much has changed since those early times, not least the modus operandi and cleverness of the killers themselves. This book isn't meant to be a scientific study or an academic thesis on serial killers or deviants, it's about complex human emotions, human behaviour that is out of control, broken minds, and broken people. It's about understanding one another, listening and using our 'sixth sense' to read situations and our fellow human beings. I stand by the reasoning and philosophy of Occam's Razor - for its absolute simplicity it has never failed me yet.

Suppose there exists two explanations for an occurrence. In this case the simpler one is usually better. Another way of putting it is that the more assumptions you have to make, the more unlikely an explanation.

Without doubt, the most important people in any crime are the victims. Where serial killers and deviants are concerned, it's the families and friends of lost loved ones who matter most. I'm not one for sensationalising serial killers or murderers of any description, nor do I agree with such behaviour. However, there is, I believe, an overarching need for us to try to understand what drives these people to commit some of the vilest crimes imaginable and a need for us to interact with and study them.

This is where my focus has been for most of the last fifty years of my life. I'm not obsessive, nor am I fixated by killers. My original aim as a child was to keep myself safe from paedophiles whose abhorrent behaviour I had to suffer on an almost daily basis. I wanted to learn what makes that sort of person behave like they do, selecting and grooming vulnerable children before selfishly defiling them. That knowledge, I believed, would allow me to help save other children from a similar fate. If I could identify and establish the fundamental causes for paedophilia, in my mind I would be able to educate criminal investigators into the behavioural signs, and in the longer term, families and society could and would feel safer. I make no bones about the fact that I hold no sympathy towards anyone who commits abusive acts upon children or vulnerable persons of all ages. Such behaviour is unacceptable in any form and deserves the most severe punishment.

I achieved much more than I ever believed possible. After such a horrific start in life, I learned to cope with trauma, creating my own survival strategy that really worked. I developed my profiling skills through studying my own father, his peer group and countless others thereafter. I learned that paedophilia isn't an illness that can be treated, it's a life choice. Like serial killers, these people develop more acute behaviour as the desire for greater excitement takes control of their sexual emotions. What may begin with (what they claim to be) 'innocently' viewing pornographic images of children online, grows into more physical deviant behaviour. The paedophile tries at every avenue to disguise his or her behaviour, living a life of lies and deceiving all who encounter them. They understand and know that what they are doing is wrong which is why they mask their actions. Many take on child-like personalities in online chat rooms, lying from the outset about their age and every aspect of their lives. When caught out by the Police, they continue with the deception, claiming it to be an accidental click that led them to the sinister website. Or if caught out by a 'paedophile hunter' sting, it's a case of mistaken identity. Later, when the Criminal Justice system clicks into gear, it escalates to become a mental health affliction, they didn't know what they were doing, were out of control or are seeking help from some support agency. They rarely confess to their crimes being premeditated, that they are in full control of their actions and that they know what they are doing is immoral, illegal and viewed by most members of the public as sick or vile.

Many of the deviant serial killers contained within the pages of this book and across the globe are paedophiles, so my progression to study, analyse and get to know such offenders was to my own mind at least, a natural one. The one thing I have learned, (and I continue to learn each day) during the past fifty years is that we are all human. That includes sexual deviants, serial killers, mass murderers, spree killers, et al. As sentient beings, we all act differently and possess different drivers, yet each of us displays a similar basic need. We want to be liked. None of us likes to think we are hated, despised or disliked by anyone, whether it be a stranger on a train, or a bus, or a neighbour or online.

The deviants I speak about are no different, they didn't set out to be reviled or demonised, it was their abhorrent behaviour that caused such emotional harm. Add to that the global media, that salaciously reports intimate details of crimes and go on to create devil like statuses along with a creative pseudonym for the offenders. So, the public's animosity and hatred towards this entity grows, until they are universally feared and disliked. It is fair to say that the 'monster' serial killer is a media invention, a tag commonly used to describe this kind of individual. The term monster helps us rationalise these people as being extraordinarily different. As monsters, they have been given a tag that allows us to demonise them, as the need to make them visibly odd and strange separates them from most of humankind, allowing us some feeling of being in control and safe in our own world.

To say this book has taken fifty years to write would be wrong, yet the experiences I have had during this period have been integral to its completion. I could probably say I wouldn't want to change any of them. Fair enough, my childhood isn't something I could ever regard as acceptable, the positive thing emanating from that is not only my survival but learning from every moment of those dark times.

The MacDonald Triad was first printed in the American Journal of Psychiatry under the heading 'The Threat To Kill' in 1963. It is also known as the triad of sociopathy and the homicide triad psychiatrist John. M. MacDonald claimed that if two, or all, of the following symptoms existed in a child then this would be predictive of later violent episodes, particularly with relation to repeat offending. Bed wetting (Enuresis) is one such trait, yet we all wet the bed as infants and children. I used to until I was close to ten years old because I was terrified my father (abuser) would enter the room at night and attack me. I lived in constant fear of that threat. The second trait was fire starting, or arson. Again, the number of serial killers who have committed such actions is limited to say the least. Another part of the triad is deliberately harming animals. There exists a wealth of evidence that shows the vast amount of serial killers do not harm animals, nor did they as children, or adolescents. On the contrary, they love animals because they don't answer them back, or call them names. They give unrequited love and enjoy being close and stroked. To add to the triad, we now have a final aspect - child sex abuse or other physical or mental abuse being suffered. Let me say at this point, never in my life have I ever considered committing murder or killing someone. Not even my abuser. The same train of thought is often incorrectly cited when discussing paedophilia, that the abused becomes the abuser. Indeed, I know of very few survivors of child sex abuse (and I've met several hundred) who have gone on to become abusers themselves. Nor have they become serial killers. Needless to say, I possess two of the traits MacDonald states are definite predictors of violence. I'm the least dangerous or violent person imaginable. To add substance to my contestation of this outdated guidance, I went on to follow a career in law enforcement and in the field of criminal justice. Actually, I'm not a serial anything. The MacDonald triad, whilst well-meaning, is now part of the past and should remain there as testimony to how science is sometimes misguided and does in my opinion occasionally get important things quite wrong. My own view is that the presence of two of those indicators might indicate evidence of childhood abuse, but taken alone they are not a predictor of someone being violent or dangerous.

Paul Harrison
July 2018

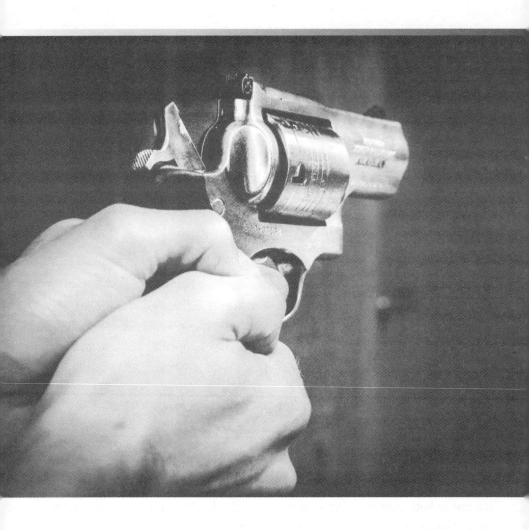

INTRODUCTION

Serial Killers! What are they all about? How do they think before, during and after their crimes? Is it nature or nurture? Have they suffered brain trauma at some point in their life that causes them to behave so anti-socially? There are so many burning issues relating to this phenomenon that one could spend a lifetime pontificating over the variables and possible answers. In this book I hope I'll be able to give you some answers and perhaps a different angle on these people, a human perception we are rarely told of, or see.

I'm the guy the press has dubbed Britain's 'Mindhunter - The Profiler'. In reality, I'm Paul Harrison from Yorkshire. I'm unique, I know that. Not only have I five generations of Police Service within my family blood line, I've also served in law enforcement on a national basis; and in Scotland where different laws are in place, frequently crossing the border as a serving officer with a professional foot and interest in both countries. I've worked extremely closely with the Judiciary at the Royal Courts of Justice, London and elsewhere, and I've been a victim of what I believe is the worst crime of all - Child Sex Abuse.

In that time, I've seen cover-ups, lies, deceit, and all too frequently how large organisations close ranks to make an outcast or scapegoat of an individual who dares question such behavior or is outspoken about it. Those who think this kind of systemic corruption cannot or does not exist need look no further than the Hillsborough football disaster. It's shameful, yet sadly the system does lie and deceive, it's how the establishment often operates and survives globally. The law does occasionally get it wrong and innocent people are jailed for crimes they did not commit. However, the serial killers who I have communicated with are not among this group. They were guilty of their crimes and although many would never confess, justice was ultimately done. There is something chilling about looking into the eyes of a serial killer verbally denying their guilt. It's as though the confession cannot be spoken, yet the eyes reveal all, they are cold and dead, emotionless and without compassion. They stare blankly into my eyes as though looking directly into my soul because their own no longer exists. It is perhaps the bleakest moment during any such interaction, and still sends shivers down my spine to this day. That kind of experience is something that science or academics can never qualify. It is raw human response and behavior.

Over the years, I've found myself questioning time and again the very basis of academic study into this subject. I personally don't believe we will find answers in datasets or from scientific theory alone. Real solutions will come through close personal studies of the offenders themselves, from crime scene analysis and from a non-judgmental approach to communicating with and understanding what makes a serial killer or sexual deviant tick. To succeed there has to be a combined approach between a variety of authoritative bodies, maximizing individual strengths and best practice to develop further analysis. Currently, there is much disagreement about freshly proposed theories, causing rifts and animosity towards certain protagonists. It's all too clear that many involved in this area believe themselves - and desire to be - the 'come to' expert, and to that end it serves their own purpose to discredit anyone else's beliefs, opinions or theories.

I myself have suffered what can only be described as online bullying from select areas of academia, who seem desperate to preserve what they view as their 'own territory' and field of expertise. It's a sad state of affairs that the vast majority of these authorities have never met or been in the same room as a serial killer. They rely on academic papers or peer studies to determine their hypothesis. As we have seen, some of that detail is drastically outdated and plain wrong. The competition to be 'the' expert is rife across the subject. It is but a few who feel threatened by others, generally the most outspoken. I class many scientists working within this arena as friends and genuine experts, people whose knowledge and experience is very real, but that doesn't mean I unilaterally agree with their beliefs, every bit as much as I doubt they agree with my own 'non-scientific' approach to serial killers and profiling.

From the very outset of my work in this area forty-plus years ago, I recall being advised by Robert Ressler:

"As human beings we all want to be liked. None of us want to be disliked or hated, that's because we have emotions and feelings. We are sentient beings.

Serial killers are no different, deep down inside they want to be liked. We don't have to like them, but we owe it to humankind to try to understand them. If we can successfully do that and create diversionary options when, at a young age the first antisocial signals reveal themselves, then we will have the opportunity to preserve thousands of lives."

That statement resonated with the fundamental rationale of my own life. From a very young age I wanted to help protect others from suffering. I wanted survivors and their families to be supported, understood and listened to. It goes without saying, that I was totally victim focused on helping people throughout my career as an English Police officer. So when I'm asked what directed me towards a career studying criminal offenders, and in particular, serial and sexually violent criminals and deviants, I am honest and open about that very reason. It's a question I've often asked myself, since it can be depressing and miserably morbid, focusing and living in the sinister world of death, murder and deceit. Everything about the darker side of humanity is uncomfortable and difficult to comprehend.

It was my own childhood. I was born into a family dictated to, and ruled by, an abusive and dominant father who possessed a deviant attitude and sinister behaviour. Putting it mildly, he was an active and predatory paedophile. As an infant I suffered greatly from this man's sexual predilection. I would be beaten and thrown into a cupboard under the stairs, and left there alone, in the dark, for hours, often days on end, stripped naked and without proper sustenance, other than what my brother could secretly pass to me in my father's brief absences.

Sitting there in the dark, I imagined all kinds of monsters and vile creatures lurking at the back of the tiny damp space. Every noise was escalated in volume when confined, causing my own innocent imagination to constantly run riot. In truth, the worst it ever got in there was the tickling sensation of spiders quickly darting over my legs, feet, or occasionally my face. The feeling of terror that these invisible beasts might eat me or take a chunk out of my skin, filled my waking hours in that place. I would sit quietly for hours, emotionally fraught with the belief I had done something wrong to deserve such incarceration, and that it was my own behaviour that resulted in such dreadful punishment. After countless periods of imprisonment in that black hole, I began to realise the severity of my predicament. Even at such a tender age I was able to recognise that my life was in danger. My father was constantly telling me I was the little boy no one wanted, he referred to me as the replacement child; it seemed that love and caring were not part of his emotional make up. From those early years, if I was to live, I had to adopt a survival strategy, a means of keeping myself from death.

It's not something that should ever be taken lightly, every victim of child sexual abuse must sense the feeling of worthlessness and fear within their own physical world. For me, it was very much a life-defining moment, a point when my true destiny was created. I was able to close down when I went into the cupboard, shut off my emotions, detach myself from my environment and fears and meditate. I'd take myself somewhere different, a place where I was happy and laughed a lot and I was content with my life. Most importantly it was a place where I could feel safe.

I knew what my father was doing was wrong, yet as a child there is nothing concrete to base such perceptions on. My own belief was created through the emotional trauma I suffered almost daily. To be beaten and defiled by someone who was supposed to love and protect and care for me, left me feeling anxious and more than a little confused. There appeared to be no logic to my abuse, it generally came when I least expected it. When at home, it left me feeling alone and vulnerable, emotions no small child should endure.

When my father attacked, he did so without remorse or guilt. He was devoid of mercy in the vocabulary he carefully selected to enhance my feeling of hopelessness and to being without support, before stripping me bare and throwing me into the cupboard to await my ultimate fate - rape. It was a living nightmare. Hell. The persistent reminders by my older brother that I had done nothing wrong, somehow kept me focused on one day escaping the clutches of the man I called my father. So, I began to learn and read him. I would carefully listen to the intonation in his voice to understand the nature and level of his mood; the deeper his voice became in everyday conversation, the greater the likelihood of him attacking me became. It was as though he needed to assert his authority vocally to whoever he was speaking with. It was his own feelings of inadequacy that caused him to take that insecurity out on me, or my brother.

I surreptitiously monitored his every movement, read his body language, eye movements, and gradually began to recognise the consistency in his behaviour when he was about to turn into someone very dark, a human monster. It became not only a challenge but a fundamental basic requirement of my personal survival, that I understood every facet of his behaviour.

As I grew older, I was more able to mentally and physically deal with his despicable actions. I began to understand that he wasn't alone in his predilection for abusing children of all ages, male or female. For me, it felt natural to look inside the soul and minds of his peers; political figures, entertainers, professionals in the Police and armed forces, and those across all aspects of the legal world. Professional types from all walks of life were actively engaged in illicit child sex abuse. Many years later I understood the reality - that I was little more than an object of desire for a seedy paedophile ring.

To be able to recognise this negative trait in other people's behaviour required sensitive skills and perception, based not on statistical detail or analytical datasets that science promotes as a necessary infrastructure to criminal profiling, but from real life human emotion and behaviour. I was able to understand the murkier side of humankind by seeking out the monster and looking it in the eye, before getting inside its mind to learn how it was created, to see how it operates, what makes it tick, and triggers its actions.

Without doubt, it's a terrifying and lonely place to be as an adult, let alone a child; confronting other people's demons and trying to understand them isn't a safe thing to do. All the time in the back of my mind sat the personal driver - to avoid self-capitulation, resulting in the (voluntary) premature ending of my life, like so many of my peers did. And, sadly, still do.

My father's profile was anything but a simple one to formulate, particularly as I had no way of making or keeping notes on him and his erratic conduct. Instead, during those early years everything was permanently imprinted in my own brain. His 'attitude' as I first called it, when I was old enough to understand what that meant, was complicated. Over the years I began to see patterns and synergies that I could connect to others of a similar lifestyle. I was forced to connect with them to understand them, so I would ask innocent sounding questions about their own childhood, family and life. They had no idea I was storing away every ounce of detail they provided. From those early communications I quickly ascertained that paedophilia isn't any kind of illness, much like becoming a serial killer isn't. It's little more than a deviant life choice. Those who commit to it, select vulnerable people as their victims. Easily manipulated children who are neither physically nor emotionally able to fight back or resist. Innocent minds are destroyed by the web of consistent lies and threats, and the shame of not only the act itself, but by the deceitful nature of everything connected to it. This is the legacy of such a crime, it leaves the child victims mentally scarred and with a lifetime of relationship and trust issues. As one grows older, the fear of speaking out against such a crime increases, as the years of indoctrination about it being one's own fault and that the system won't believe such claims becomes a harsh reality.

Initially that was the case for me; but then one day after hearing of yet another suicide linked to child sex abuse, I decided that enough was enough. It was time to take my future in my own hands and take it where I wanted. I joined the Police Service because I wanted to make a difference, I wanted to help victims of crime and get up close and personal with offenders and understand what drives them towards criminality. I was interested in serial offenders, shoplifters, burglars, car thieves who were in and out of the Police cells like revolving doors. Such people would be charged, bailed to appear at the local Magistrates Court then, a few weeks later, they'd be sat in front of me being interviewed for identical offences. I began to dig deeper into their domestic and social lives, engaging them in conversation and listening to their life stories. Each one was very different, and soon I was compiling profiles on individual criminals in my area. Armed with such knowledge, I was able to gain an understanding of what the drivers were for their actions. For many it was survival, stealing to sell on and get money to pay the rent or put food on the table. For others it was drug/substance or alcohol related, and for others still it was learned behaviour, passed down by a parent. I quickly learned that the support networks that are supposed to help these people were turning their backs on them, leaving them to their own devices. Where many criminal justice services were concerned, convicted felons were a Police responsibility only. When I highlighted these failings to such bodies as the local authority, I was called a troublemaker, a loose cannon and a rebel, for not keeping quiet about the systemic failures. Thankfully, senior Police officers saw the merit in what I was doing and supported my efforts to help reduce crime and develop partnership networks where everyone had to accept their responsibility. The first time I professionally used my profiling skills remains a memorable one. I was called to attend the scene of a suspicious death, where an older female had been found dead in her home, a council flat. The woman lived alone in the specially-adapted property which was originally two semi-detached houses. These had been made into four flats, two upstairs and two on the ground floor. The lady lived in one of the upstairs properties and access was via an external staircase which was exposed to public view.

The dead woman, who was regarded as fit and healthy, was last seen alive the previous evening, walking home with two shopping bags full of provisions. A neighbour saw a light on in her lounge at around 10.00 p.m.; the curtains had been drawn. The following morning, a neighbour called to visit the lady. This was a daily routine and happened like clockwork at the usual time of 8.30 a.m. Using a spare key she had under her sole control, she entered the flat and found the woman dead on the floor of her bedroom. She was naked.

Lying on the floor of the hall was her nightdress, carefully laid out by someone to give the appearance of a human form. A pair of tights stuck out of the bottom hem. Below them was a pair of slippers, with the feet of the tights tucked into each respective slipper. Inside the nightie a pair of knickers had been placed around the pelvic region and a bra where the breasts should be. Traces of human secretion were evident on the nightdress - semen stains.

These were the days before DNA was regarded as an evidential tool for investigating Police officers. Scenes of Crime Officers were busy taking photographs of the scene and the clothing. The woman's body showed no sign of external bruising or injury, except at the wrist and upper arms, where finger bruises were evident. Someone had gripped these areas very tightly. Her bed had been laid in which suggested she had retired to bed before her death. She had clearly got up to answer the front door, and her attacker had entered or been allowed access.

The area where this had happened had been blighted by a series of burglaries. It started with garden shed break-ins, followed by garages then houses. Now, there was a body. The pattern of criminal behaviour, if this was the same offender, had deteriorated. I carefully examined the flat and saw no evidence of burglary or forced entry. Indeed, there was very little in the way of disturbance, except the victim's purse, which had been deliberately tucked down the back of an armchair. This was examined for fingerprints, but no alien prints were found on it. Credit and bank cards remained inside the wallet part of the purse flap. The only thing that could be ascertained as missing was money. A bank withdrawal receipt showed she had taken out fifty pounds from her account the previous day. She had spent just £21 pounds doing her shopping. With no notes and no small change present, it seemed obvious that this had been taken by whoever had entered the flat.

Death was later confirmed as a heart attack, as evidence of murder seemed non-existent. On returning to the Police station, I reviewed the crime reports on all crime in the area covering the previous twelve months. I was able to add three sexual crimes to the property crimes list. Two older women and a young girl had all been independently attacked and sexually assaulted in the darkness of night, in the street, by an attacker wearing a balaclava over his head. The attacker had run off along the street when each victim screamed out.

I later revisited each of those crime scenes to look at the layout of the area, access egress being an all-important and integral aspect of the crimes. Based on informed conclusions I had calculated from my review, I was able to confidently state that the offender we were looking for was likely to be a male teenager who lived locally, or at least within geographic striking distance of each crime.

The previously reported burglaries had smaller items removed; other larger items such as lawnmowers etc had been left untouched. This showed me that the offender had no vehicle access since these items were of greater resale value than a few screwdrivers and boxes of screws and nails. Entry into the sheds had been by brute force and occurred on each occasion between 8.30 p.m. and 11p.m. That seemed to indicate it was someone active between those times. In fact, every crime occurred between those times. A teenager might be roaming the streets in the early evening, potentially right up to 11.00pm.

Two of the victims of sexual assault were around the same age group as the murder victim; they had been returning from an evening playing Bingo in the town centre and had caught a late bus home. The first victim of the sexual assault was a young twelve-year-old girl, who had been attacked one winter evening. I suggested that this was the offender's first public act and crime of a sexual nature. He was practising his art, seeking greater thrills from his behaviour as the first attack was clearly inexperienced. The deviant nature in him had identified vulnerable targets, meaning he was likely to be either young, or small in stature, or both.

In the case of the dead woman, he had no worries about being seen climbing the external staircase to the woman's flat. Thus, I determined it was someone local who would not look out of place. Furthermore, the victim clearly recognised him as she had answered the door and let him in. I felt it was more than likely that the offender had entered with a view to raping her. He had grabbed her by the arms and pulled her into the bedroom where she had suffered a heart attack and died.

The offender then stripped her bare, laid out the nightwear before masturbating over it. He then took money from her purse and tucked it down the back of the chair before leaving. He had then walked back to his own home which I predicted would be nearby.

Within 24 hours, I was sitting looking at the person of interest. He was a fifteen-year-old boy, lived with his mother within 150 yards of each crime. A search of his bedroom identified boxes of screws, nails, and screwdrivers and knives. Mild pornographic literature was found under his bed mattress. Tucked inside his jeans pocket was £29 in bank notes and some small change. During the interview, conducted with his mother present, he denied any wrongdoing until presented with the evidence seized from his bedroom. I later ascertained that he had lived alone with his single parent mother since birth. He felt he had been abandoned by her as she went out to work different shifts in a local factory.

"All of my friends have normal homes, a mum and a dad. My mum won't tell me who my father is, because she doesn't know. She was a slut when she was younger. My mates have everything, computers the works, they go on holidays. I have nothing, I don't even have a television in my bedroom. So I decided to get some money to get those things for myself. I used to break into neighbours sheds and outhouses and steal smaller things that I could sell at the flea market or in school. When I became bored with that, I started breaking into people's homes. At first it was scary, but then I got better at it and I'd go into the bedroom while the people slept in their beds. The thrill I got from doing that was unbelievable. It is the ultimate power.

I accidentally saw a woman getting undressed in her bedroom at night, she'd left the lights on and the curtains open. I felt myself getting aroused and began to play with myself. That's when I wanted more than the thrill of breaking and entering, I wanted sex. I was certain that woman knew I was there, right outside her bedroom window watching her, she did it on purpose I think. I guess you can blame my attacking those women on her behaviour, she created this in me. I never harmed that old woman though, she just slumped to the floor when I told her to take off her nightie. She was making gasping sounds and couldn't talk. Her face went a funny colour. I stood and watched, I wasn't scared or anything, but I could hardly go and get help. Then she stopped doing anything, I thought she was pretending to be dead so I'd leave. I shook her a bit to try to wake her up, I grabbed her by the upper arms. She didn't wake up. Seeing her laid there with no clothes on I got myself all worked up. That's when I got the idea to frighten whoever found her, by laying out the nightie and underwear. I'm not certain whether I masturbated over those clothes or not."

Because of the technique I used to determine the type of person who was most likely to have committed those crimes and I got it right, and through further successes through the same process, my Police colleagues thought I must be something of a psychic. I soon had a force nickname - 'The Profiler'- and I was elevated to some kind of fantasy superhero status. I was offered all kinds of remunerations from colleagues who wanted to know my secret, or to train them how to use profiling to their own benefit. It wasn't something I felt comfortable about, since my own skills had been honed since I was a child and they weren't easily transferrable. It wasn't magic, it was second nature to me.

A short time later, I was asked to look into another sexual offender case. This time, the man was a disguised flasher who exposed himself to lone female joggers in a park. It was a horrific crime for the victims, since he would jump out of bushes or from hiding places and confront them. He wore sunglasses, and a hoodie covered most of his head and face. Various undercover Police operations had been carried out to try catch the offender, without success. The incidents were getting more frequent as the matter began to cause serious concern to local communities, especially female joggers. A number of men were stopped for simply being in the park, and soon complaints of Police harassment came from innocent men who had been questioned by officers on several occasions. There was a need to catch this miscreant before his crimes deteriorated into more serious sexual deviant behaviour.

I spoke with victims and witnesses and along with Police intelligence reports was able to get a better understanding of the offender. He was described as being around 6ft tall, muscular build, and two witnesses had managed to get a look at his hair as he ran off, they described it as being a ginger colour with waves and curls, cut in service style short back and sides. As he got near the park exit, one had seen him remove his hooded sweatshirt and thought he was dressed like a security guard with a white shirt and shoulder epaulettes and dark trousers. He then ran off down an adjacent road and disappeared from view.

I looked at the timings of the crimes and determined that they seemed to coincide with the timings of shift patterns in the emergency or security services. This fit with the uniform description provided by one of the eye witnesses. Naturally, it's a huge thing to accuse someone of something without supportive evidence. So I was reluctant at that point to say it may be emergency service personnel. Randomly, I spoke with a senior detective and asked if I could look at Police officers home addresses and the respective shift patterns of those officers. Reluctantly, he agreed but swore me to absolute secrecy. Within a few hours, I had my person of interest. One of my colleagues!

I handed over my investigation dossier to the senior officer, and provided a statement regarding the evidence supporting my claims. I was shown a photograph of the individual and sure enough, he had ginger coloured hair that was wavy and with pronounced curls. The individual was called in and interviewed. He had no defence and went sick, claiming mental illness, bullying at work and depression as the cause of his alleged behaviour. The important thing here being, he never admitted the crimes, yet equally he never denied them. He left the interview, went sick, and never returned to Police duties. He was never prosecuted and the incidents of flashing stopped thereafter.

It goes without saying, that when my peers learnt of what had happened and rather than being upset with a colleague who was displaying serious sexual deviancy, there was a handful who viewed me as the enemy within, a snake in the grass. Incredibly, various rumours began to circulate within the ranks that I practiced black magic, or I was in league with the criminals and was carrying out my profiling due to the insider knowledge I possessed. Nothing could be farther from the truth. Profiling didn't sit comfortably with many, including the senior hierarchy. It became farcical, as when I was called in for annual appraisals or interviews, I would have two senior officers present. I was advised that this was in case I began to 'inadvertently exert mind control powers over them and managed to manipulate their thoughts'. This was the modern Police force in action, experienced officers above the rank and file. They viewed me as some kind of witch!

When I offered to provide a briefing on the topic of profiling, this was denied due to some officers thinking it was a hypnotic trick that could be dangerous. No matter how hard I attempted to explain and justify profiling, there existed a wall of denial. It was easy to see how corporate pressure and peer intimidation could cause alienation as I was ready to stop what I was doing and walk away from the Police altogether. It was only when I attended a further crime, a rape, that I decided to stand my ground and to use my skills to help people and not to worry about how my fellow professional colleagues felt.

Rape is a disgusting crime, the negative trauma it has on the victim and their loved ones is immeasurable. There exists a million-and-one protocols and sensitivities when dealing with such an offence, not least support and understanding for the victim. When I looked into a series of sexual assaults that had occurred within one relatively small area over a period of a few months, I realised the likelihood that one predatory offender was highly probable. To think we had several deviants suddenly operating at one time in this same area was improbable. Especially since the modus operandi was similar in each reported case.

With crimes such as these there is high probability that many associated incidents go unreported. So local intelligence and community feedback is of vital importance.

Local enquiries had proved fruitless and there was nothing coming back from the Police intelligence system. It was commonly believed that the offender, or offenders were travelling into the crime scene areas, committing the attacks then driving away from it. Potentially into a different Police area.

From the outset, I found that theory full of flaws. Whoever was committing these crimes knew the area well, they didn't accidentally stumble across the victims. They were targeted. Assessing the images of each victim I could list several physical similarities, hair colour, style, facial features, they looked alike, and social interaction. They mixed within a small geographic radius, drank in the same pubs and in at least two instances, knew other victims. These people had undoubtedly been stalked by their attacker.

Their own testimony provided me with an insight into the masked offender, who attacked from behind, threatened with a knife and had a strong West Midlands accent. He used foul and offensive language and breathed heavily. His breath smelled of stale cigarette smoke and alcohol. His hands were rough, and he had bitten down fingernails; he also had a nicotine stained index finger on his right hand. The estimated age group varied between 45 - 60 years old.

What made this deviant different was his actions on leaving the crime scene. He would tell the victim to lay facing the ground, to slowly count to 100 before getting up and leaving the area. A number of his victims looked up and saw him running away. First he backed away before circling them twice and running off towards a nearby road. His escape route. A white van was, a short time later, seen to drive off at speed. The man's gait was not an athletic one, he seemed to run in a stiff manner, showing that it may be an older person.

My first act was to visit the last venues the victims had visited before the attack. I was in plain clothes and accompanied by a fellow detective. The first bar we entered, I saw a man who instantly caught my attention. His behaviour was outlandish, gregarious almost, and he shouted out to the two or three other customers in the premises, 'I smell bacon', meaning the pigs (Police). I looked at him directly in the face and saw guilt etched across it. I approached him and asked what he meant by the comment? He said it was joke as we looked like Police officers. So I hit him with it.

"We are investigating a serious set of crimes, relating to sexual assaults on females." His eyes dropped from their contact with mine and he backed away. "What type of vehicle do you drive?" I asked.

"None of your business mate, instead of coming in here on the piss, why don't you get your arses out there and catch the rapist?"

"I never mentioned rape. Now tell me, what type of vehicle do you drive?"

"A white Transit van," he replied.

I casually glanced down at his fingers, the nails were bitten down and the index finger of the right hand was nicotine stained. I knew it was him, but there was hardly sufficient grounds for an arrest. So I opted to walk away and go to speak with the manager. We talked in whispers, arousing the man to come and stand nearby to listen to what was being said. Minutes later, I turned to him and asked if he'd seen anyone acting suspiciously in the bar or area. He was overtly helpful and offered all kinds of suggestions about our unknown suspect. I allowed him to continue until he began talking about the crime scenes and information that had never been put in the public domain.

As we left the bar, I turned to my colleague and told him to ask the individual to come outside to speak with us for a moment. Minutes later he was under arrest and made a full confession of his attacks under caution and interview. The Police prosecutor (it was pre-Crown Prosecution Service) found it difficult to understand how I had identified the man as the attacker. No matter how many times I justified my suspicions, he couldn't find a way to decipher it. Thankfully, there was no public trial, so I did not have to explain or justify how my suspicion was aroused, since it was a guilty plea. He was imprisoned.

Back in the day, it was called copper's instinct, now, it seemed that my colleagues believed it to be some form of sorcery. Again I began self-analysis, looking at my own perception of everyday situations and people. I realised I was looking at many things differently from others. I call it 'back to basics', a place where the human mind is not intoxicated by marketing propaganda or having the beliefs of others forced onto us. I have an ability to cleanse my mind and look at things from a basic perspective. At crime scenes I place myself in the offender's shoes, and then I follow in the victim's footsteps. It had also been called gut instinct or a sixth sense. Fundamentally it's looking at the obvious solution.

The individual in the bar aroused my suspicions due to his actions. I had noticed a white Ford Transit sat at the rear of the car park on entering the property, however it never registered a point of suspicion. Yet inside my own mind it had done just that. So, putting the man in the van he became a suspect. His demeanour, build and the state of his fingers added to my suspicion. I also knew that offenders liked to stay one step ahead of the Police investigation and often got themselves involved, providing details to divert Police suspicion away from themselves. This individual displayed all of these traits within five minutes of meeting him. I was shocked afterwards, when my hugely experienced detective colleague said he had not a clue that the man might be connected in some way. He described my talent as 'special', though I'm not altogether certain that was in a complimentary way. My legacy was being created for me by the opinion of others.

It goes without saying, in those early days, there were occasions when I got it wrong; not wholly, but I misinterpreted obvious signs. Thankfully not seriously so, and no one was hurt or escaped justice as a result of this, but it was sufficient for me to question my own ability. When I reviewed why this happened, I soon realised it was down to not having the full facts before making a judgment call. I learned from those mistakes and made sure they never occurred again. The pressure to get results was causing me to react before making a full assessment. It was time for me to take control of my skill and manage it as opposed to allowing the system to use and abuse it.

Within a year, my efforts had not only caught offenders, they had helped rehabilitate them - over a dozen offenders who went on to lead good purposeful lives. I constantly added more relevant detail to my profiles, as I gradually created a picture of regional criminality, its causes, its remedies and more importantly, I was able to learn from the offenders themselves. Such aspects as the criteria for being a victim of non-violent crimes like domestic and commercial burglary, car theft, and later, more personal and intimate crimes such as sexual assault and robbery.

I examined every aspect of the offenders' lives, from diet, sleep patterns, fears, wishes, expectations, through to relationships. I then progressed to studies of the demographics and geographic area in which they lived, highlighting the pattern of their behaviour before, during and after a criminal act. I was soon able to determine the different modus operandi of them as individual criminals. It seemed perfectly clear to me that the individual crime scene portrayed the offender's personality, which ostensibly is a further aid to crime detection. As individuals, each of us has our own personality and style; the cars we drive, how we dress our home or ourselves reflect this. It's something wholly unique to each one of us. Likewise, a crime scene will be dressed by the offender. A pattern of actions that, if one studies the profile correctly, can often be as unique as a name. What my profiling didn't do was personally identify offenders. The profiling work was supported by good investigative work and intelligent questioning and reading of witnesses and of the offenders (when apprehended) themselves. Such was my success rate that I soon earned a good reputation among my peers, who unofficially would ask me to look at crimes they were investigating, to give them some direction for further enquiries. I was so passionate about, and believed so much, in what I was doing that I produced a paper to be read at an Association of Chief Police Officers conference. In it, I highlighted the benefits of criminal studies and profiling:

"If we are to understand criminality in all its forms we must walk in the offenders' shoes - male or female, adult or child, they are driven to crime by a variety of reasons. When one connects with the mind set of these offenders it exposes a whole new field of criminal intelligence and understanding. Areas for development where investigating Police officers can begin fresh lines of inquiry in unsolved cases. The psyche and mind set of these offenders differs according to the target, the mens rea will adapt to the geographic surroundings. Yet, their behaviour (actus reus) rarely alters.

A crime scene for example, should be viewed as a painting and scrutinised by the human eye, it can be read and reveal clues about the offender type. As human beings we all possess our own unique personality. This is reflected not only in how we live, but in all other aspects of our life. The style in which we dress, the cars we drive, the music we like, the entertainment we prefer, and in particular how we decorate our homes, apartments or rooms. This is the painting to which I refer. Each sequential offender leaves visual clues at serious crime scenes, and at domestic burglaries et al. By this, I mean not simply those identifiable by Scenes of Crime Officers (SOCO), but those which provide us with a glimpse of their personality type. Police officers should be trained to read these, if not, they should be more aware of how to protect crime scenes so that persons with the skill set to read such a location, can do so knowing it hasn't been inadvertently compromised.

From a proactive perspective, we can then develop an approach to identify and catch potential criminals of all types, at a young age and provide intervention options to introduce structure and discipline to their lives. Teaching moral boundaries and the rules of society is a fundamental basic of a child's development. Failure to do this can lead to a breakdown of domestic and social structures, abhorrent behaviour, alienation of the individual by his/her peers, and a collision course towards anti-social behaviour and initially, low level criminality which will deteriorate to become more frequent serious criminal activity.

Ultimately through partnership collaboration and education, together we can make a positive difference to crime reduction across all of our communities, all by understanding those groups at a basic ground level, the family unit, and addressing any highlighted issues correctly. Police interaction with communities is paramount to improving awareness and receipt of good quality intelligence regarding the nefarious activities of those involved in criminality. More bobbies on the beat, with professional responsibilities for communities is something we should never lose sight of. This builds trust and unity and of course people talk and the Police officer listens. Community spirit and respect is at the hub of this work and we as a Police Service can create and engender that."

In addition, I provided individual de-personalised case studies to support and qualify my work. The feedback I received to my paper was supportive, yet negative. Those who did respond commented on the need for additional 'financial and human' resources to be able to develop such a programme. This wasn't viewed as a political priority and would not be something the respective forces would engage in any time in the near or the distant future. Effectively, because it meant additional work and monetary support, and it wasn't about fresh money 'coming in' from central and local government, it was quickly forgotten about.

I was devastated, as I believed this genuinely was the way forward. Undeterred I began to compile profiles on convicted sexual deviants, identifying commonality in their behaviour and modus operandi. I took the conscious decision to continue my work as it became a focus for my future career.

The deep-rooted desire within me to know more about criminals, particularly sexual deviants and paedophiles, since it was primarily vulnerable children I wanted to protect, continued. Getting people to talk openly about child sex abuse back in the 1980s was impossible. Fellow Police officers struggled to discuss or mention it, and the term was (and still is), generally whispered when such an offender was brought into custody.

It was a sudden death that introduced me to my first non-personal incident of paedophilia as a Police officer. An infant had died in its cot and I was first officer on scene. So little was known about cot death back then, that as Police officers we were duty bound to treat it as a suspicious death and independently question the parents as suspects.

I was devastated by the scene, and it was clear that this was not a malicious incident. It was what the medical examiners said, a cot death. The parents were inconsolable and their five-year-old daughter was completely lost in the situation. I worked hard to support the couple and attended the infant's funeral at their request. Thereafter, I would pay the occasional visit to see them and to check how they were getting on. It was during one such visit that I noticed actions that sent alarm bells ringing in my head. I saw the little girl sat on her father's knee, her eyes had a bleak, almost dead appearance. Gone was the happy little girl who ran around full of laughter and life. She now looked depressed and frightened.

As I sat talking to the couple, I saw the father's hand in what I can only describe as a 'wrong place'. He was touching his daughter inappropriately. Confronted with this situation I had no option but to address it. I asked him to stand up and come with me to the kitchen. There I spoke to him about what I had witnessed. He went bright red and told me he wasn't happy with my accusation and asked me to leave. The one thing I wasn't going to do was leave the little girl in danger. I told him I wouldn't leave and I was seeking back up from specially trained officers. There was an uneasy stand off for about twenty minutes until my colleagues arrived. The little girl was removed and medically examined, confirming my suspicions that her father was abusing her.

It was during the subsequent interview with the suspect that I began to delve deeper into his background and life. I expected to find childhood and adolescent correlations between him and my own father. There were none. This man had come from a middle-class family, had seemingly displayed no deviant behavior throughout his life and had not come to Police attention for anything. The more I talked with him, the more detail I extracted.

As we communicated further he visibly slipped back into conversation mode. His body language relaxed and his posture opened up. Suddenly he was talking about his childhood, referring to an uncle who touched him and generally made him feel important and wanted. His own father wasn't tactile and didn't show much emotion towards him. At school he was popular with girls younger than him, and he then admitted touching and interfering with them sexually. He'd bully them into not reporting it. As he grew older he was able to manipulate children (girls) into coming with him, and again he used threats to control them. I was sickened by what he was telling me yet managed to maintain an air of professionalism and a non-judgmental approach. He wouldn't provide personal details such as victim names or locations, and when I spoke about such matters he closed up. Ultimately, he confessed to touching his daughter and was jailed for 3 months for this offence. So far as I know he never discussed his deviant acts with anyone again.

On release from prison he didn't last long; his ex-wife and her family constantly pursued him, until eventually he committed suicide. News of his death caused little emotional trauma across the community and few people attended his funeral. I did, not out of respect but because I suspected other like-minded criminals may turn up to say goodbye to one of their own. I was right, four convicted child sex offenders turned up. One had travelled hundreds of miles from Doncaster. Since I was dressed in civilian clothing, they had no idea I was a Police officer as I talked with them about the dead man. Afterwards we shared a drink in a local pub where I gathered much in the way of profiling intelligence from them, before they dispersed back to their own areas of the country. This detail was passed to the appropriate authorities and Police forces.

I knew I'd put myself in a precarious situation, confronting the very people I despised as a child and man. However, it was a risk worth taking as I wanted to know more about their backgrounds and history which they openly talked about. None of those men felt it was wrong to abuse children, they all said they did it because they wanted to and because they chose to, and it made them feel good. Some were predators and stalked their victims in playgrounds and parks before finally committing the vile act. Not one of them had been abused as children, and three held down highly paid careers. My profiles were adapting new formats, now I was dealing with sexual perverts and deviants. It came as no surprise that the fundamentals leading towards criminality altered little. There existed common denominators emerging from everywhere I looked. This wasn't by accident or by coincidence, I was getting all of this new information through conversations with different types of offender.

It was while reading a newspaper article that I first learned of the FBI work in this very same field, criminal profiling. With no such thing as the internet or modern technology available to me, I was forced into libraries in an attempt to glean more information about what was taking place in Quantico, Virginia. Sadly, other than an address I found little that could help me, so I did what I thought best, I wrote to them.

To be honest, I never expected a response. Why would the groundbreaking FBI Behavioral Science Unit wish to engage with me, an English cop, and discuss my own profiling work? A few weeks later, a brown manila envelope dropped through my letterbox - the envelope was clearly post marked Quantico, Virginia. Excitedly, I opened it and read the contents. They were interested, and not only that, they wanted to know more and liaise with me about my own work and experience. Once I was verified as a Police officer and I confirmed they too were genuine, we exchanged general information. There followed telephone calls with different agents, not least in my opinion the greatest profiler of them all, Robert Ressler. The duration of the calls got longer and longer. The rest, as they say, is history. I achieved my ambition of working with serial offenders and the leading profilers in the world of policing

In all honesty, I enjoyed an exemplary and fulfilling Police career with more than my fair share of unique experiences. My career path followed the route I wanted, I worked extremely hard, kept my head down and set about making my mark by making victims of crime feel valued, safe, and supported. Whether it was as a uniformed bobby, a dog handler or as a crime writer, I always gave my all. I've been engaged on dangerous firearms duties; provided close protection to people like King Hussain of Jordan on a visit to the United Kingdom; worked in undercover intelligence as a football hooligan; and as a security advisor attempting to gain access into top secret Ministry of Defence establishments across the country. On one occasion having breached MoD security I got inside a top secret building, only to be confronted by three Rottweiler guard dogs handled by their respective patrolling soldiers. I never stood a chance and ended up in hospital, torn to shreds. Lesson learned. I've been threatened with death by criminals on several occasions, none of whom were aware I was a copper. Anyone who believes that the British Police force offers no exciting roles is very wrong. Britain remains the best and most respected policing structure in the world, and I'm proud to have been an integral part of it in a career covering three decades. However, my opinion did understandably alter several years after my medical retirement.

In 2006, I suffered a breakdown after I was sexually assaulted in a lift at night by a senior political official who shall remain nameless. I had been holding a large, paper-filled box, both hands grasping it close to my chest. I gave no thought to it at the time, but this left me vulnerable to a predatory deviant who attempted to take advantage of the situation. A knee to the head and a few expletives aimed directly at the person in question let them know it was unwanted attention and unacceptable behavior. In response, I was told 'dare report it and you'll lose your job and I will personally destroy your reputation'.

As I stepped from that lift my legs turned to jelly as my childhood trauma surfaced for the first time. Thankfully no one else was present to witness me falling apart, for an hour or so I sat sobbing uncontrollably and couldn't understand why. Over the years, I had got deep inside the minds of some of the world's worst and most notorious serial killers and never once felt intimidated or frightened. Now a sexual predator had deliberately touched me through my clothing, and I was in bits. That was it, the moment I had been dreading all my life. The floodgates opened as memory after vivid memory of my childhood came pouring out. I tried to fight it, and worked hard and long hours in the role I was then employed in. I even reported the sexual assault. On doing so, I was again threatened with professional destruction. This time I was alienated, as an entire organisation closed ranks and I was made a scapegoat, made to feel stupid, inferior, unwanted, pathetic, impotent and hopeless. Eventually, I could hold back no longer, I spiraled into a mental decline and meltdown. I had no idea how I was functioning, or what I was doing until I could do it no more. I was examined by professional medical people who advised me I was having what is more commonly referred to as a full mental and nervous breakdown.

For the first time in my entire life, I was forced to tell someone intimate details about my childhood. That was hard. Then the prescribed drugs kicked in and to be honest, the following five years are a complete blur to me. Those closest to me tell me I tried to take my own life several times as four decades of living and operating in the darker side of humanity took their psychological toll. Eventually I plucked up the courage to report my childhood abuse to the Police.

I expected a sympathetic professional approach and response from the Police. Instead I was confronted by some of the worst policing and safeguarding children experiences anyone could suffer. Failure after failure by the relevant authorities at one point even saw me accused of being a paedophile offender, as I was instructed not to go near my own grandchildren. The child protection body paid to help me went into absolute denial about the errors. It was a devastating period and left me feeling an outcast and abandoned. For a time I wished I'd never reported it.

Eventually one Police officer showed professionalism and my case was progressed, my father was arrested and described by the interviewing officers as cold and 'serial killer-like' in his emotionless animosity towards both myself and my brother. At one point he said he only had one son, and that I didn't exist. Step up the Crown Prosecution Service who deemed his old age and health condition meant it wasn't in the public interest to prosecute him. He would be dead before going to trial. That was it, the case was closed. From that day forth, no one from the Police, victim support or any other agency has contacted me. As in my childhood, I was abandoned, left to deal with it on my own. Thankfully, I had a good family to help me through.

Incredibly, after everything I endured as a child, and my breakdown, I believe I'm a reasonably well-balanced individual. I have my moments, I won't deny it, however I now love what I do and have many more exciting adventures ahead of me yet. My entire life has been spent looking for human monsters, be they child sex offenders, murderers or serial killers. I've met way too many, communicated with them and somehow managed to get inside their heads. That's a human experience, learning about emotional trauma and crime drivers that can never be understood or rationalised in the world of number crunching or data analysis. People react differently to the situations life throws at them, my own life is a positive example of that. As humankind we are all different, emotionally, physically and mentally. As you'll learn throughout this book, people don't always conform. I certainly didn't as a youngster. Many can't or won't be labeled or put into a scientific class or academic box. We all have a story to tell. In a series of one-on-one conversations I have heard the most chilling stories of all - those of the vile people we call serial killers.

ONE

Serial Killing - The Early Days

Murder and deviant behavior aren't modern day phenomena, they've been around in different guises since time immemorial. The bible and other religious texts apart, we have original regional folk lore and fairy tales which undoubtedly depict acts of murder, cannibalism, torture, rape and child abuse. Take 'Sleeping Beauty' for example - in Giambattista's 1634 version the handsome Prince finds her asleep and proceeds to rape her! In the original version of the 'Pied Piper', the hero rids a town of rats by playing music from his pipe and drawing them to a river. When returning for payment, the town folk refuse to pay up, so he leads three children down to a river and drowns them.

'Snow White' is another dark tale, the original version sees the Queen ask for her liver and lungs which are to be cooked and served up for dinner that evening. Later in the story, she is awakened by the movement of the cart on which her body is being carried by the Prince who believed her to be dead and wished to have his own way with her. The Grimm version sees the Queen forced to dance to death in red hot iron shoes.

'The Tale of Bluebeard' by French author Charles Perrault, refers to a wealthy man who meets and marries a beautiful woman. She is brought to live with him in his luxurious castle; however, there is one room to which she is allowed no access. Naturally, this captures the young woman's imagination and she becomes desperate to find out what lays inside. Her husband's attitude changes as trust is lost. When Bluebeard is called away from the castle, his wife unlocks the room and is stunned to find several corpses of dead women, all previous wives he has killed!

Myths and legends are a further source of potentially serious serial killer activity.

Sadly some allegations of crimes have been accepted as fact. Take the case of Gilles de Rais. Born in 1405, in France he is remembered as a hero, who in 1435, fought alongside Joan of Arc, in what is known as the Hundred Years War, and defeated the Kingdom of England and its allies. It all sounds very credible until rumours began to emerge of a dark and sinister side to his nature. He was accused of abusing, raping, torturing and killing up to 200 children. His criminal reputation undoubtedly inspired the myth of Bluebeard.

This is where it all gets a little murky as the brave soldier suddenly finds his integrity trashed. According to legend it seems that in 1440, a serious argument between Rais and a cleric at the Church of Saint-Étienne-de-Mer-Morte took place, resulting in the abduction of the said priest. After a brief time, the church was forced to launch an investigation into the matter. It then emerged, as a result of this religious investigation, that over the previous eight years, Rais had been engaging in sordid and deviant acts with children. The Church, supported by secular lawmen, interviewed staff and servants who knew him better than anyone. Soon the church declared that he had raped and murdered close to 200 young children, mainly boys. To authenticate this, two French clerics testified that he had identified individuals who practiced alchemy and demon-summoning, as he wished to learn the art for his own devices. Their claims continued and became even more fantastic. On one occasion they said that he once procured the body parts of a young (virgin) boy child as a sacrifice for the summoning.

The church was and remains a powerful and influential body. One can only imagine the terror and intimidation his household staff felt as they were threatened with the taking of their own lives during ecclesiastical interrogations. Alleged confessions were forthcoming, as two of his servant staff confessed to abducting children for him. Others told how he would masturbate over the living bodies and sexually interfere with and molest innocent and terrified young boys before chopping off their heads and eviscerating their bodies. There were reports of child beggars who visited his castle disappearing. The church did a thorough job of destroying the reputation and integrity of Gilles de Rais, leading to his arrest. Under threat of torture he is said to have confessed all, with the following being a small part of his admission of guilt.

"When the said children were dead, I kissed them and those who had the most handsome limbs and heads I held them up to admire them. I then had their bodies cut open, the sight of their inner organs spilling out was a delight."

On October 26, 1440, at the age of just 35, he was hanged. As grisly as it sounds, there is little substance to the tale, certainly no hard evidence. It seems more likely that the church took exception to his abduction of one of their clerics and his outspoken comments relating to religion and decided to silence him for good.

Also in the 15th century, Vlad Tepes, Prince of Wallachia –more commonly known as Vlad the Impaler or as the inspiration for Dracula - murdered hundreds of people to avenge the killing of his father. Having spent much of his early life in a Turkish prison, upon his release he discovered that his father had been betrayed by his people and buried alive by Hungarian soldiers.

Recognising that many of the noblemen who served under his father were involved in the betrayal, he invited all those he suspected of involvement (about five hundred) to a great feast at his home. Afterwards, he had his soldiers charge into the room and run through with lances every single nobleman present - they were impaled where they sat. With the bloody corpses left and held in place by the stakes, Vlad is said to have finished his own dinner before dipping bread into the blood collecting beneath the bodies and eating it. The lust for blood and euphoria provided by the power of the kill drove him on.

Vlad consistently used the same modus operandi to lure people to his house with the offer of a feast, then he would kill them. Anyone who refused would be killed on the spot. In a form of ethnic cleansing he set fire to villages where the sick and poor lived, leaving no survivors. Estimates indicate that Vlad killed, or had killed on his instructions, anywhere between 20,000 - 100,000 people. The real figure will never be known. An undoubted sadist, he is recorded as boiling people alive and forcing relatives and close communities to eat the victims' flesh, and poisoning water sources to kill off entire communities. He died in battle.

More recently, in 17th century England, individuals like the Witchfinder General, Matthew Hopkins, were creating their own imagery of criminal types. In this instance, witches. Hopkins travelled much of East Anglia and the Midlands areas of England seeking out individuals who bore the behavioral and physical similarities of witches elsewhere. This was based on his own, flawed profiling model. Hopkins himself is likely to be the world's first serial killer, since his own direct and extremely corrupt actions were responsible for the deaths of three hundred-plus innocent people. Hopkins attempted to veil his actions, and those of his partner in crime John Stearne, with respectability, by stating he was employed by Parliament as Witchfinder General to hunt down and have witches executed or put to death. His title and actions were never officially bestowed by parliament, but the authorities where he travelled openly welcomed him, paid him handsomely and celebrated the deaths. The Witchcraft Act did not come into place until 1735, so Hopkins' actions were entirely unlawful. Without any shadow of a doubt, Hopkins can be recognised as one of the world's first serial killers.

Very little is known of Hopkins' childhood. He was one of six children, and his father, James Hopkins, was a Puritan Clergyman, and vicar of St John's, Great Wenham, Suffolk. One can imagine that young Matthew was raised in a strict religious household with many rules and discipline. The family itself would have some privilege and seen within the community where they lived, as a connected part of the middle classes. Therefore, he would be educated to a reasonable standard and raised to have manners, be polite and with an understanding of moral propriety. The entire family would be under public scrutiny, so it's likely that childhood pranks and general misbehavior, which were natural and part of the development of young children, were missing from their life. Religion and the church were indoctrinated in the childrens' psyche from a very young age since it provided a decent level of income and living for the entire family. It's fairly obvious that each member of the family had a personal responsibility to James Hopkins to be respectful and an underlying expectancy of being on one's best behavior at all times. Within such a disciplined domestic environment it's likely that laughter, playfulness and the right level of positive emotional support were lost in the midst of religious practices. In essence, Matthew and his siblings were raised in what was likely to be an emotionally sterile home. We know that in today's society, this very often leads to periods of anti-social behavior as the child grows resentful of the parents and society in general, because they feel restricted and alone through not understanding emotions. This was certainly reflected in Matthew's brother, John. He went on (more likely he was pushed into the position by his parents) to become Minister of South Fambridge in 1645 but was removed from the role within a year for neglectful working practices.

Matthew himself began to rebel. He claimed in his book 'The Discovery of Witches' (1647), not to have moved far from home to gain his Witchfinder experiences. He left home and later moved to the village of Mistley, where he established himself (through wealth) as a gentleman, mainly through 'ill gotten' gains. He purchased The Thorn Inn. According to legend, he had previously trained as a lawyer, however, there is no evidence of this to be found anywhere, other than the manner in which he eloquently spoke in pseudo-legal terminology at the kangaroo-court witchcraft trials he cleverly manipulated.

Such was the self-initiated power he yielded that no one in authority dared challenge him (even the Magistrates presiding over the trials were in fear of him) during his murderous rampage. He was eloquent and a master of twisting words to his own advantage, creating profiles of typical witch-like behavior and presenting this to the courts as proven and solid evidence of witchcraft. Nobody it seemed dare question his authority and accepted his word as gospel. Matthew Hopkins was emotionally cold, ruthless and without empathy for his victims who he often randomly identified wherever he was called to. He was paid handsome amounts of money that financially set him up for life, for what can only be described as his own version of social cleansing.

Eventually, some authorities did speak out against his practices, pointing accusatory fingers in his direction and claiming that he himself had been overcome by the powers of evil. In essence they claimed he had become a Witch/Warlock in his own right. It was the classic 'takes one to know one' mindset. His days were numbered as society throughout East Anglia in particular turned against him. Moving back to Manningtree, he died at his home on 12th August 1647 of what is believed to be pleural tuberculosis. He was buried within hours in the consecrated ground of the graveyard of the Church of St Mary, in Mistley Heath. The church is long gone although the land, and presumably the final resting place of one of the world's worst serial killers, remains. Locals don't broadcast its location or openly talk about it to visitors or researchers; it's a dark and morbid secret they wish to keep locked away where it belongs as part of the unwanted history relating to the darker side of humanity.

It's easy to assimilate Hopkins' crimes with those of a more modern serial killer. Over three hundred years later, in 1970, Charles Milles Manson (nee Maddox) was convicted of first degree murder and conspiracy to kill seven innocent victims. Although he didn't physically kill any one of those people it was deemed at his subsequent trial, that the murders had occurred as a result of his sole coercion and manipulation. Right through to his dying breath in December 2017, Manson continued to deny his involvement in the murders. Discussing this and his innermost thoughts, he emphatically told me;

"I ain't physically killed no-one. Not ever, Paul. This system of ours can't decide what to do with me. I'm like a bad smelling fart that won't go away, so they set me up for those murders. The system is corrupt, it's all about covering up their own sins. It's not justice, there is no such thing as that, it's about them and others

making sure they are all fine and dandy in their big homes and flash cars. You're part of that movement, how does that make you feel? The stories they put out about me, they're pure bullshit, made up to make me look evil and bad. I maybe a bit of a loony at times, but I am not evil. Do you know how it feels to walk in my shoes? The devil is scared of me, and God doesn't want to know me. Yep, I'm on my own in this big bad world, if you want some advice, look after yourself and your own, because sure as hell the system will take from you, but it won't look after you.

I'll tell you something else, facts that no one dares talk about. It's the damn system that is creating bad people, manufacturing serial killers as they call them. Take a look at those people's lives, their shitty childhoods, beatings, torture and rape. Did anyone ever try to help or step in and try to stop it, or even understand or try to help? Nope, they turned their backs and ignored it because they were more concerned about protecting themselves. The people in here, other killers, rapists, the evil people that society despises, they are bonded by their lousy childhoods and upbringings, most of them resent authority because it let them down. Put that out there and let people understand that it's their children who will someday kill other children. They may as well put blood stained knives in their hands at birth."

TWO
The Media, The Monster & Profiling

The so called Jack the Ripper murders committed in London, England in 1888, are probably the most analysed series of events in the whole of criminal history. The Police at the time were clueless and have subsequently been maligned for their failures to catch the killer. Efforts ever since by criminologists, true crime aficionados and self-proclaimed 'Ripper experts' have failed to convince a global audience as to the identity of their preferred suspect; there's even been questionable evidence 'produced' in a suspect's diary. The murders of Jack the Ripper are now an industry in their own right.

Sadly, in the hundreds of years since, the crimes have been sensationalised and misreported and we are unlikely to ever confirm the true identity of the miscreant who murdered and disemboweled an unknown number of street sex workers in Victorian Whitechapel. It's a sad indictment of the case that the victims have in many instances been dehumanised by the media and often pale into insignificance when the case is regurgitated in the press. Policing and criminal investigations were very different then. Basic and naive with little or no forensic support, it was a process of learning new skills from fresh criminal activity. So when this series of murders occurred, it was breaking into new territory for law enforcement and from a killer's perspective.

It was Dr. George Bagster Phillips, the divisional Police surgeon who first made efforts to identify the group of persons from which the killer might have come. Because the modus operandi was so unique he studied the wounds inflicted on the victims (wound pattern analysis). Essentially, he was attempting to identify the offender's personality through examination of his murderous behaviour with the victim. In the case of Annie Chapman, he believed some level of professional skill was present in the execution of the attack and wounds. What intrigued him most was the succinct manner in which she had been disembowelled with clean precise incisions. He was suggesting the killer may have possessed some level of anatomical or surgical competence.

At Chapman's inquest, the coroner for the South East District of Middlesex, Dr. Wynne E. Baxter, commented to Phillips: "The object of the inquiry is not only to ascertain the cause of death, but the means by which it occurred. Any mutilation which took place afterwards may suggest the character of the man who did it."

Thus, some realisation that a body or a crime scene can give some clues towards the character and type of person who had committed the crime was hardly unique or new, but it had at least been accepted, by some professionals at least, as a useful forensic tool to enhance detection.

The situation became more confusing when Phillips's colleague and fellow Police surgeon, Dr. Thomas Bond, was professionally involved in the case. He stated with some authority, that the killer showed not the slightest clue of anatomical knowledge. He went on to suggest that the killer would be: "A man of solitary habits, subject to periodic attacks of homicidal and erotic mania, with the character of the mutilations possibly indicating satyriasis".

Bond claimed the gaping wounds and cuts to the bodies of each victim were not conducive to medical awareness or dexterity. Two medical experts, contradicting one another. What is clear, is that no medical official, then or now, has considered the killer's emotional state at the time of the crime. We can't possibly understand unless we are in the mindset of that offender, and that means genuinely understanding the social, professional and domestic aspect of the killer's life. Then we have to understand why that individual chose to kill. We are all human beings and our brains react and respond differently to all manner of situations. What we can say is that each attack, except that on Mary Jane Kelly, was swiftly executed, the murderer was hampered by poor street lighting and was literally working in the shadows. Crouched over a prostate body, that person managed to achieve their own personal euphoria through the kill and the mutilations. In addition, working outdoors, at night and seriously running the risk of being seen, the killer must have been listening out for passers-by or potential witnesses who might identify him. What we have here is someone who is on emotional high alert while at the same time experiencing the thrill of their actions.

The increase in the severity of the injuries inflicted in the attacks tends to support the actions of a serial killer. On the night/morning of the so called 'double event', the killer failed to satiate their desire upon being disturbed after killing Elizabeth Stride. Evasive action occurred, and they left the scene, blending into the background and becoming almost invisible. This indicates someone with local knowledge, who knew the streets and geography of the area; and it had to be someone who looked like the average person in the district, since anyone looking 'different' would have stood out. We have no Royal carriage or horse and cart or top hatted doctor with a Gladstone bag, just someone who fit perfectly with the surrounding environment.

Thereafter, the killer came upon the Mitre Square victim, again showing a potential route of foot travel back into Spitalfields, escaping the chaos that was undoubtedly emerging behind him and avoiding Police heading towards the crime scene from both Leman Street divisional headquarters and the Police station in Commercial Street. The killer actually headed into a different Police area, as they entered City of London Police territory. The victim was Catherine Eddowes, who took the full brunt of his deviant nature. The killer then headed back into Spitalfields, depositing a blood-stained piece of material in a doorway en route. Clearly some blood matter would be present on the killer's clothing, therefore we can see that they were not going to stray too far, keeping to the darker, more ill-lit streets and alleys back to their place of residence, which by deduction must have been local.

Finally, Mary Jane Kelly was literally taken apart by the killer in her own lodging room in Dorset Street. The killer was clearly invited there by the victim, therefore despite the fear and terror running through the district and her own professional community, she clearly felt safe being alone with that person. Once inside, she was killed and horrifically mutilated. On leaving, the killer locked the door by reaching through a broken window to secure it. This indicates someone who was aware of this - someone who has just committed one of the worst crimes in the history of humankind calmly carrying out the act of securing the door using prior knowledge. Thereafter, the trail goes cold. I still maintain, as contentiously now as in my book 'Jack the Ripper - The Mystery Solved', that Joseph Barnett is the most likely candidate for the killer. Until real evidence to the contrary is revealed then I stand by that assertion.

The reality of the Ripper investigation in Victorian times was much the same as in present times - it was often influenced by the press. Forget the detectives, they were simply being marshalled by senior hierarchy who, in turn were dancing to the tune of the politicians, who themselves were responding to newspaper articles keen for a new angle or take on the murders. Even HRH Queen Victoria found herself embroiled in political discussions about the murders. It was the press who first revealed the label the killer had allegedly given to the crime (Jack the Ripper) after he supposedly sent a letter to them. It's much more likely to be the creation of an inventive journalist looking to strike fear into London, resulting in the newspaper increasing its sales and the journalist's stock rising likewise.

Tags or pseudonyms for serial killer murders are a popular feature across the media, sensationalising the attacks with the same purpose of London's Victorian press, to sell copies.

A case where the press potentially jumped on the labeling bandwagon is that of the killer best known as 'The Boston Strangler', who was originally dubbed 'The Green Man' by the media. This killer was carefully selecting his victims between June 1962 and January 1964, when he committed a number of sexually-related homicides in the city of Boston, Massachusetts. Officers from the law enforcement department were quick to connect the crimes and claimed they were the work of the same offender. Despite this, their investigative efforts could identify no viable suspects. Keen to bring the case to a successful conclusion, the decision was made to bring together a group of skilled individuals who through psychological assessment of the crime scenes, could draw a profile of the type of individual who might be committing these crimes. A psychiatrist, a gynecologist, an anthropologist, historians, Police officers, clinicians and other professionals examined the crime scene evidence and created what was known as a 'psychiatric profile' that they believed matched the person responsible.

This unique committee formed the opinion that the crimes were the work of two offenders and not a single killer. They arrived at this conclusion as there was two distinct type of victim, older and younger women. They believed there was evidence of psychosexual behaviour in these groups. In the older group, the women had been strangled and killed by a man who hailed from a dysfunctional family background, who was possibly raised by a controlling and domineering mother. As a result of this issue, his animosity and hatred towards women was formed, the inability to hate or hurt his mother was therefore focused on older women. His domestic life was a lonely one, he was likely to have lived alone and in his own mind held the belief that if he could conquer the issues created by his domineering mother, then life, love and relationships would be normal.

The younger women in this series of crimes were murdered by a younger, homosexual male, possibly a close ally of the killer of the former group. He had killed as a result of his sexuality and blamed this group of victims for the years he was forced to suppress (hide) his own sexual tendencies and possibly to prove his own masculinity in some way.

In April 1964, Dr Brussel was invited to assist in the investigation, and at once produced his own profile. From the outset he disagreed with the findings of the committee. He claimed there was no evidence to show two offenders, he said the crimes were the work of one person. In November 1964, Albert DeSalvo, was arrested for the 'Green Man' rapes, so called because the offender wore a green set of outer clothing. He later confessed to his psychiatrist of 'The Boston Strangler' murders to his psychiatrist, later recanting this confession, saying it was made under duress.

In 1973, he was stabbed to death in the prison infirmary. A man by the name of Robert Wilson was brought to trial for the crime, but a hung jury failed to convict him. Curiously, no one was ever convicted of the murder and to this day it remains unsolved. The case of 'The Boston Strangler' was closed.

Almost a quarter of a century later, after a fresh forensic investigation, serious doubts have been cast over DeSalvo's guilt. It has now been proven that DNA (semen) samples found on one of the murdered women do not match that of Albert DeSalvo. The crime scene evidence from the murder of 19-year-old Mary Sullivan, the last victim in the series, failed to match or associate with De Salvo. He was innocent of that woman's death. The DNA belonged to someone else, a different killer! Further evidence of DeSalvo's innocence in this particular murder was revealed when the press were told that Mary Sullivan's hyoid bone had not been broken. In all cases of strangulation this bone is broken, therefore contradicting DeSalvo's recanted version of events.

In 2013, to silence their critics, the DA of Suffolk County authorised the exhumation of the body of Albert DeSalvo. A few days later it was confirmed that the DNA (semen) found at the Mary Sullivan crime scene directly matched Albert DeSalvo's. Despite this 'official' claim, there is a growing belief that DeSalvo was innocent.

Books, TV films and movies continue to be produced about the case of 'The Boston Strangler', whose actions - and above all pseudonym - struck terror across not only Boston but the whole of the US. Was he guilty?

In my own opinion, there are so many different profile patterns and behavioural actions attached to this case that it seems highly unlikely that DeSalvo, if guilty, was the sole killer. Then we have the alleged confession; major parts of that contradict the crime scene and the medical reports on the bodies of the victims. The taped statement made by DeSalvo contained no new information or evidence, it was material that could have been lifted from and read in the newspapers of the day. Much of the detail was absolutely wrong. It seems more likely that the pressure to identify 'The Boston Strangler' became a heavy burden for the investigating authorities and they were willing to accept any confession without examining it in detail as it meant they had their man.

Over the years through their choice of killer nicknames (see APPENDIX), the media has been responsible for creating mass fear among communities. It's not only English-speaking countries who are fascinated by giving these people's actions titles, it's a global phenomenon.

Globally, serial killers are given gruesome and terrifying pseudonyms by the media based upon their murderous activity. For example, 'Bible John', who terrorized Glasgow in the 1960s, dumping bodies of his female victims in isolated spots, dressing the crime scene to shock, and leaving a used tampon beneath the victim's armpit. Each victim was picked up at the same dancehall (Barrowlands) before being killed. The case remains unsolved but his spectre still haunts that city. The 'Green River Killer' (Gary Ridgway) was so called because his bodies were mainly found close to or in the river. Or 'The Sunday Morning Slasher' (Carl [Coral] Watts) who killed on a Sunday morning and made a bloody mess of each of his victims. 'The Night Stalker' (Richard Ramirez) prowled the hours of darkness selecting his Los Angeles based victims. 'The Butcher of Rostrov' (Andrei Chikatilo) was so named because of his predilection for cutting up his victims. The list goes on.

The nicknames are meant to shock and horrify us, yet in a subliminal way they also lead us to believe that the people who commit such crimes are hugely different to us. The monsters are first created in the mind of the reporters who write and update news story lines covering the crimes and investigations. The more sensational the killing the more papers are likely to sell. It's a vicious cycle where the killer feeds the media. The media cannot always be blamed for its reporting. In some instance, such as 'Zodiac', the killer writes to the press requesting front page coverage, even resorting to a type of blackmail and threatening to kill innocent children if he doesn't get newspaper coverage.

The reality is, Zodiac was very likely a loner with social issues who in childhood had endured some kind of trauma, and someone who was denied compassion, love and good nurturing. His targets as a killer weren't personally selected, in the main they were loving couples in remote areas. Something in those situations aroused anger within him, maybe because he was alone or had suffered the loss of a loving relationship at some point in his formative years. Whatever the situation, from his behavior, it's clear that he desperately needed to satiate his desire to be loved or to be someone. Zodiac became his alter ego, and so infamy followed but it did not provide round the clock love. He claimed in writing, to have killed many more victims in a show of grandiosity, and continually maligned the investigating San Francisco Police. For me, this shows someone with a grudge against the police. Perhaps he was someone who felt some form of injustice towards them, punished or jailed for something he didn't do, something that was life-changing. Alternatively, it may be someone who was in law enforcement and had felt slighted or demeaned in some way, overlooked for a specific role or promotion for instance. The mocking of the Police was consistent throughout his reign of terror, and this defines much about the killer's mindset. Certainly, Zodiac took risks, and he must have known the region extremely well to be able to evade capture. Similarly, Zodiac always seemed to be one step ahead of the Police investigation - if he was part of that force, he would be aware of which direction the investigation was headed.

The murder of taxi driver Paul Stine was another random attack, this one in the street, during the hours of darkness. The attack probably took place close to his home since he wiped the cab clean of his fingerprints before casually walking away from the crime scene. These actions are of a disciplined individual who knows where he is headed and believes he can escape the law. What type of professional possesses such feelings of superiority? Most killers flee the scene as quickly as they can, especially as this wasn't the dead of night, but late evening. Zodiac seemingly remained calculated in all he did and didn't stop or hesitate about which direction to take after this kill - he walked off somewhat confidently, even though some blood staining would be present on his hands and parts of his outer clothing at the very least.

The crime itself was likely to be an assertion of his masculinity since he was being publicly maligned for killing young women, and two of his male victims, although seriously injured, survived, calling into question his clinical ability and strength. He needed to assert his strength and power over a grown man, albeit Stine offered no resistance and was shot in the head from the rear seat of the taxi he drove, so no physical altercation actually took place. The kill provided Zodiac with the euphoria he yearned and in his own mind at least, proved he was a seasoned and ruthless assassin.

Zodiac then arranged the body and removed a trophy (a piece of shirt) from Stine's body. To confirm his prowess and to instill shock in the public, he then sent a piece of the blood-stained shirt to the press, all to keep his name in the papers and to give him a sense of power and control over an entire city, if not a nation. Was he calculating? Or just plain lucky?

Ex-cop Joseph James DeAngelo, the suspect in custody for the Golden State killer and East Area rapist crimes, had six years' service in the Police. He was dismissed from the Auburn, California Police Department for shoplifting, having served in both Auburn and Exeter. Clearly there is a great amount of sexual deviancy present in these crimes and premeditation, so we have an offender who is in every way a human nightmare on a horror film scale. In addition to sexual attacks, he used physical and mental torture to instill fear into those he did not kill. How could someone with such clear deviant behavior enroll, serve and blend into the culture of the Police? It has been claimed in the press that De Angelo is suspected of committing upwards of fifty crimes, including his first two murders during his three-year stint in the Auburn Police Department. His nom-de-plume (Golden State Killer) was awarded to him by journalist Michelle McNamara who maintained interest in the case with her outstandingly factual reporting, and her book of the same title.

No one suspected him of anything sinister, showcasing his 'chameleon-like' ability to blend in and become almost invisible. Police officers across the globe are not the paragons of virtue they have been made into. They too are human and have their own personal needs. There are cases of law enforcement officials 'going bad'. The vast majority, however, are outstanding law-abiding peacekeepers wishing to make a positive difference to society.

Curiously, about three months before the big arrest in the Golden State Killer case, I drew up a profile of the wanted felon. Based solely on what accurate information I could find, I compiled a skeletal profile of the type of person I would consider a suspect, or to be a potential person of interest. Practical awareness of law enforcement behaviour and discipline were prominent. It was nothing that jumped out at me, albeit I was able to highlight the possibility it might be someone with military history and or with, an association to Policing in the region. It was clear this individual was calculating and knew the district well. Hence the arrest and background of this type of suspect came as no shock to me.

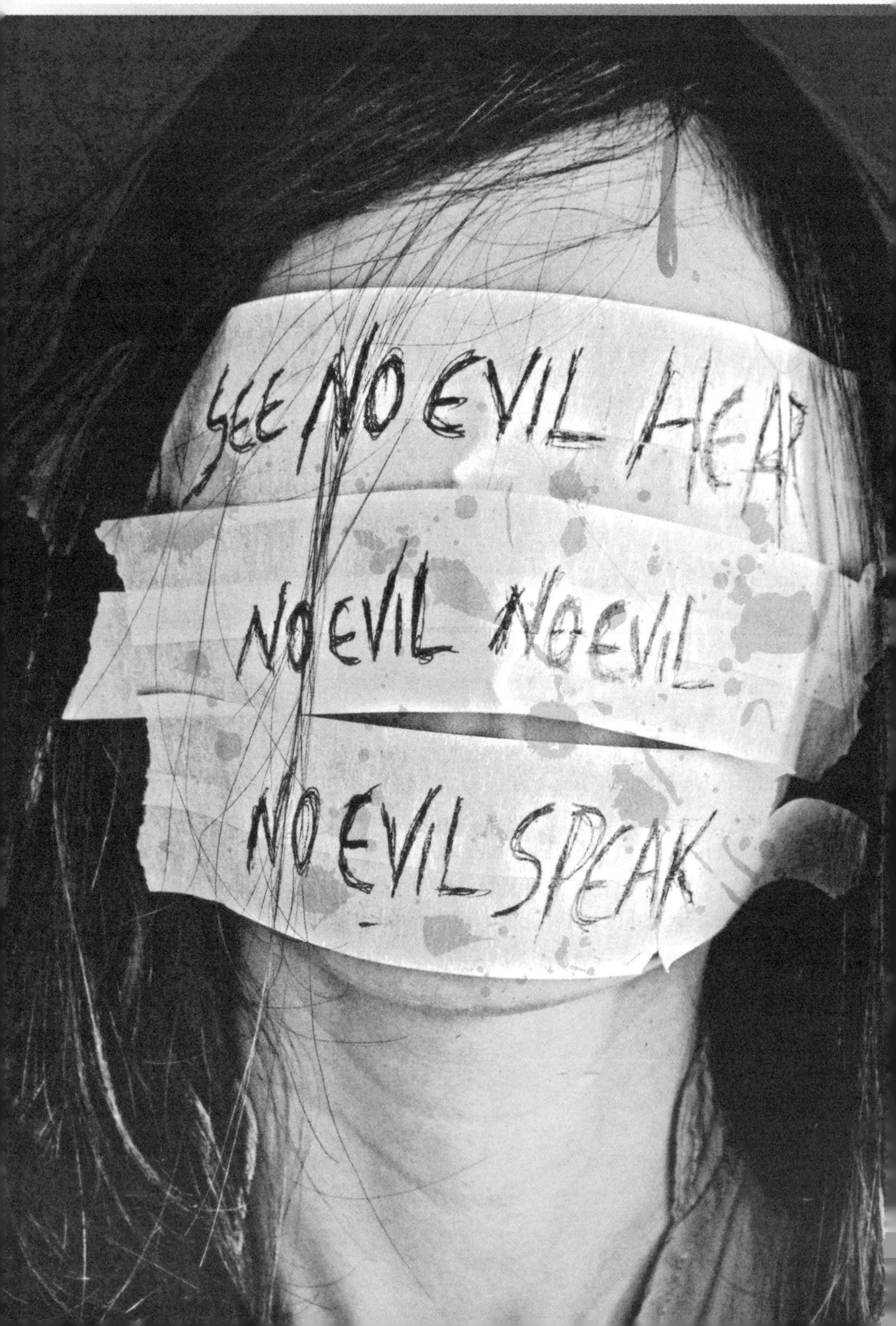
SEE NO EVIL HEAR
NO EVIL NO EVIL
NO EVIL SPEAK

THREE
Behind A Painted Smile!

"I never killed no one, though I figure the Clown could have!"
John Wayne Gacy

Chicago, Illinois in the 1940s was a changing place, becoming a more diverse community as Hispanic immigrants began to arrive. The vast majority came from Mexico and Puerto Rico, as well as Cuba during Fidel Castro's rise in the 1950s. The city produced 20% of all America's steel (10% of the world's entire production). In December of 1942, the world's first controlled nuclear reaction was conducted at the University of Chicago as part of the top secret Manhattan Project. This was a place where lots was going on, including murder. Gangsters ruled the streets, as the Outfit, once led by the infamous Al Capone, continued its stranglehold on the country's wealthy and famous – for example, the Hollywood extortion trial found eight associates guilty of conspiracy and extortion. During this decade, the Outfit boss, Frank Nitti, publicly committed suicide on the Illinois Central railroad track. Al Capone and James 'Jimmy the Bomber' Belcastro died, and 'Bugsy' Siegel was murdered. In addition, the so called 'Lipstick Killer' was running amok. This individual infamously left a message scrawled in red lipstick on the wall of one crime scene:

"For heavens
Sake catch me
Before I kill more
I cannot control myself"

The police initially believed the killer to be a woman, mainly because of the use of the lipstick to scrawl the message. The press seized the opportunity to give the mysterious murderer a pseudonym and so 'the lipstick killer' became a real life monster and terrified much of Chicago. The press was relentless in their reporting of the crimes and raised the fear level by discussing other unsolved murders of women in the region.

On 7 January, 1946 the city went into freefall as James Degnan discovered his six year old daughter, Suzanne Degnan, was missing from her bedroom, again, in the North Side district of the city. The Police searched her room and found a crumpled piece of paper. It was a note from the kidnapper advising the family to prepare for a $20,000 ransom. They were instructed not to notify the police or the FBI, and await further messages.

Shortly before 7pm. that evening, Suzanne's severed head was found less than a block away; it was floating in a sewer catch basin with blue ribbons still tied in her hair. The following hours had further gruesome revelations, as the child's legs and torso were found and recovered from separate locations in sewers nearby.

After this murder, the Degnan case became the first national crime sensation of the postwar era. The media across the country reported every new detail and flooded the city in search of a new story or fresh developments. The Chicago police were under pressure to catch the sadistic killer. Over the days and weeks that followed, thousands of men and women were questioned and alibis examined. All known sexual deviants and violent offenders across the city were closely looked at and their modus operandi and movements during key times investigated. Several serious suspects were arrested and later released without charge.

The authorities were desperate to find the killer and at times it seemed to overwhelm them.

Dreadful mistakes began to creep into the investigation as after each arrest, the state's attorney, William Touhy, made the dramatic new announcement that the killer had been caught and was in custody. The suspect remained so for 48 hours before being released without charge; no evidence existed against him, and he refused to confess. His guilt was suspected by the Police through association with the building only.

Months passed by, as gradually the Police exhausted every lead they had. Ultimately at the beginning of the summer 1946, all they had was a few smudged fingerprints that had been found by the FBI on the ransom note. Touhy was if anything persistent. 'This is one crime that is going to be solved' he asserted to the press. When I discussed the case with the convicted killer, William Heirons, he told me:

"My childhood was good, average I suppose you'd say. I was happy anyway. I was creative and used to draw a lot. I had one hell of an imagination and I remember sitting telling my young brother science fiction tales, rockets, space that kind of thing. I really enjoyed repairing things, as I say I was useful in many different ways. Despite that, there was a lot of bad stuff going on as well. I wasn't very old, maybe 12 when I started to steal. It wasn't a case of greed or anything like that. It was more a case of having to do it. I used to deliver groceries for a local store. It was always being drummed into us by the business owner that if the money we took from deliveries was short at the store, then we wouldn't get paid. I was short changed by a customer but couldn't prove it and when I told him the bastard wouldn't have it. Later that day I was still on my round when I saw an opportunity to steal and get some of the shortfall money back. An open purse was laid on the side inside a chain locked apartment. So I reached inside and slipped out a dollar bill. I got away with it, and of course the store keeper kept the money if you were ever overpaid.

Stealing became a way of life after that, it was easy and I became obsessed by it, I wanted to be rich and this was an easy way to acquire cash. My folks, they weren't rich or well off even, just hard working and normal, but they provided for us, the kids. It's funny looking back at it now, the things I was taking, stealing were quite bizarre and random, though they were always valuable and had a decent resale price. I took guns, radios, cameras, small clothing items like underwear and socks and then sold them on for decent money.

It was the June of 1942, I was 13 then when I first got caught and arrested for breaking into the basement locker of an apartment block not far from our home. When my father found out, he went mad and I got a good beating for doing it and bringing shame on the family. He couldn't understand why I was doing it so I told him I first got the idea from the comic books I read. Fictional stories where crime was exciting, acceptable almost. Things went from bad to worse from thereon in. I ended up in court and was found guilty on ten counts of burglary, they sent me to a semi-correctional school in Indiana.

The next summer, I was at it again, stealing and breaking into property. I never considered that the cops would have my fingerprints and knew my M.O. So they soon caught me and I was sent away again, this time I went to Peru, Illinois.

When you're locked away in these kind of places, you have few options, sure you can become a pain in the arse and argue with staff and question the system, but that does you no good. So I took the other alternative, I got my head down and studied hard. When I was 16 I won a place at the University of Chicago, it was an experimental scheme that was open to gifted students like me.

I enrolled in a bachelor of science course as I wanted to become an electronics engineer. I wanted some independence and to get away from the discipline of home, so I moved onto the campus. It opened up a whole new world for me, I was surrounded by intelligent likeminded people, who taught me lots of things: how to dance and I even learned how to play chess. With my savings which were made up from previous bouts of stealing, I managed to buy a radio phonograph, and began to collect records which were mainly South American or classical music.

The other thing I liked was girls. Boy, I went through them at a rapid rate. I had a lot of girlfriends. That made me fall behind on my studying and academic work. No matter how much I tried, I enjoyed the thrill of committing crime and I started to steal again. A few of the girlfriends I had ended acrimoniously and they called me names and put nasty untrue stuff out about me. I couldn't get it up, and things like that. It was all lies. I started to hate them and I felt that all women looked on me as some kind of joke. I was angry, upset, and felt I needed to get revenge. That forced me look at life, and people differently, I started breaking into people's homes again. Then I connected with one girl, I wanted to impress, and keep her.

I had a lot of savings at the post office from my ill gotten gains. I wanted to withdraw about $1000 as I was going to treat this girl well. It was sometime in June I think (26th) an afternoon in 1946 I went to the post office to cash my bonds. I slipped a revolver, (stolen from another break in) into my pocket as with so much cash on me I needed some protection from street robbers. The damn post office was closed leaving me with no money for my date. So I decided to get it from a break in. I knew one particular house held the funds in cash that I needed. I had barely started when someone saw me and yelled for the cops.

I needed to get away before I got caught, so I managed to get away and ran into another building nearby. I climbed the back stairs and hid. The cops were there quick and I mean quick, pretty soon I was cornered by two of them. I was scared and didn't know what I was doing, I was in shock. So I pulled up the gun and pointed it at them."

At this point there is some confusion about the facts. One of the Police officers confronting Heirens, Officer Timmin, claims that the cornered man pointed the gun and pulled the trigger, however, the revolver misfired. Heirens denies trying to shoot. The second officer (Constant) fired off three shots at Heirens with his Police issue revolver. Heirens didn't want to die and tried to attack the officer, leaping down the stairs towards him. The pair struggled and rolled around on the floor grappling. Enter Abner Cunningham, an off duty Police officer. Seeing what was taking place he tried to help his colleagues. Snatching up a stack of flower pots, he smashed them over Heirens head several times. By the time the third pot had broken, William Heirens lay on the floor unconscious. He was disarmed and taken into custody.

"I know I did a lot of wrong things in my life, but I did the lesser things through necessity. I don't honestly know what caused me to start the nasty stuff, I won't say the word. I admit doing them but you know I've thought about it a lot over the years and still I can't say why? I'd get a thrill breaking into people's homes and on occasions I'd see people asleep in their beds or sat in chairs. I'd get a kick of excitement, euphoria when that happened, I could feel my heart pumping loudly in my chest and often wondered if those people could hear it too.

'I don't think the name calling by women helped me much, I was at a low point in my life and I never trusted people much after that. Did that make me do those things to women? Probably, though I was usually caught during a break-in so I had to silence any witnesses as I didn't want to go to prison. That's what happened each time. I wanted to make a lot of money, easily and quickly, efficiently, if you like. So kidnap seemed easy. I never meant to harm the child, she saw me I know she did. I silenced her there and then. I got scared and decided to take the body away with me. That's all I'll say."

William George Heirens died on 5 March 2012 at the University of Illinois Medical Centre, Chicago, Illinois.

The Lipstick Killers series of crimes impacted on everyone in the city, not least the nine year old Robert Ressler, the man who went on to become an inspirational lead at the FBI Behavioral Science Unit, who took a great interest in the case and its mental and physical effects on the community, if not the city. He resolved to become a cop and fight crime as a result of it.

Another Chicago youngster was to become interested in these crimes He was born into a dysfunctional family environment on St Patrick's Day, 17 March 1942. The family was of Polish and Danish ancestry. The father (John Stanley) was an auto repair machinist and a veteran of WWI and an inveterate alcoholic. The boy was the second of three children; he had two sisters. Being the only boy his father viewed him differently, through negative eyes and often alienated him from the family. He would regularly beat the boy mercilessly for the smallest indiscretions and at times for no apparent reason. On one occasion at least, he rendered him unconscious through the brutality of the assaults. His mother (Marion Elaine) was no physical match for her husband and when she tried to intervene and stop the beatings, she too would suffer. This wasn't all. He was abused by a family friend at the age of nine. The friend was a contractor mate of his father's who would take him for rides in his truck and assault him, fondling and playing with his genitalia. When he was in grade four, he suffered blackouts and it was believed he had a heart condition which meant he could not play active sports. He was overweight, uncouth and often mocked by his peers who often referred to him a 'stinky.' He continually sought validation in all he did, especially from his father; none was ever forthcoming. His ill health forced frequent absences from school and he generally became a bit of a loner in his early school years.

That boy was John Wayne Gacy. When he was six years old, Gacy stole a toy truck from a neighborhood store. His mother made him walk back to the store, return the toy and apologize to the owners. His mother told his father, who beat Gacy with a belt as punishment. The following year, the father was informed that his son had been caught fondling another boy and later, with another young boy, he had interfered with a little girl. The father was angered so much that he whipped him with a razor strop as punishment. After this incident, his mother attempted to shield her son from his father's verbal and physical abuse.

In his early teens he was a 'peeping tom', spying through open curtains at women and children getting undressed for bed. The thrill of this soon disappeared and he wanted more, it was time to move onto physical interaction. He practiced minor sexual assaults on younger children and threatened them with death if they told anyone.

He left the family home and moved to Las Vegas, Nevada, in 1962 where he found work within the ambulance service as a mortuary attendant. He lived and slept in a bed behind the embalming room. Obsessed by the dead bodies he climbed inside a coffin and interfered with the corpse of a young boy, caressing and cuddling it while it was held in the mortuary. He was shocked by his behaviour and enjoyed it, he felt sexually aroused by it. Frightened and confused he left Las Vegas after just three months and went home after his mother pleaded with him to return because his father's bullying and excessive drinking was making matters worse. He enrolled in the Northwestern Business College from which he graduated in 1963.

He found a job as a management trainee working at the Nunn-Bush Shoe Company where he was soon promoted to the position of manager of his department. He fell in love and married a co-worker, Marlynn Myers, settling into a typical life in middle class America. They had two children. In the 1960s he joined the Jaycees - The United States Junior Chamber, a voluntary organisation aimed at providing opportunities for young men to develop personal and leadership skills through service to others. By 1965 he had risen to the position of vice-president of the Springfield Jaycees.

He committed his first sexual rape in 1967. The boy was the son of a fellow Jaycee who had been groomed and tempted back to his home where he sexually assaulted him. Several other rapes and assaults of young boys followed. One victim, Donald Voorhees, reported the assault and his father reported the matter to the Police. Arrested and questioned, Gacy did his level best to satisfy the Police of his innocence. There was no conclusive proof of the attack, however the Police went ahead and indicted him on the charge of sodomy. He hired an employee to beat Donald Voorhees and to try to force him not to testify at the upcoming trial. The assault happened but Voorhees reported that also, resulting in a further arrest and charge. In December 1968 at his trial, he was found guilty of sodomy and sentenced to ten years' incarceration at the Anamosa State Penitentiary. His devastated wife soon divorced him in 1969 whilst he was imprisoned.

In prison he was the model prisoner, and joined the inmate Jaycee chapter. In June 1969, Gacy first applied to the State of Iowa Board of Parole for early release: this application was denied. In preparation for a second scheduled parole hearing in May 1970, Gacy completed 16 high school courses, for which he obtained his diploma in November 1969. He was not told that his father had died until two days after his death. When he heard the news he collapsed to the floor, sobbing uncontrollably, and had to be supported by prison staff. He requested supervised compassionate leave from prison to attend his father's funeral in Chicago, but his request was denied.

He was released on parole after just 18 months and he returned to Chicago and tried to rebuild his life. He never spoke of his past and got on well with those he connected with, neighbours liked him and he was viewed as a pillar of the community where he lived. He met another woman Carole Hoff, a divorcee with two daughters, and remarried. He turned into a sexual deviant, and was actively engaging in wife swapping, prostitution, pornography and to some extent, drugs, since they loosened peoples' morals and made them easier to take advantage of.

Part of his voluntary work in the community saw him entertaining sick children by dressing up as a clown. He would throw parties for his neighbours, and everyone who knew him at this time fell for his charm offensive. Meanwhile, his darker side continued to thrive as his lust for sex with young boys continued to grow. He had moved on from rape to killing his victims, ensuring their silence and protecting his identity. In 1974, he started his own painting and decorating service (PDM Contractors). Keen to make something better of himself he took a real interest in politics and offered the free services of his decorating business to members of the Democratic Party. Around this time, his predilection for sex with young boys and brutality saw his relationship with his wife deteriorate until she left him after he confessed to being bi-sexual; they divorced in 1976. She ensured his reputation and integrity was called into question by alerting everyone to his sexual preferences and his use of violence towards her, supporting rumours that he was sexually assaulting his younger teenage employees.

A teenage boy, Robert Piest, disappeared from the area in 1978. It transpired that he had told his mother he was going to speak to a local contractor about a potential job vacancy he had heard of. That contractor was PDM Contractors. Gacy was a person of interest. The Police were made aware and obtained a search warrant to his home. In December 1978 Police discovered 29 dead bodies buried in the crawl space beneath the house. He was held at the Police station and eventually confessed to 25-30 murders since 1972. In April 1979 he told the Police they would find Robert Piest's body in a lock on the Illinois River. A further four corpses were deposited into the Des Moines River.

Gacy was charged with 33 murders and his trial commenced in February 1980. He claimed insanity and was therefore not responsible for his actions. Several psychiatrists were duped into believing him to have been insane at the time of the murders and now unfit to plead at his trial. Others were not so easily convinced by his behaviour, and the trial went ahead. The jury reached a guilty but sane verdict and he was sentenced to death for 12 of the thirteen murders on 13th March 1980. He spent several years on death row at Statesville Correctional Center where he was executed on 9th May 1994.

That's where I found myself preparing to sit opposite serial killer, John Wayne Gacy. Waiting inside any place of criminal incarceration, whether to speak with a prisoner, or to simply visit, is not a pleasant experience. Naturally, they are full of individuals with sinister intent, angst-filled offenders who all too often claim their innocence and recount establishment cover ups. I recall reviewing my case file on this individual, and no matter which way I glossed it up, it made for a harrowing read. However, I wasn't there to judge Gacy as he had already been tried and convicted of the worst offences imaginable in a court of law in 1978 by a jury of his peers. He now faced execution by lethal injection.

My purpose was different. I was trying to make some sense of his life and identify what had driven him to the crimes he committed. I was about to meet one of the world's most reviled criminals, a man whose name still arouses emotional contempt and strikes fear into some to this very day. Background knowledge and awareness are imperative, so I thoroughly checked every aspect of his life to make sure he wasn't being manipulative or simply lying.

One person who preferred anonymity, whom I met during the information gathering stage of this profile, was a mother who knew the family well. She told me:

"They seemed to have a picture-perfect life. Outwardly, in public anyway, the parents seemed to be a loving couple who cared for and raised a healthy family. John Senior was a hard-working man who held down a good job. They had a good home and Marion, the mother was attentive to the children's needs. Sure, her husband could get a bit handy with his fists, and beat the boy whenever he did wrong, and occasionally his wife for interfering in that process, but they weren't bad people. The boy, he was different from a young age. A nightmare kid, cheeky, foul mouthed, a bully and strange in a perverted kind of way. It wasn't hard to see that he would turn out different to the other kids on the block. He seemed to enjoy time on his own, whenever he played in a group of kids he would cause trouble. Touch some of them in places children don't need to be touched. You know, sexually. A few parents were forced to comment to the family about his inappropriate actions. He'd get slapped and beaten right in front of us for doing those things, but it made no difference. He took the beatings in his stride and then went out and did the same thing again."

His own mother (Marion Elaine) said of him:

"John wasn't a bad little boy, he had all the love and attention any child could want or need. His downfall was his arrogance, he couldn't bear to think he was wrong about anything. He'd challenge anyone if he thought they were wrong. That used to upset his father, a lot. He struggled in relationships for most of his life I think, he never took to girls at all, it was always boys and we suspected his homosexuality long before he confessed to feeling attracted to boys or young men.

His father was a proud man and he tried his best to beat it out of him but despite John being different, his father still loved him, it might not seem that way, but he cared about him no matter how he behaved.

He had his own way of thinking and doing things, he was an achiever, always looking to better himself and be well thought of by everyone who knew him. I think he was desperate to be accepted, he'd often say he didn't feel connected to anyone. Sometimes I think he was too smart for his own good. Really though, he just wanted everyone to like him, I suppose that's what he wanted anyway. I was shocked when I heard what he had done, we all were, he was a son, a brother, a father how could he hurt and kill those young boys? Normal people don't even think about things like that, let alone do them. It wasn't our fault he did those things yet sometimes it feels like we are being punished for his sins. I feel so much sympathy for the families who have lost little ones."

I was disturbed from my thoughts with the clanging of metal security doors, and in walked Gacy. Somewhat older and fatter than I had imagined, he seemed calm and in control. Small beads of sweat were evident on his forehead, and he looked a little anxious. I was surprised that the first words he uttered related to his innocence and insanity.

"I'm innocent, you know that, right? Yes, innocent. It seems curious to me that I was never judged insane by the psychiatrists who interviewed me. I have children of my own, I love children. It seems to me that the state is setting me up, those bodies, they could have been in that house all along, before I bought it I mean. There is no evidence at all that connects me with these crimes, other than the bodies being found under my house."

I reminded him that he had made a full confession and instructed the Police where to find other bodies, so what he was saying didn't add up, and wasn't impressive.

"Those statement were made under duress, extracted from me by force, not physically but mentally. They threatened to do things to family members if I didn't confess. Where's the evidence if I did it? The Feds have got nothing, this whole thing has been framed with me as the patsy."

Again, I explained my purpose and reiterated that I wasn't there to judge him or to condemn him with my opinion. What I wanted was to get to know him, to try to understand his life if he was prepared to share it with me. He smiled when I explained this.

"You might regret that, getting to know me I mean. I have had some very dark times and experiences in my life. I can take you to places in my mind that no one has ever been, only me. Are you prepared for that, prepared to stand at the entrance of hell and to walk through it with me?"

I nodded in agreement and reassured him that I too had experiences that were black and terrifying, so I was mentally capable and strong enough to cope with wherever he led me.

"Do you know what it's like, can you even imagine how it feels to be hated and despised by your own father? Every part of my life as a kid and older, I spent trying to impress him, seeking his validation in everything I did. Not once did I receive it, every time he dismissed me as though I was some kind of amoeba. I desperately wanted my father to love me, to have pride in me, show some interest in what I achieved. All I ever got was beatings and name calling. Look at me, I'm not small, I'm strong and can handle myself. Stinky he would sometimes call me, stinky! What the hell was that all about? Do I smell? Did I smell back then? I must have because other kids called me that name too. I'm asking you, do you think I smell?

I've had a shit life really, it's a problem when no one believes in you or your ideas. The relationships in my life have been bad, no they've been really shit. I've got few fond memories of my relationships with women, they all let me down. It got to the point where I was ready and waiting for them to dump me like an old wreck of a car. I don't think I can be blamed for any of my relationships going wrong, I was a good guy, business people liked me, they asked me for advice. I was well connected in my day. It was with one eye on taking up politics myself. I could have been a great politician, a leader. I have this thing about me, persuasiveness, I can get people to do things. That's the sign of a leader, delegating to others.

Not now of course, I'm long past those days. Politicians know jack all about anything really, they look after themselves, not the people. I was never like that, I put the welfare of others first. Even in here, I reply to every letter I receive, I give the writer the courtesy of reading the letter in full and reply honestly. I get marriage proposals all the time, women wanting to connect with me. Give me a man anytime, there's no agenda with male pen pals.

I'm not a danger to anyone, I never have been, I'm innocent, it's about time the politicians saw sense and took me off death row, what useful purpose will it serve to execute me, I'm an old man. I'm going nowhere. All I want to do is paint, to tell my life story through my drawings and paintings. It's cathartic putting it all into a picture - a permanent image is better than a thousand words. You've asked me if I became another person when I dressed as a clown? I'd say so, the most important thing about being a clown is getting the right balance between being happy and sad. Be too happy and you scare the kids, be too sad and they'll get upset themselves. What you do is look for sympathy, so you play like a clown would, stupidly, then when something goes wrong, a balloon bursts or you pretend to hurt yourself, they come close and give you a hug because they feel your pain. It's not easy doing that, but it was something I could do okay.

The kids loved me as a clown, especially when I got up to my antics, dancing and singing and getting my magic tricks wrong. The mother's loved it too, they'd come over and give me a kiss on the cheek and a hug, that was nice, I used to think. Do you honestly think that if I was what they say I am, a serial killer, a paedophile, that I would be able to control myself around the kids I played with as a clown? Actually, I recall there was a couple of hairy moments, when the kids made allegations against me, saying I touched them. There was no truth in it, attention seeking, and I was able to convince the parents that nothing unusual had happened.

I believe, that when the real day of judgement comes, I'll do okay. A few regrets yes, but nothing major. Right through my life, I've had to fight for everything I got. I don't want or need material things now, just my paints and colours, those are what make John Gacy happy.

A prison guard told me that I looked like a 1950s gangster, hard and tough, someone who looks like they are in control. I like that, the thought of appearing in control. Because I am not, I put on this act, it's like when I put on my clown outfit, I played that role. Well, the person the world sees, me, this is not the real John Gacy. I am anxious sitting here now, I could cry. The real John Gacy sits in his cell alone, thinking about life, his life and how different it could and should have been.

I don't feel any remorse, what am I supposed to be remorseful of? I haven't done *anything wrong. I can't feel sadness or sympathy for the families who have lost a loved one, because it's nothing to do with me. I have enough sadness in my own life to contend with, let alone take on someone else's. Does that make me cold, calculating, evil? I don't know but that's how it is. When I needed someone to tell me it was going to be okay when I was kid, no one did, I had to pick myself up and sort myself out. I had to learn how to cope and lead my own life.*

Sex is an awful thing, wicked. It leads to all sorts of trouble doesn't it? Broken marriages, rapes, murders even. They called me a deviant once, which I didn't like, I'm not one of those types. It's wrong that we get hurtful names attached to us like that. A bit like Stinky, that really hurt me, it made me paranoid for a time. I did get my own back on the boy who first called me the name, let's just say he couldn't smile, or open his eyes for three weeks after. Looking back, I think I needed the right people to respect me, now I'm shut up in this place, where no one respects anyone else. Life is just a game, a never-ending cycle of repetitive garbage. We are born, go to college, leave college, get a job, get married, have kids, grow old and die. Once you realise that, you should try to enjoy the bits in between life and death. Travel is something I didn't do but I would like to have tasted different cultures. I did learn new skills, and every so often I would jump off the carousel of life and take a deep breath and enjoy the moment. Society expects us all to act in a certain way, to abide by rules, the problem is, the people who create those rules are corrupt, they have designed them to protect themselves. I jumped off the carousel of life regularly, and I enjoyed it. Those are the moments to remember before you are sent into the next life. Those are what I'll be thinking about. What a bitch of an existence it's been. What a shit of a life."

He was narcissistic to the end. I didn't think he smelled but it seemed relevant that something as innocuous as that would remain deep inside his mind throughout childhood, adolescence and into his later years. It was significant and showed how he clung onto negative comments about his appearance, that potentially created part of his insecurities. In those opening minutes I learned a lot about Gacy, he yearned for validation from everyone, a need to be wanted, to be liked, and to be respected.

"I wanted to be a cop when I was younger, I couldn't stand to see all those young lives being wasted and thrown away by laziness and wasted on alcohol. I'd have made a good cop I think."

FOUR
Regrets? I Have None!

"I sure as hell made a laughing stock of the Feds." - *Kenneth Harrison*

Every so often you read case files that send a shiver running down your spine, a certain chilling aspect to a crime that causes you to gasp or shake your head in disbelief. This particular case was one of those. Boston has had its fair share of drama over the years, not least the fearsome Boston Strangler, a homicidal maniac who hunted down women and killed them in their own homes. The killer I am about to discuss is someone who also prowled the Cradle of Liberty, though his body count was far greater than the Boston Strangler, and many other well-known killers of this era. Yet he remains something of an unknown in the annals of criminal and serial killer history.

The Paramount Hotel was situated on Boylston Street, Boston. An eleven storey building, it offered cheap and relatively tacky accommodation to its transient clientele. On the ground floor was a bar, popular with a certain type of punter, mainly sailors whose ships were docked in the busy harbour. In essence it was men looking for cheap thrills and sex. The area where the Paramount was located was known locally as 'The Combat Zone', Boston's red light district. The surrounding streets contained adult bookstores, bars and venues such as Club 66, the Naked I, and the Two O'Clock Club.

It was around 6.30p.m., on the night of 28th January, 1966, when a huge explosion rocked that part of Boston. The night sky was filled with dust and flying debris. The pavement outside the Paramount Hotel collapsed and those in the area quickly realized that the explosion had emanated from the basement of the Paramount.

Inside the building, the bar was a scene of utter devastation, as its floor gave way and dropped into the basement. Walls and debris collapsed onto the guests who moments earlier had been enjoying a drink and some adult fun. Some were crushed to death, others suffered terrible injuries as flying glass whipped through the air from windows shattered by the explosion. Outside, shop fronts were in ruin; it was a scene of total devastation. Suddenly further loud bangs were heard, followed by a sharp whoosh as flames shot out of the basement. Fractured gas mains ignited, with flames reaching up to thirty feet towards the heavens adding to the mayhem.

The Boston Fire Department was quickly on scene, freezing cold weather making conditions more treacherous. Hoses froze, and many trapped victims were screaming for help as the burst water mains were saturating them in water. The fire crews bravely battled on to try to get the fire under control and eleven bodies were removed from the aftermath of the explosion.

A full investigation into the fire was carried out, and with the aid of the Boston Police Department it was ascertained that a known arsonist had been in the area on the night in question. He was an immediate suspect, but with other evidence coming to light, a case against him was never conducted. The fresh evidence was damning, as the cause of the explosion and subsequent carnage was blamed on a crack in a gas main beneath the hotel.

The press were keen to speak with survivors and witnesses and one individual seemed more than happy to cooperate. Kenneth Harrison explained how he had been sat in the bar with a female companion for the evening. He told journalists, "I reached out for her hand and nothing was there, she had gone through the floor. Then suddenly I was in the cellar, too, and I could see her arm sticking out of some wreckage."

Four months later, on 24th May, 1966, the body of a little girl, six year old Lucy Palmarin of South Boston, was pulled from the water in Fort Point Channel (site of the Boston Tea Party). A terrible accident said those who learned of the incident. The matter received little or no press coverage and like the explosion was written off as a tragedy.

It was to be three full years before the people of Boston were shocked into a far greater realisation of these tragedies. Matters took a turn for the worse on the 15th June, 1969, in a telephone call received by the Boston Police:

Police: "Boston Police."

Caller: "My dear, at the corner of Washington and Kneeland Street, in a construction site...There'll be a man down in the water, dead...The Giggler...ha ha ha ha ha."

Officers were dispatched to the scene, where they found the dead body of thirty-four-year old Joseph Breen partially submerged in a water-filled hole on a construction site precisely where the caller had described. He had suffered major head trauma that did not appear to be accidental.

Investigations were carried out on the construction site and in the neighbourhood, but with no witnesses or evidence, the Police were left with nothing to work with. There was nothing to connect any of these incidents and the Police cannot be blamed for not linking them. Then on 26th December, 1969, a young boy, nine-year-old Kenneth Martin, left his home in Dorchester, informing his mother that he intended to head into downtown Boston to buy some Boy Scout equipment. A young age for someone to be allowed out on their own and to go shopping in a busy city. His mother quite correctly questioned the need, but he pleaded with his mum to allow him to go. Since Kenneth was a sensible lad and trustworthy, his mother acquiesced and agreed to let him go. It was a decision she forever regretted as this would be the last time she'd see her son alive. When he didn't return home later that afternoon, she called the Police.

A thorough search of the area was carried out and a number of officers from the 'Juvenile' team investigated the case. It was as though he had disappeared without trace and two weeks later every lead had gone cold. Then, out of the blue, a telephone call was received by the Boston Police Department from an individual who informed them that the body of Kenneth Martin could be found under South Station. Simultaneously, they heard from an informant that young Kenneth had been seen in the company of a drifter known as Kenneth Harrison who was known to Police.

A team of officers went to South Station, a vast area of disused tunnels, catacombs, storage rooms and a bowling alley where Kenneth Martin had occasionally worked as a pinsetter. Kenneth Harrison was also known to frequent the bowling alley. The finger of suspicion was now well and truly pointing directly at this individual.

The suspect was arrested the next day in Providence, RI. and whilst travelling in the Police vehicle to Boston he confessed to murdering Kenneth Martin, claiming it was an accident. He didn't stop there, he continued to make other confessions to the Police, claiming to be The Giggler. In November 1970, Harrison was convicted for the murder of Kenneth Martin and sentenced to life imprisonment. Thereafter in 1972, he was sentenced to further life stretches for the murders of Lucy Palmarin, Joseph Breen and Clover Parker.

When I later sat and communicated with this character, he openly talked of his crimes and life:

"Don't you think it's kind of freaky that we have the same surname? Harrison, you know we could be related somewhere down the line. You might be related to a serial killer, how would that make you feel? Pretty shit I'd guess, huh?

"I grew up in Mission Hill, Roxbury. I wasn't stupid you know, went to eighth grade. I was clever, intelligent. I was a cook but finding the right work got tough. You lose your job and you're out on your own. You have to prove your worth to new employers, prove you are capable, that you are someone special. I washed pots and dishes and odd jobs that they needed doing. I got fed up with the way those people (prospective employers) treated and spoke to me, like I was stupid or a vagrant or something you'd scrape from the sole of your shoe. It was wrong, they made me angry and want to hit back at the world.

You know I set that fire in the Paramount Hotel, that was me that did that, I killed those people. I'm not going to tell you how, but I did it, yes, I was responsible. The cops knew because I told them, I confessed but they never took me to court on that one. Maybe because the last time they did after I started a fire in Dorchester, they lost the case and I walked. After the Paramount fire I know they (Police) saw me nearby and they must have read my statements in the press. I was teasing them because they couldn't pin it on me and make it stick. Some of those cops, they didn't like me, they'd blame me instantly when something bad happened and I was close by.

Back in '67, I was employed as a cab driver, it was around May of that year I think, when I picked up, and gave a ride to a little girl, Lucy Palmerin. She was fun. We drove around for a bit, and I talked to her became friendly with her. I parked up and we played around and I was giving her piggy back rides. Next thing I knew I was looking down at water, and I saw her floating in the Fort Point Channel. I guess I must have thrown her in."

He was laughing smugly at this point.

"With Joseph Breen, we had been drinking in a bar, maybe a few bars, I can't remember. We decided to leave and buy a bottle of liquor to take out with us and drink. Joe wanted to get a taxi and told me I had to pay. He'd got the liquor I think, he wouldn't give me a drink, so when we got down into the construction

MIND GAMES

site, I pushed him into a hole. I didn't know it had water in, well maybe I did, but I didn't think it would be that deep. He went under and started gurgling as he came up for air, so I hit him over the head with a rock, every time that son of a bitch came up for a breath I'd hit him on the head again. Then he didn't come up. I waited to see if he was kidding, but I knew he was dead. Then I rang the cops, it was the early hours of the morning around 1.30 a.m. I guess. I said they'd find the body by The Novelty Bar. I was drunk and laughing, giggling so much. I thought it would be funny to give myself a name, that's when The Giggler came to be; the cops tried to steal it from me, saying they invented it, but it was me. Shit like that is important, if cops can lie about stuff like that then they can lie about anything.

It made me feel good killing people, all those people who laughed at me as a kid or for being down and out, a drunk, I got them really spooked being The Giggler. They weren't laughing at me then. The old lady (Clover Parker - 75) I pushed into the water off the Broadway (Bridge). I remember how worried she looked when she asked me if I'd mind linking arms with her to escort her over the bridge. It was slippery outdoors and the bridge was dangerous in those conditions. We got to a certain point and I could see the river below us. It was calling out for me to toss her in, so I did it. She didn't know anything about it, it was quick and I watched, she never resurfaced.

I don't want to talk about my childhood right now, I was able to look after myself. I guess you'd call me the runt of the litter in that neighbourhood. I was always the one the others would pick on, at home, at school, anywhere and everywhere. That's why my life turned out as it did, I never really felt settled at anything. I don't know what respect is, it doesn't exist in my world it's a bit like love, it's just a word. In the newspapers, the witnesses they called me 'pudgy'; that's offensive, I'm not pudgy, am I?

I admit, I had this urge to kill, I still have it now, not all the time just every now and then. The medication helps control that now. I wanted to strike back at society I guess. It came easy to me and I always took the easiest option. Water is so powerful you can't beat it as a way to kill. Did I enjoy killing those people? Of course I did, it wasn't like I was doing it every other day. They (the cops) asked me if I did any more, killings I mean. I can't be sure on that. I don't think I did but my memory is all over the goddamn place now so who knows?"

This was man rightly destined to die in prison. In the end, he couldn't wait for death to come naturally; he committed suicide on 20th April, 1989 at Bridgewater

State Hospital for the criminally insane. The real issue with this case was the disconnect between the crimes. The modus operandi and victim type changed. There were long intervals between the killings and the act itself (with the exception of Joseph Breen) was made to look accidental. Even the explosion at the Paramount Hotel was written off by investigators as a mains failure.

Harrison himself admits the urge to kill and his animosity towards people in authority, those who gave him menial tasks to prove his worth. As a drifter he knew few moral or legal boundaries and the fire starting (arson) charge for which he was taken to court, was one of his first acts at striking back at society. It's highly likely that further offences can be attributed to him before the individual killings started, it's clear his level of criminal activity escalated the longer he was free and able to continue with it.

Another killer who piqued my interest was possibly the worst of his kind. A sexual deviant so devoid of emotion or empathy for any of his victims, that he often shocked himself when recounting what he had done.

Baltimore, Maryland, is a city I like. The inner harbour area is teeming with restaurants of all types where one can sit and enjoy a relaxing or formal meal overlooking the ocean. A diverse, and in the main, welcoming community, it's a great place to visit. It's also a place with a dark criminal history.

In 1995 Joseph Roy Metheny, a wood yard worker with a services background, turned his attention to murder. He claimed it was as a result of discovering his crack addict wife had left him and taken their young son with her. It was the classic 'Dear John' letter. Metheny, who lived in a trailer in the wood yard, had found the note along with a threat not to try and track her down as she would report him to the Police for previous acts of abuse he had carried out on her. Metheny weighed in at close to 500lb and was a well-known pugilist in and around the bars of South Baltimore.

On the night he returned home to the note, he visited a remote bridge close to his home where he believed crack addicts and dealers used to hang out. He was naturally upset that his wife had left him, filled with rage, he felt humiliated that she had run off. He knew that several homeless camps were to be found near the bridge, places where street sex workers looked for business. In truth, Joe had been hanging round these places for several months. On this night he desperately wanted an encounter with the crack dealers, not to buy from them, but to cause them serious harm; he blamed these people for his wife's addiction and ultimately for leaving him. Approaching the bridge, he could hear voices whispering in the night close to where he stood. Looking round, he saw two men drinking and laughing - they were drugged up vagrants. 'They'll do' he said to himself. Joe felt the pent-up anger that had raged within him for much of his life erupt. Pulling an axe from the back of his pick-up truck, he approached the two men and killed them both, chopping at their bodies until they barely resembled human forms. He was arrested, charged and tried for the crime. However, he was acquitted due to the lack of evidence.

His anger never dissipated, yet the lust for killing continued. This time a few months later, it was two local street sex workers, who he lured back to his trailer. Cathy Ann Magaziner (45) and Kimberly Spicer (26) agreed to a threesome. Once inside his trailer, he got the women to undress and mentioned tying them up and enjoying some bondage; they happily agreed. Bound, gagged and unable to defend themselves or scream, he strangled then stabbed them to death. Afterwards, he carefully chopped up their bodies, stripped the flesh from their bones, and stored it in a freezer nearby. The skeletal remains he buried in the woodyard.

It wasn't long before he was again arrested and charged with first degree murder times two. A potential victim had managed to escape from his clutches and ran for help at a nearby gas station. The Police were called and soon Joe was in custody. In December 1996, the Maryland authorities charged Joe Metheny with the murder of two women and he confessed to further murders, including those of another female and a male. He later went on to claim there were at least ten victims.

He had enjoyed the taste for blood and savored the power over life and death that killing provided. He was sick of people laughing at his huge frame, calling him names and abusing him. He was fed up with the sycophants who sucked up to him because of his size, he knew these people were telling tales about him behind his back. With his wife gone, Joe had no one in his life who he genuinely trusted.

At his 1998 trial and conviction, he begged for and received a death sentence. This was later overturned on appeal, and instead he was handed two life sentences without parole. In response, he commented:

"The words 'I'm sorry' will never come out of my mouth, for they would be a lie. I am more than willing to give up my life for what I have done, to have God judge me and send me to hell for eternity."

There is a much darker side to this case, for as well as holding down a job at the wood yard, Metheny had a second occupation - he ran a burger stall on the side of the highway. The human flesh he stripped from his victims was put through an industrial mincer and mixed with animal meat and made into burgers, which he cooked and sold to the public. He called these The Metheny Magic Burger.

When one views the prison images of Joe Metheny it's not difficult to see why so many people were frightened or intimidated by him. If there was an archetypal look for a serial killer, then this man has it. A giant of a human being, he had a propensity to be overbearing and if allowed to get away with it, a bully. Yet the individual who looked at me across a table was anything but that. He was open, honest and commented on his life and crimes as though it was everyday talk.

"I grew up the hard way, in the slum districts of Baltimore, you learn to look after yourself from a young age just to survive. I am a bit of a gentle giant really, at school I tended to be isolated by school friends because of my size, no one wanted to know, especially not the girls. I struggled with relationships because of my appearance and that really got to me.

Then came the older boys, they'd all want to pick a fight with me. I saw it as a way to win over a few of the girls, so when these boys picked on me within a few seconds it would be over; I'd batter them, really batter them. I believed that the girls would see me as some kind of warrior, tough, strong and someone to be around. But they never did, instead they'd turn on me, and start hitting me. I never retaliated but I always got into a lot of trouble from such situations. The teachers would blame me, and the girls would lie and say I hit them. I never did though.

My parents weren't really interested to be honest, they just let me do as I liked. So I did. I studied hard at college then joined the US forces and served in Vietnam for some time. I was popular out there because my fellow servicemen would say they could hide behind me in combat.

Afterwards, when I came out, all I wanted to do was find a wife, settle down and start a family. I picked the wrong woman, she was not what I would call straight forward, complicated would be better, but I won't say bad things about her because she bore me a child and I respect her for that. We seemed to argue a lot, all the time, I was out working hard, delivering pallets for the yard, then coming home at night and she'd often be out of it on drugs, off her face. After a while she wanted more money and more drugs. I couldn't deal with it and once or twice in our arguments I hit her. After that she'd be fine for a few days, no demands, no going out and selling herself, she was a good wife. Then the need for drugs would kick in again. Vicious cycle of death in my opinion. Yeah, I tried it a few times but I'm not a crack head or a druggie. I don't have an addictive personality.

I'll admit that when she left me, my world fell apart. I loved that woman, but she tore our family apart and left me alone and upset. It's hard at the time because you can't think straight, you can't think about what tomorrow might bring. I drank a lot to try to block out what had happened. I blamed the dealers, the people who sold her the crack, they were the cause of our break up. I needed to show them that what they were doing was destroying America. I used to go out to where I knew they'd be and beat the hell out of any I found dealing. It never got reported because they didn't want the cops prying. I literally had a license to kill.

The act itself gave me a sense of power, I got a rush out of it, it's way better than sex. I know it was wrong and I shouldn't have done any of it, but I got a sense of satisfaction from it, I enjoyed it. I can't give you any other reason, I did it because I wanted to and because I could.

You've asked me about my little sideline, it's not my place to go over that, you'll just have to guess. I did strip flesh off the bodies and I feel sad for the families who heard about all the other shit I done or may not have done. Like having sex with a victim's skull, that kind of stuff is personal, it's not for families to hear. I wouldn't want my family to hear any of that shit, and I'd be mortified if they did, but the press guys, they love it don't they? They make up what they don't know. No harm done as I'm not getting out of here, ever. So it's not offensive to me, but for the families, it's shit.

Of course, if I was a cannibal I'd know a lot about the taste of human flesh. I used to sell real roast beef and pork sandwiches, and why not, they were very good. The human body tastes very similar to pork. If you were to mix it together with other meat, I'd guess no one could ever tell the difference.

Oh, to hell with it, here goes. Yes, I killed and butchered their bodies up. I cut the meat up and put it in some Tupperware bowls then put it in a freezer. I buried the remains in several shallow graves in the woods behind the company. There, you have it now. I'm sick, a bad person, I know I need help, but I don't get it. I think about it every day, what I did. I can't say I'm sorry if I'm not, or if I don't feel it. I wrote a full confession once, admitted it all, everything.

I just want to go, I want to die. Inmates here, they say to me, you're the main man, the worst killer ever. I tell them straight. Look, this wasn't about being number one or anything else, it was about me, I don't want books, television films or documentaries about my life, because that's private shit. I did this because I wanted to not for any other stupid reason. Not to be infamous or leave a legacy. I did it because I could. They don't understand it.

So, I tell this to my special visitors only, so you're nothing unique okay. Just recall, the next time you're headed down the highway and you come across an open-pit beef stand, or burger truck that you've never seen before, make damn sure you think about this story before you take a bite of that sandwich, as you never know what it is you might be eating."

He was laughing at this closing remark, but he got no recognition or response from me. I sat deadpan, looking straight at him. He rose, a huge frame of a man, not particularly healthy, just big, fat almost, but certainly intimidating. He winked a goodbye, "Take care, big man," he commented before disappearing through the security doors. I considered for a few moments how frightened his victims must have been when he towered over them in a rage.

Joe Metheny was found dead in his cell around 3p.m. on Saturday 5th August 2017, at the Western Correctional Institution in Cumberland, Maryland. The death was briefly investigated and showed it was of natural causes, a heart attack.

I saw from the brief glimpse I got into his life, how affected he had been by his appearance and size. It had been an issue for him since he was old enough to recall. The only time it was positively viewed was during his time in the US armed forces. Those who knew Joe Metheny speak of a man who could make you laugh, was often good fun to be around, a man who looked after his friends. They also stated he became extremely uncomfortable when women joined others in his company. Almost as if this was a trigger for his behaviour. There were some who explained that whenever a woman was there, his language suddenly became vile and they would often find themselves the brunt of his abusive jokes.

There can be no doubt that his masculinity, the macho image he outwardly portrayed, was damaged beyond repair when his wife left him, taking their son with her. He never got over this, and this seems to be the trigger for more aggressive and abusive behaviour generally. His victims posed no threat and were killed not to silence them but because he felt empowered by the act, it gave him a sense of control.

Interestingly, I recently carried out a social experiment with audiences of volunteers, around two hundred each time. The idea was to identify the world's worst serial killer. I provided profiles on fifty such randomly selected individuals. I offered no criteria for the 'worst' tag. The experiment was carried out ten times in the space of two months. Each time, Joseph Roy Metheny was nominated by participating audiences as the world's worst serial killer.

FIVE
Mommie Dearest!

"Mothers are everything, they nurture, they love, they do what's best for their kids!" - *Henry Lee Lucas*

It's a difficult task getting into the psyche of a serial killer, walking in their shoes and visualizing what they saw and felt throughout their lives. As with all human beings, some are more open than others and allow you access. It's not mind therapy or hypnotism, it's through conversations and listening intently to what's being said to you. Many play mind games with you, teasing you, lying about events to shock and maintain control of the conversation. Others are openly confused about their past, issues in their childhood that added to the confusion of their everyday lives.

Born in Amarillo, Texas, on 10th August 1933, to a young law student who was forced to put him up for adoption, my next case study had an extremely sad and difficult start in life. As children we need to consistently feel loved and supported in all we do. Part of that involves understanding the rules of life, moral and domestic boundaries as well as social interaction and behavioural skills. For much of this we rely on our parents to teach us the correct habits and skill sets to set us up for life in schooling and beyond. We never stop learning and adapt to each new crisis or situation as best we can. Imagine then the confusion in a young child when they are born a boy, but their parents treat, dress and speak to them as a girl. It's a difficult concept to grasp let alone understand. However, this is the situation that faced a sweet young boy known as Charles.

Given up for adoption, he was soon in the system awaiting new parents who it was hoped would provide and care for him. One couple, Fred and Delle Albright had insisted to the adoption authorities on wanting a little girl. It defies all logic that the authorities ignored that fact and instead offered them the opportunity to adopt a little boy. Presumably the adoption took place out of desperation after the couple had been informed they would drop down the list of families awaiting to adopt as a result of turning an offer down. Outwardly, at least, his new adoptive parents seemed like good people, they were well respected in the local Amarillo community and few had anything bad to say about them. Fred Albright owned a grocery store, and his wife was a teacher, so it seemed that Charles was being provided with the best possible start in life.

Unfortunately, as in many instances like this, things were not what they seemed. Behind closed doors things were different. Delle Albright was a strict god-fearing woman who herself had not had the best of lives as a child. She was often left alone to her own devices, using this time to study and explore as young children often do. This led her into trouble in the home as she dressed in her mother's clothing and wore make up at a tender age. She would often naively make up her toy dolls, plastering them in lipstick and foundation, and ultimately, they looked more like circus clowns. Caught in the act by her parents she would occasionally suffer beatings and be verbally abused. Through much of her adolescent life she was denied the opportunity to wear make up at social occasions. Such scars, rather than serve as lessons in life, remained with her as she internalised them and allowed them to fester.

Now she had her own child to raise, those suppressed emotions began to resurface. The suffering and anguish she endured she could now force onto someone else, her own adopted child. Over a period of years, she physically abused her son, not only beating him if he spilled milk or food, she would tie him to his bed for days if she deemed his behaviour bad enough. In the afternoons when he was due to take a nap, he was regularly tied to the bed and denied food. The abuse took other forms, too - he'd be called names and treated like a wild animal. One of the punishments was to lock him in a pitch-black room. Terrified he would sit in the dark and was told not to make a murmur. On other occasions he would escape the family home any way he could. Having been tied up in the rear garden like a dog, he would be left to play there. He was able to slip out of his bonds and would often go to the fence and speak to people walking past the property. Some he asked to lift him over the fence, so he could play. Most left him in the yard, realising the dangers he faced as a small child beyond the boundaries of the family home. When this was discovered, he'd be locked inside his bedroom.

This was cruel, controlling behaviour by a woman entrusted to care for school children, a school teacher with deviant habits and devoid of compassion for the child she had promised she would raise in a safe, caring environment.

Events took a turn for the worse as Delle decided that Charles would become the little girl she had always wanted, the child she could make up and dress in pretty dresses and clothing. He was given his own doll to play with, which in today's terms might not be seen as wrong or odd, but back in the 1930s such behaviour wasn't acceptable, dolls were seen as toys for girls only. He was dressed in girl's clothing and often had ribbons tied in his hair. His aunty would often visit and stay to look after him, she would dress him likewise and lock him in his bedroom to play. This wasn't a child receiving all the right messages. Charles Albright was a child in turmoil, full of angst and desperate to be himself, a little boy.

Despite this peculiar abhorrent behaviour, Delle did love Charles, there were times when she would sit and kiss and cuddle him as though he was a doll. If he hurt himself she was there to make him feel better, it was a juxtaposition of emotions he was forced to endure, loved yet hated. The dressing up as a little girl continued until his teen years, when his life began to change, if possible, for the worse.

In 1946 he had stolen from a local store and was caught red-handed. The Police were involved. His mother was hugely embarrassed by this, it didn't reflect well on her professionally or as a mother. Distraught, she made him apologise to the store keeper and offered to take his punishment, blaming herself for his behaviour. Once again these were conflicting messages the boy was receiving, he could do wrong and his mother would take the punishment; his poor attitude towards other people and lack of discipline became more prevalent now. Despite his mother's best efforts, he was now known to the authorities for the wrong reasons. The level of criminality deteriorated as the acts he committed escalated as he searched for greater excitement with each crime.

As a teenager, his parents bought him his first gun, and soon he was wandering through woodland and fields shooting small animals and birds, squirrels and rabbits. As this act became more banal he took it to new levels, enjoying the thrill of the kill and the power it provided taking these creatures' lives, yet part of him wanted more. He wanted a reminder of the excitement he felt, so he took to taking these dead animals home, and in the basement of their home he started to learn from his mother and a mail order course, the basics of the art of taxidermy. His mother would often help him and showed him how to carefully disembowel the creatures and prepare the bodies for the stuffing process, how to use the correct tools for each act. For hours on end Charles would sit in the basement learning the craft. In his own mind not only was he taking lives, he was resurrecting them. Sadly, no matter how hard he tried to recreate a lifelike pose, the procedure fell flat on its face as his mother refused to pay for glass eyes which would finish off the work giving it an element of reality. Instead, he was forced to either sew the eyes shut or to sew buttons onto the head. It made a nonsense of his best efforts and it was something that was to stick with him.

As a freshman at North Texas State College, Charles found himself an integral part of a student burglary ring. Along with his college peers he carried out a series of break-ins and burglaries on local stores, stealing all kinds of different merchandise. The Police quickly ascertained the culprits and visited the college. The boys went into denial and claimed their innocence. A search of their dormitory rooms revealed a large quantity of the stolen goods under Charles Albright's safe keeping, stashed in various hiding places in his room. He continued to deny any involvement and said he was looking after the property for someone else. The authorities didn't believe his story and he was prosecuted for the crimes, serving just six months of a two year sentence.

His criminal activities continued, as he kept stealing. On one occasion he took $380.00 from a cash register. He was arrested, and the Police later recovered from a search of his property two handguns and a rifle worth over $111.00. Another time, he visited Arkansas State Teacher's College with the intention of burgling the premises. He broke into a girls' dormitory and stole nude pictures he found there.

His behaviour was becoming more erratic and sexually motivated. He caught crabs from a local street sex worker and began referring to women as being dirty, filthy.

At one point he cut the eyes of a friend's ex-girlfriend from a number of photographs and pasted them onto walls and onto the photograph of another girl's face. He began dating Bettye Nestor who worked in the school Presidents office and persuaded her to steal keys for various parts of the establishment, allowing him easy access to continue to steal. He married Bettye on 27th December 1954, who by then was a school teacher. Meanwhile, mainly down to his attitude, he couldn't hold down a regular job. He worked as a hair stylist, was an illustrator for a time then became a bullfighter, the idea of killing and torturing an innocent animal no doubt appealing to him. Nothing lasted, and he was seen as something of a waster.

In 1968 he forged papers from Arkansas State Teachers College, changing grades to As and Bs, first giving himself a Bachelor's degree, and then a Masters, a crime for which he was sentenced in Hunt County to three years' probation. Bettye, his wife with whom he had a daughter, had suffered enough of his behaviour and divorced him.

His criminal activity continued, and he was sentenced to a further year's probation in April 1979 for theft from a Dallas store. The following year saw him imprisoned for theft and damage to another Dallas store, cutting through a chain allowing him to exit the store with a shopping cart full of goods. He was loading this into his truck in the car park when he was confronted by the store manager who called the Police.

In 1981 his mother Delle passed away and he began the search for his natural mother, eventually visiting her. A short time later, he was accused of molesting a nine-year old girl. He denied that accusation but later accepted a guilty plea to stop further issues from rising. As a fifty-one-year old man he was later convicted of having sex with a fourteen-year-old girl, showing his deviant nature to its full and his lack of respect for women in general.

In 1987, his father, Fred, passed away resulting in him inheriting almost $100,000 from their estate. It's also around this time that he meets and moves into the home of a woman called Dixie Austin. Despite his minor wealth he forces Dixie, who worked at a gift shop, to fully support him and to pay all the household bills and expenses. His behaviour was becoming a real concern not only for Dixie, but for his neighbours, as he would often mow the lawn wearing just his underpants. He began to collect books about serial killers, reading them from cover to cover and constantly talking about them.

Then, a street sex worker named Mary Lou Pratt was found dead in a South Dallas street. She had been shot in the back of the head and her remains had been posed to reveal her breasts. The body was discovered by local children playing - initially they believed she was a manikin lying in the road. The body was quickly removed by the authorities and taken to the local hospital where an autopsy was ordered. It was then that medical officials made a terrible discovery. Mary's eyeballs been carefully removed with such care and precision that medical experts declared that whoever had done this to her might well have medical qualifications or be a doctor of some sort.

The finding of a thirty-year-old, Dallas street sex worker in almost the same location a short time later barely made the pages of the press. Rhonda Bowie had been stabbed to death and her body left in the street. Again, her breasts had been left exposed. The Police carried out initial enquiries but with little to go on the case was soon forgotten. A further street sex worker was found dead. This time, the victim was a thirty-five-year old woman who had been shot in the back of the head. The eyeballs had been removed from the body which had been dumped in the South Dallas area.

On 10th February 1999 the body of another street sex worker was found in a South Dallas street. Susan-Beth Peterson was thirty-seven-years old, and as in the case of the previous victim, she too had been shot in the back of the head, and her eyeballs carefully removed.

Less than a month later, a third victim was found in the South Dallas county area. This time it was Shirley Elizabeth Williams, a forty-one-year old street sex worker who was found on 19th March. Her body had been dumped in the block of 2800 Bentley Avenue (Charles Albright lived in block 1000 of nearby El Dorado Avenue, Oak Cliff). The dead woman's eyes had been skillfully removed.

The Police investigation had to go back to the start, with the finding of the first body, that of Mary Lou Pratt. Witness reports were double checked and re-examined by detectives on the case. Officers then remembered a somewhat innocuous incident that now might have some association with the investigation. They recalled a man who used the pseudonym 'Speedee' who had been stopped by patrol officers. In his car was a prostitute. No harm had been caused to the woman who was more distressed by the Police presence than that of the driver's. Officers decided to run a background check on the driver. It was Charles Albright. A short time later, a woman had visited a local Police station and asked to speak to detectives working the murder investigation. She told them of a Charles Albright who would regularly visit her whilst she was at work, asking for dates. She eventually agreed to a date and was to regret it. The man was not all he had seemed, he was aggressive, rough and in her own words, mean. He had told her he was a professional conman. A photograph the Police had of Albright was shown to other witnesses; one woman who had seen one of the murders as it happened identified him as the man she saw kill the victim.

With this weight of evidence, the Police obtained a search warrant and visited the home of Charles Albright. There they had found the same miniature scalpel-type knives that would be used for surgery. These, they surmised, were what had been used to remove the eyeballs from the victims. DNA samples were collected and provided a connection; a solitary pubic hair had been found at the scene of one of the murders and matched his DNA. A number of red-coloured condoms were found in the house, similar to those found in the street next to the third victim.

He was eventually charged with the four Dallas murders. Typically, in an attempt to clear up other unsolved crimes, the authorities looked to (inappropriately in my opinion) associate him with other murders, two in Arkansas, and many other unsolved murders across the region, none of which he was charged with.

At trial the jury convicted him of just one of the murders, that of Shirley Williams, and he was sentenced to life imprisonment. There are those today who maintain his innocence in the Williams case, including Albright himself. He denies any involvement with the murders.

"What kind of person would do that? Why cut out their eyeballs? I don't know the purpose behind it, unless that person thought the woman wouldn't be able to see without their eyes in the next world...That's just ignorant. I don't think anybody would want to keep eyeballs...That would be the last thing I would want to keep out a body. It might be the head or a hand or something if you were a sick artist and you thought the woman was fabulous, you might not want to see that beauty go to waste...If I decided to be a serial killer I'd be a good one, I wouldn't get caught."

It's clear from his antecedents and life that Albright had and still has a fascination with eyes, whether that emanates from his childhood and the use of buttons as replacement eyes or by virtue that he viewed his own blood line mother as a prostitute. According to myth, Oedipus tore out his own eyes after sleeping with his mother. Was Albright somehow punishing her and his adoptive mother through the killings?

For many people who knew him when he was free, he was a nice, kind man who was attentive to the needs of others. Many have good things to say about him, even though his behaviour could at times be shocking, such as the lawn mowing in his underwear. One individual said: "He was so kind and generous and he was always giving our daughters gifts."

Almost all said they couldn't imagine him being a killer. This is the typical reaction of most people when a killer is unmasked, personality is not a good base for judging anyone. The outwardly respectable model is evident in this case, as opposed to the homicidal transient model. There are far too many connections between crime scenes, modus operandi and Charles Albright. Since I'm no believer in coincidence, that the crimes ceased after his arrest speaks volumes. While the state didn't prove the case against him in the murder of three of the unfortunate women, that doesn't, in my opinion, prove his innocence. Nor does it mean he hadn't killed others. Charles Albright will remain a criminal enigma, as a creative talented artist he once painted images of dead women. Why? Was it a subliminal message relaying his guilt?

Undoubtedly, at times Charles Albright felt humiliated by being dressed as a girl by his mother. Historically, there has always been rigid gender roles, so this would have made any child's experiences in such a world all the more traumatic and it is known that humiliation does contribute to violence. This perhaps is a precursor to why these people did what they did. We need to go back into the 1930s once more, to further understand how it affects not only the child but to understand how the stigma continues into adulthood. Often with catastrophic results.

Every so often evil finds its muse and the consequences are horrific and the next case displays this perfectly. Our first offender was born on 5 March 1947 in Jacksonville, Florida. His mother was hardly a paragon of virtue, she was physically and mentally abusive towards her child, and dressed him in girl's clothing from a very young age; she also called him Susan. That in itself must have been confusing to young Ottis Elwood Toole who went on to struggle with his own sexuality. His father, an alcoholic, abandoned the family when Ottis was young, leaving his mother to raise him. Toole's grandmother was there to help raise the family, though how good an influence she was is debatable. She was an active Satanist who exposed him as a child to various Satanic beliefs, practices and rituals, such as self-mutilation, incestuous sex and robbing from graves and graveyards. Her favourite and special name for Ottis was 'Devil's Child'. To be fair to him, Toole's childhood was at best complicated and he also suffered from mild mental health issues, as well as grand mal seizures caused by epilepsy. As a youngster he was infatuated by fire; he went on to become a serial arsonist and was sexually aroused by the intensity of the damage caused by fire. At the tender age of five, he encountered his first sexual experience when he was raped and forced to have sex with his father's close friend. At the age of ten he revealed to his mother and other family members that he was gay, and then began an ongoing episode of child sex abuse where he was raped and suffered incest by family members and their friends. An unhappy child, he left home as soon as he could, and while much of his life between 1966 and 1973 is unknown he claimed he was a drifter moving around the South West United States, supporting himself through prostitution (male and female) and crime.

"The whole sex thing as a kid, that was the pits. You have no control over what adults do with you when you're little, they smile and kiss you fondly, while at the same time they're fiddling with your bits and probing you with their fingers. I

hated every minute of it. Then they'd make you do things to them, it's terrifying. There were times when I wanted to kill myself because of how they made me feel. I'd often run away from home to get space, sleeping in old abandoned houses or huts, I was safer in those places than I was at home. How sad is that?

I'd say we were the family from hell, each one of us was tainted in one way or another. My sister abused me, everyone was at it like it was normal. It made me who I am today, who I turned into, a killer. That's not good. All the devil worship and things like that, it was freak city. I was told there was no heaven, only hell and that if I wanted a good place in hell then I had to commit terrible crimes now in this world. Is that the kind of stuff children should be taught?"

When he was just fourteen years of age, he was accosted and propositioned for sex by a travelling sales man. Toole agreed to go with the man to a remote area where the assignation could take place. Once there, both got out of the car and started to undress. Toole hung back and waited for the ideal moment when he could beat the man up. With the man partially clothed, he knocked him to the ground and kicked at him, he then jumped into the car, and ran over the body until his victim was dead. He was never arrested or charged for this crime and we only have his word that it actually happened.

"The desire to kill was in me from my childhood, I knew I was different, I hated being around women, because they would touch me and make me feel uncomfortable about myself. Ask me to show myself to them, men didn't do that kind of thing, well not all the time. I had few options and had to work my butt to get some money to survive. I did what it takes and hated it. Everyone left me behind, they done me over then dumped me, alone and feeling sad. I guess it got to the point that people abusing you all the time has to stop, so I took that guy down, mowed him down with his own vehicle. I didn't feel guilty or sad afterwards, he was a filthy pervert, he deserved it."

In 1964 he was arrested for loitering, looking to pick up gay men for sex. He moved to Alaska and it was while he was living there that he became a prime suspect in the murder of Patricia Webb in Nebraska, whose body was found shot and hidden beneath a hay bale on April 20th, 1974. She was naked apart from a quilted blue jacket, one of over 140 XL jackets that had been specifically distributed by a Kansas manufacturer as part of a promotion. Webb had been shot six times in the head and four times in the body by a .25 caliber pistol and a .22 caliber weapon. Her mouth had been taped shut to prevent her screaming for help.

It was later claimed that she was to testify in a narcotic case as a narcotics informant. Thereafter information was revealed that the Police had been looking for her for several days, after she'd gone missing from an adult book and cinema store along with $30 in cash, fifty-one pornographic magazines and an office machine. The Police were quick to state that she was not a suspect but had worked at the store when the items had gone missing, and for obvious reasons they needed to talk to her. They were also interested in speaking to an individual, a man, who was seen hanging around in the store on the night in question. Realising he was in the frame Toole moved on, this time to Boulder, Colorado.

There, in the same year, he became a person of interest in the murder of thirty-one-year-old Ellen Holman. Again, he fled, this time back to Jacksonville with the allegations of murder still hanging over him. In his most bizarre act yet, there he met and married a woman who was twenty-five years older than him. The relationship lasted just three days after she found out his true sexual orientation. He later claimed it was an attempt to try to hide his sexuality. In 1978 two evil worlds collided, when Toole met with a man in a Jacksonville soup kitchen. As the two chatted it was clear there was a physical attraction. The stranger with whom he was striking up a relationship was another drifter, his name being Henry Lee Lucas. In those early conversations the men excited one another with deplorable tales and sexual innuendo.

"I'm always getting asked about Henry, he was one tough cookie. Cold hearted, and always looking to make a few bucks at someone else's expense. I never saw anyone as good as him at breaking into a house with no one hearing him. He had a way about him when he was doing that, it made me admire him, respect him. There was that other devil side to him as well, the one that killed all them people, he reckons it's in the thousands and I believe him. He could be laughing with someone one moment then shooting their brains the next. That's the kind of guy he was. No guilt or emotion, as long as he was okay then we got on just fine.

I can't remember how many I killed, I was more of a coward, I needed a reason, Henry did it because he liked it. The quickest and easiest way to kill is through setting a fire in a property, a house or factory or anything like that. It becomes engulfed very quickly and you hear a few screams to begin with, then the voices stop and you can smell it, like cooked ham. I know it's not normal to talk about death like this but it's a fact of life, we are all going to die my friend, even you.

You've asked me if I think my childhood affected me as an adult and turned me in a serial killer? My mother dressed me as a freakin' girl and called me Susan, so what do you think?"

Henry Lee Lucas was born on 23rd August, 1936 in a one room log cabin in Blacksburg, Virginia. He was the youngest of five children to Viola Dixon Waugh, a street sex worker and Anderson Lucas, an alcoholic father. He would claim that his mother regularly beat him and his brothers for no reason, using a wooden plank as a method of inflicting pain.

"At one time I was beaten so badly that I lay in a coma for three days before coming round. Mother would make me sit and watch her having sex with her clients, committing the most awful things before my young eyes. She would encourage me to join in and to touch myself in front of them. It wasn't a good place as a kid. Then she started making me dress in my sister's clothing, like a little girl, she'd take me out into the street and town dressed like that. It was humiliating I tell you. I used to get angry with her about it, but she had no compassion, she didn't care she thought it was funny. As for my father, well he taught me nothing. He collapsed drunk one night, he was outside and froze to death in the cold; typical of his life, always on the edge. I'm not sure what to make of my childhood, it was really shit if I'm honest."

The family and domestic environment that surrounded Lucas was hardly a supportive one. He was never shown a mother's love or the nurturing side of family life. Instead he was viewed as an object of derision. It's saddening to note that he was being publicly displayed by his mother, so many other people must have been aware of what she was doing to this unfortunate child, and at this point in his life he was but an innocent child. Yet no one stepped up to the plate to help or question what was happening, instead they turned their backs on it, allowing it to continue. Their failure effectively created an angry human being who turned into a killer.

During a fight with his older brother, Lucas was stabbed in the eye with a knife, the wound went untreated until infection set in, causing its medical removal. This was an obvious opportunity for the authorities to step in, yet once again they did nothing. He was given a glass replacement which ultimately caused him to suffer further.

"Don't get me wrong, I could look after myself but when you have a whole group of people laughing at you, calling out names because of my glass eye, it hurt

me a lot. I hated them, I hated the teachers who did nothing to stop it. Eventually I would lose it with anyone who looked at me funny. I became a loner not only because of my glass eye, but because I was seen as an angry boy who no one wanted to deal with.

I can't remember the exact date or year, it was in the early 50s when they say I first killed someone, a girl called Laura Burnsley. I confessed and gave the cops a good motive, but it was all bullshit. I didn't kill that girl, if I did I've forgotten there's been so many over the years, they merge together in my mind. I was more of a burglar, housebreak whatever you call it, I got a thrill of being in someone else's space. Going through their personal goods and taking some away with me."

Lucas was committed on a dozen counts of burglary in 1957 and sentenced to four years imprisonment. Escaping in 1957 he was soon recaptured and spent the next two years in prison. On release he went to live with his half-sister, Opal, in Tecumseh, Michigan. Whilst he had been incarcerated, he got friendly with a pen pal, and was engaged to the woman. His mother came to visit him at Opal's, and soon learned of his ambition to marry this younger pen pal. She was enraged and demanded that he drop all relations with the woman and return home with her, she was old and needed him to take care of her. Henry was having none of it and a physical altercation took place, during which she was stabbed in the neck.

"All I remember was slapping her alongside the neck, but after I did that I saw her fall and decided to grab her. But she fell to the floor and when I went to pick her up, I realised she was dead. Then I noticed that I had a knife in my hand and she had been cut."

The reality was very much different, he left his mother bleeding to death on the floor and it was Opal who found her and called the emergency services. She was still alive when Lucas ran off. She later died of a heart attack as a result of the trauma from the injury.

He took off, first to Virginia before returning to Michigan and was arrested in Ohio, where he was charged with second degree murder. A plea of self-defence was rejected by the court and he was sentenced to a spell of twenty to forty years imprisonment. Incredibly, he was released after just ten years, due to prison overcrowding. After a spell of drifting he met with Ottis Toole in Jacksonville.

Despite his relationship with Toole, Lucas was a sexual deviant of the worst kind, his behaviour knew no boundaries. The two men had moved in with Toole's family, and soon Lucas was having relationships with his partner's young niece Becky, who had mental health issues. He took off with Becky and eventually killed her in Texas.

By the time of his arrest in 1983, Henry Lee Lucas had killed several times, alongside his partner in crime Ottis Toole. The arrest was for a lesser crime, the unlawful possession of a firearm. Research of case files indicate that he was denied basic rights, behaviour, that if proved today, would jeopardise an entire case. He was denied basic rights such as bedding and even at times wasn't allowed to wear any clothing. It was the type of bullying he had suffered throughout his life, and explains why, at one point he attempted suicide. Whilst being held, he confessed to three thousand murders during his entire life. The vast majority of his confession was fake, and it was proven that he could only have committed at most six hundred and fifty. To have committed all three thousand would have meant him driving over 350 miles a day every day, an impossible feat as he was incarcerated for many years, during which some of the killings occurred. Forensic psychologists with whom I have discussed this case in depth, claim that this fake aspect of his life was constructed to gain national infamy; like an attention seeking child, he wanted people to take note of him.

"I know I was a heartless bastard, I'd kill them, then keep going until I got bored with it. I felt detached from my body, like it wasn't really me doing those things. Like I say, as though I had left my body. The more you look at them, it's as though that person wasn't dead so you keep stabbing at them and imagining that they aren't real and they're not dying. It wasn't anything to do with shocking the cops or the people, kids or whoever found them, it was all about me, how I felt. It was what I was good at, that's why I'll always be known as the worst killer of all time."

Lucas was convicted of eleven murders, and Toole, when he was arrested, of seven murders. Both men tried to support each other's bizarre kill count claims, but their stories didn't tally or match the facts.

Toole was a sadistic murderer every bit as much as his sidekick, Lucas. One homicide positively linked to him was that of George Sonnenburg, a former lover whom he barricaded inside a house before setting fire to it. Ottis Toole died in prison on 15th September 1996. In 1998, Governor George W. Bush commuted Henry Lee Lucas's sentence to life in prison. He died of heart failure in his cell in 2001.

SIX
Deadly Dames

"We are very much more than man's equal." - *Aileen Wuornos*

If there was ever proof that serial killers are created and not born evil, then our next group of offenders are just that. When you spend so much time studying these people, staring into the abyss and beyond, delving deep inside their minds, listening to them, looking on as you see genuine tears streaming down their faces, you gain an understanding that goes beyond any academic or scientific thesis. It's at such emotionally dramatic times that I recall the victims of the crimes, the families and friends left behind as a result of the killer's work. That puts everything in perspective; in my opinion, serial killers deserve no sympathy based solely on their criminal activities. The monster is generally male. However, generic or typical associations mean little when it comes to serial murder. Killers come from all denominations, a diverse group that comes in all shapes and sizes and from both sexes.

I'm often asked who are the worst, male or female killers - this chapter will hopefully provide an insight into my personal thoughts regarding this question based on actual experience. Holding conversations with serial killers is very much a challenge, it's not like sitting with a friend or for a job interview and chatting through everyday life and professional experience. When such a situation arises, it begins as a game of cat and mouse. The offender is generally reticent to talk openly and teases, dropping in the odd dramatic quote or comment to get some kind of emotional or physical reaction. A cringing face, a shake of the head or a tut or a smile even, might be sufficient to cause them to switch off and disengage.

It's about being non-judgmental and for the duration of the conversation at least, treating the killer as a fellow human being, as an equal. Sometimes that's difficult and it can be awkward listening to the often savage tales of life and death. Sometimes you just want to scream out in horror, yet you can't, you must absorb it, compartmentalise it and lock it away where it deserves to stay, deep in the darkest recesses of your own mind.

Dealing with morbidity such as murder for prolonged periods does affect one's own mind set. Trusting anyone, even family members, becomes a real issue as you see a dark side to everyone you meet. Pretty soon you realize how precious life actually is, yet it's difficult to embrace it when you spend so much of your life exposed to the worst human actions. There is no magical on/off you can flick to suddenly block such traumatic memories. Once you've been told something, it's there, right in your mind; there is no delete key.

From the outset of my journey I wanted to understand why these people did what they did, what was it that created such hatred and angst within them to not only harm or kill a fellow human being but to destroy them? It would be wonderful if we could place them in a box that makes it clear to the masses that 'these are serial killers'. But does that mean the rest of us are 'normal', and what makes the serial killer different from us?

When it comes to moral discipline and rules, we learn those from an early age, the infant stage where we unintentionally soak up knowledge and store it away, recalling it whenever we need it. This pattern continues throughout our lives. As infants we are taught the difference between good and bad, right and wrong, positive and negative, the term evil is something we come to fear, it's never really explained what it means as it is used as a coverall when bad things happen to people. I remember as a teenager seeing an old lady being harassed by two young boys; as I approached to intervene, she snapped at them calling them evil little red devils. The boys were shocked and stopped in their tracks before running off, it was the term evil that resonated strongly with them. They recognised what they were doing was bad. I went to offer my support and help, and half-expecting her to be relieved I too was stunned when she looked to me and said, "fuck off, I don't need your help."

I had a preconceived idea that she needed help. I was wrong, I had typecast her and the situation. Likewise, we are told to respect the laws of the land, that Police officers are paragons of virtue who can be relied upon to always do the right thing. To protect us, to defend us, not to discriminate and to recognise good from bad, with the 'bad' being punished for their criminal behaviour or actions. In most instances, that's totally correct, the Police do a great job, yet as in all aspects of life, there exists a rogue element whose main goal is to look after themselves.

Over the years I've heard countless real-life tales of Police officers lying, falsifying testimonies, dishing out beatings and generally abusing the authority vested in them by the law and the courts. It was indoctrinated in me as a trainee Police officer, to be a good cop you have to think like a criminal. It's a thin dividing line that separates legal from illegal. Every cop who joins a force initially does so with the right intentions, to maintain law and order. Yet over the years they experience heartache, sadness as skepticism creeps in and they begin to view the criminal justice system and people within it differently. Miscarriages of justice, cases kicked out of court, dangerous offenders given lenient sentences, or worse walking free, it all takes its toll. It's easy to see why some cops go feral and use the system to their own advantage.

The first time I heard of the next case was well before any trial proceedings took place, I was researching numerous felonies when I came upon this one. There was nothing outstanding, yet something felt different about it. When you think of the term 'serial killer' a different character type is formulated in our thoughts. Generally, it's a domain dominated by males, who we perceive to be cold, calculating psychopaths or sociopaths. There's an over-indulgence of violence, sexual deviancy, arrogance, narcissism and manipulation, and perhaps in true Hitchcock movie style, an overbearing mother figure in the background.

When seven victims are all men killed in a tight geographic area and the modus operandi seems to match - and the crimes are committed in the space of one year - one begins to speculate that a serial killer with a grudge may be on the loose. Background checks into each victim reveal little, there are no obvious reasons for their execution, no dark dealings or gang type connections, no financial issues or debts that might lead to them being killed. They appear to be people simply getting on with their lives. With that avenue closed, new lines of investigation open up, in particular, the motive or reason for the kill. In serial killer terms one year is a relatively short space of time, some killers stop killing at regular intervals until the investigation or public interest winds down, then starts again. Here the killer didn't leave too many intervals therefore the desire or the driver to kill has never dissipated, indicating a serious grudge or vendetta against men in a specific area. It's at this point that you start to look at potential female offenders, as for a motive, perhaps someone who in their own mind at least, has suffered at the hands of men.

Sounds easy and uncomplicated on paper, but it is rarely that straight forward when working an investigation.

It began on 1 December 1989 when a motor vehicle was found abandoned in Volusia County. Checks revealed that the owner was Richard Mallory, a fifty-one-year old from Clearwater, Florida. He was the owner of an electronics repair shop. Some twelve days later his body was found several miles away, dumped, and wrapped in a carpet, in a heavily wooded area. He had been shot three times.

Six months later, on 1st June 1990, the naked body of forty-three-year old David Spears, a construction worker from Bradenton, Florida, was found on a dirt track road in Citrus County. He had been shot to death, with six bullet wounds to his torso. Identification came as a result of dental records. His truck was later found abandoned on Interstate 75.

Thirty miles south, and just five days later, on 6th June, 1990, the naked remains of Charles 'Chuck' Carskadden, were found a few miles off Interstate 75 in Pasco County. A part time rodeo worker he too had been shot. His badly decomposed body revealed nine small caliber bullet holes to the upper chest and body. The state of the body decomposition meant that no fingerprints could be taken from it nor the estimated time of death.

On 4th August 1990, the decomposing body of a fifty-year old sausage salesman, Troy Burress from Ocala was found in woodland in Marion County. He had been killed by two bullet shots.

The fifth victim was found on 12th September, 1990. Charles Humphreys, a fifty-one-year old former Air Force major and Police Chief was found in Marion County. He had suffered multiple gunshot wounds to the head and body, he was fully clothed leading investigators to think this might be a different killer, since he was also a child abuse investigator for the state of Florida. It was initially thought this might be a clue to the killer's identity. His car was found in Suwannee County.

Peter Siems was a retired merchant seaman who spent much of his time committed to Christian ministry outreach work. His car was found in Orange Springs on 4th July, 1990. Witnesses claimed to see two women leaving the vehicle after it had crashed off Interstate 15. The women were arguing with each other and threw empty beer cans into roadside bushes. The emergency services were called to attend and came across the two women nearby. They questioned them. However one of the women became angry and cursed them claiming to know nothing about any crashed vehicle. They allowed them to leave the area. The vehicle was traced to Siems, whose body was never found.

The witness who had seen the two women crash Peter Siems's car was able to help Police come up with a composite sketch, which was released statewide.

Then, on 19th November, the body of sixty-two-year old Walter Jeno Antonio, a part time security guard and a member of the Reserve Police, was found partially naked in Dixie County. He had suffered four shots to the back of his head. His car was found five days later in Brevard County.

In addition to the composite sketch, fingerprints found on jewellery removed from the bodies of the dead men were linked to a known offender, a convicted street sex worker known as Aileen Wuornos. She was arrested while drinking at The Last Resort bar, a biker bar on 9th January, 1991. The Police had tracked her down to an area of Port Orange, Florida where a task force took over to consider if she had had contact with a woman known as Tyria Moore. The woman had in fact been her lover. It was when Moore had seen the sketch released after the Siems murder, and its likeness to Wuornos that she decided she wanted nothing more to do with her and left her a few days before her arrest, returning to her sister's home in Pennsylvania. The break-up of the relationship deeply hurt Aileen who tried to drown her sorrows and did little other than drink until the time of her arrest.

Moore was tracked to Pennsylvania and arrested in connection with minor charges against her criminal alias, Lori Grody. Wuornos trusted her girlfriend implicitly and never once thought that she would betray her. Moore had other thoughts and soon she was beginning to reveal information about Wuornos. She agreed to work with the authorities in obtaining confessions from Wuornos in exchange for protection from prosecution relating to the murders. She agreed to give evidence against Aileen in court. In recorded telephone conversations, she got the friend she was betraying (for the right legal reasons in her own mind), to confess to the murder of Richard Mallory. A week later, on 16 January 1991, Aileen Wuornos had verbally confessed in such conversations to six of the seven murders.

During subsequent interviews with Police, Wournos claimed that the murders had been in self-defence and released Moore from having any involvement in any of them. Aileen Wuornos was then charged with the murders. When it came to the first murder, the Richard Mallory charge, she claimed that he had raped her, and she had killed him while defending herself with the .22-calibre gun she had with her. It was later revealed, but not at trial, that Mallory was known to be a violent man who frequented sleazy clubs and bars, strip clubs and often used the services of street sex workers. It was also identified that he was on the verge of bankruptcy and had spent some time in a mental institution following a charge of attempted rape. Was Mallory's treatment of Wournos the trigger for the murders that followed, the tipping point in her life?

"I told the cops several times that I was raped, I even visited the station and reported it, not with Mallory but with the other men. Those bastards raped me, beat me and paid me nothing. The cops weren't interested, they didn't want to know because it was Aileen Wuornos. There comes a time when you can't take any more shit, you have to stand up for yourself, earn respect. That's what I did. I defended myself.

Don't ever portray me as some man-hating lesbian bitch who killed just to rob, or robbed to kill. That's rubbish. It's like a fairy tale and is a long way off the truth. People peddled that shit for a fast buck. What I did, what they say I did, it went much deeper than that. My life is a joke, no one ever listened to me, no one cared, no one wanted to know the suffering and pain I had. Now, the bastards have to listen, not because they give a shit about me, it's their own self-preservation they are worried about. They'll all lie until they're sick. Film rights, selling stories and personal details, lies, about me and my life to movie producers and for their books. They have made me into a monster, truth is they created this fucking monster, you all did, I am a product of you all. Now when you are confronted by your sins, you don't want to fucking know! The movie will be a downright lie. The truth will hurt them that's why they've made me out to be something I'm not.

You know, by definition, I am not a murderer. Murder by law has to be willful killing. I'm not even a serial killer. Yes I've killed a series of men, every one of them deserved to die, they were attacking me, they wanted to hurt me for their own needs. So what did I do? I defended myself. None of this was premeditated, my only planning was to go out and get some money through selling myself to them. I didn't wake up one day and think I'm gonna go out and kill a guy today.

I've been treated like dirt all of my life, no one cares about Aileen, just my closest friend, she cares. Everyone is out to make money off me because I'm notorious, I'm a female serial killer, America's first they say, well that's a fucking lie as well. I hope one day civilisation will recognise it isn't civilised at all. My entire life has been tormented by evil, now they call me evil. I was a woman defending herself that's all. I know not all men are evil, but most have it in them to be like that where sex is concerned. I think about dying and going to heaven, I've spoken with my maker, he understands. I want it done with quickly, so these bastards can't make another penny from me. When you put this in your book, your analysis of me, will you tell it as I said it or will they make you pull it and peddle more lies about me? I hope you'll say it as I meant it to sound. They've fucked me over.

Do you know, I was physically sick after I did what I did, defend myself. Yes, me the monster, Aileen Wuornos, vomited at the thought of killing someone. It didn't make me feel good about myself or proud, it gave me nothing but a feeling of emptiness that those men, some of them had families and they were cheating on their wives and kids. Liars, deceitful. Why would you do that if you genuinely loved someone? It's the road to hell I can tell you, it's only gonna end in heartache, and it did. They were trying to attack me."

Imprisoned, investigators began to sift through her antecedents and life, and it was a harrowing tale that continues to shock many who hear it. Originally born Aileen Carol Pittman, her parents, Leo Dale and Diane Wuornos, were highly dysfunctional. Her father was a known psychopath and a convicted child molester, who eventually committed suicide. Diane Wuornos literally abandoned Aileen and her brother, who were adopted by her maternal grandparents. It's a sad indictment of society to learn that her grandfather was also a well-known predatory paedophile. From an early age he sexually abused Aileen. He encouraged her to have regular sexual relations with her brother. At the age of nine, schoolteachers became aware that she was exchanging sexual favours with pupils for drugs and food. Instead of addressing this, they did nothing about it.

By the time she was fourteen, she was pregnant and was told to leave home and move into a residence for single mothers. When the child was born it was immediately removed from her and given up for adoption. Returning to her grandparents' house, she was often forced to sleep rough. In the middle of winter she'd sleep in abandoned motor vehicles and even made a shelter in nearby woodland where she slept. Adult and local parents were aware of the situation and her plight, yet no one did anything to help or support her. This was a child who from a tender age had been abandoned by her mother, prostituted and pimped out by her grandfather to all and sundry. A little girl who at no time in her life had encountered genuine love or care. The child she bore was then removed from her causing further emotional issues. When her grandmother died, she became a burden to the grandfather, who threw her out on the streets, having to provide for herself, she operated as a street sex worker.

It goes hand in hand that through the life forced on her as a child she became involved in criminality and fell in with all the wrong people, associates who sexually abused her and sold her favours to others. In 1974 she was arrested for driving under the influence and for disorderly conduct. She failed to appear at the hearing.

It was in 1976 that she met wealthy 69 year-old yacht club president Lewis Gratz Fell. Seeing an opportunity to better herself she wholeheartedly threw herself into the relationship. They married the same year. It was to be a brief marriage, as her anti-social behaviour was innate and she couldn't control it. She claimed her husband was violent towards her and on one occasion she beat him with a tyre lever. Hospitalised as a result of the attack, he pressed charges against her then filed for divorce.

By 1981, her crimes were escalating in nature, she was involved in the armed robbery of a convenience store. Arrested and remanded in Police custody, she was sentenced to prison and released in the June of 1983. Further crimes occurred over the years that followed, drunkenness, deception, theft were all common in her behaviour pattern, as she had no respect for authority or other people's possessions. The sad fact of the case is, she had little respect for herself. A named suspect in the case of the theft of a revolver, in 1986 she was charged with car theft, showing false identification, resisting lawful arrest, and for threats with a firearm. The Police found a .22 pistol and spare ammunition she had hidden in the car. It was around this time that she began a lesbian relationship with Tyria Moore, they remained a couple until it ended in 1990.

During the trial and afterwards a number of serious allegations of Police misconduct began to surface. Wuornos claimed that Tyria Moore and a number of Police officers involved in the investigation, had been making movie deals with producers and authors wanting to document her life.

One Marion County Police officer claimed that he was harassed at work following the discovery that several officers within the force had been planning to elicit the help of Tyria Moore in obtaining full movie rights to Aileen's story. A state attorney's report supported this claim, however; since no signed documents were ever located or evidence found that money had been exchanged, the repercussions were deemed minor. A Police officer investigating these allegations, received a threatening note, and his home was burgled, with case files relating to Aileen Wuornos and investigator files destroyed. Nothing else was disturbed or taken during the crime. The Police didn't take the crime seriously, claiming it was deliberately set up to reflect badly on them. Aileen Wuornos was handed six death sentences for the murders she had committed. Closer to her execution, she rescinded every previous statement and was clearly now in a mentally agitated state. She denied her crimes were in self-defence and agreed with every aspect of the prosecution's case. Something inside had snapped, and it was clear she did not believe what she was saying. It was like a carefully rehearsed act, and distressing to see a woman who had been so outspoken about her defence suddenly collapse and give in to the system she constantly defied. On 9th October, 2002 at the age of 46, Aileen Wuornos was executed by the State of Florida through lethal injection.

No matter which way one reviews this case, it sits uncomfortably on the social conscience. On the one hand, Aileen Wuornos deserved to be punished for her crimes, she killed innocent men and left families with a lifetime of devastation as a result of her actions; for that she warrants no sympathy. Yet on the opposite side of the coin she was consistently failed by a system that refused to help her as a child and teenager when she most needed it. A system that declined to accept responsibility for its failings, yet saw opportunities to abuse her further, to glorify and sensationalise her crimes without her knowledge. That she changed her plea from self-defence to premeditated murder at the last ditch says more about the system failures than it does Aileen Wuornos. From family members, through to school teachers, medical staff, Police officers, lawyers, prison guards, courts, the press, alleged friends, lovers, she had lost trust in the human race. Most had deceived her, independently used her at every stage of her life. She must have been left with a feeling of emptiness, alone and despised. Ultimately, in the end, she had no one she could rely on, or to turn to.

We can take no satisfaction from any aspect of this investigation, it is an abject lesson about systematic failures of the establishment. A place where support networks are meant to engage and help vulnerable people. That Aileen Wuornos was vulnerable as a child and later in adulthood, is without question. The more serious question is why these obvious failures were consistently allowed to happen over a period of five decades? More worrying is the question, are we denying a child somewhere a voice because we can't be bothered to listen or act, or have we pinned a label to their character or personality type thus blocking them access to support? Is it happening to a child somewhere right now? We can only hope not.

As a serial killer, Wuornos displayed some of the more common characteristics we expect to see in such a person during their life time. Dysfunctional childhood, child abuse of the very worst nature, bullying, alienation, lack of love and compassionate support, lack of discipline, no moral boundary awareness, addictive personality, silenced, ostracised, labeled, ignored, accessibility to criminal behaviour from a young age, rewarded for morally inappropriate behaviour, lack of respect for adults and persons in authority. Indeed, if one can imagine a childhood so harrowing and a life devoid of love, then this it.

Our next killer is a genuine 'black widow'. James. E. Goodyear, was a Sergeant in the United States Air Force, a proud man he was physically fit and strong. In June 1971 he returned to his family home in Orlando, Florida, from a tour of duty in South Vietnam. Within weeks of his return he began experiencing vomiting, tiredness, nausea, dizziness and general feelings of weakness. His condition deteriorated over a period of weeks and he was hospitalized on 13th September, 1971. Under the care of Dr. R.C. Auchenbach he informed him that he had been suffering from these symptoms for about two weeks. Over the three days that followed, despite his best efforts, Dr. Auchenbach was unable to save Goodyear's life, and couldn't determine the cause of his condition. Goodyear died as a result of cardiovascular collapse and renal failure.

At the time of his death, no toxicological tests were performed as there was no reason to suspect foul play or poisoning. Living in the same house as Goodyear and his wife was a woman by the name of Debra Sims. She was to later tell the authorities that Goodyear had grown progressively more ill, and she had witnessed him suffering severe hallucinations. The matter was quickly forgotten and life for the household moved on. His wife, Judy Welty, and their son were now alone. Fortunately, Goodyear had taken out a good life insurance policy, meaning that on his death his surviving wife would receive a handsome cash payout. To commemorate her late husband's name, she legally changed her surname to 'Buenoano' which in corrupted Spanish means 'Good year'.

The couple had a son, Michael, who was born on 30th March. In 1979, he suddenly fell ill, his symptoms included paraplegia. His mother did her best to care for him and on 13th May, 1980, she took him out canoeing. During the time on the water the canoe rolled and overturned, trapping Michael in place. Unable to set himself free due to the weight of his heavy arm and leg braces, the boy drowned. Again no suspicious circumstances were identified and he was buried without any Police investigation. Once again, Judy received an insurance policy pay out and moved on with her life. At this stage she had collected around $240,000 in payouts.

By 1983 she had moved on sufficiently to pair up with another man, John Gentry. The same year, he was severely injured when his car exploded outside the family home. It was clear that the explosion was anything but accidental, and soon the Police began to investigate the circumstances. They spoke with Gentry who told them he had no known enemies and couldn't think of anyone who would try to harm him. Shortly after the explosion, he had contracted a cold and began taking Vicon C vitamin capsules given to him by Buenoano. Soon he began to suffer severe convulsions, nausea and vomiting so decided to check into hospital where he recovered. Upon returning home Buenoano continued to give him Vicon C, once again the chronic symptoms returned.

On hearing this the suspicion of the detectives was immediately aroused and they began to look at the spouse, Judy Buenoano, carrying out background checks on her. They were surprised when discrepancies in her life story began to emerge. They ascertained that in November 1982, she had told friends that Gentry was suffering from a terminal illness; no such illness had ever been diagnosed for a perfectly fit and healthy man. Police became more suspicious when he told them he was being cared for by Judy who was giving him vitamin pills to aid his recovery. The officers asked to see the pills and were handed the bottle to take away for examination. The results were shocking; they contained traces of arsenic and formaldehyde. Judy was clearly trying to poison her partner.

As a result, the Police requested the exhumation of the bodies of James and Michael Goodyear, who they suspected might well be victims of poisoning too. They were initially refused permission to proceed as further evidence was required.

However, Goodyear's body was exhumed in 1984 and examined by Dr. Leonard Bednarzyck. He determined that arsenic levels in the liver, kidneys, hair, and nails indicated chronic and acute exposure to the poison.

Further investigations into her past revealed some shocking findings. The death of a previous boyfriend, Gerald Dossett, in 1974 was deemed to be by natural causes. However, he had suddenly fallen ill, complaining of nausea and sickness and dying the same year. Then in 1978, her boyfriend Bobby Joe Morris had died suddenly. As before, no one suspected foul play and the matter was never formally investigated. Buenoano had moved in with Morris and passed herself off as his wife to purchase insurance on his life. Morris died after exhibiting similar symptoms to James Goodyear. Morris's remains were also exhumed in 1984 and toxicological examinations revealed acute arsenic poisoning to be the cause of death.

In August 1984, Judy A. Buenoano was indicted for the 1971 murder of her husband, James E. Goodyear. She was later convicted of first degree murder in November 1985 and subsequently sentenced to death. She was then convicted for the murder of her son, Michael.

At trial the prosecution called Dr. Thomas Hegert, the Orange County Medical Examiner who performed the 1984 autopsy on James Goodyear, who testified that death was the result of long term arsenic poisoning. Two other witnesses gave evidence, stating that Judy had often laughingly commented that she was lacing her husband's food with arsenic. One of them also claimed that Buenoano, after hearing about an argument between the woman and her husband, suggested to her that she should increase the life insurance on her husband, and then kill him. Poison, such as arsenic, could be readily purchased at the grocery store. It was damning testimony.

Prosecutors in Colorado also found evidence that she had poisoned Bobby Joe Morris in 1978, however they did not proceed with charges because she had already been handed the death penalty for the murder of her husband in Florida.

She appealed against the death penalty, claiming that her legal representative had failed to properly investigate her background and mental health. She claimed that she suffered an impoverished childhood during which she was transferred from foster home to foster home because of her mother's death, but also that she suffered abuse from several of the foster parents.

To support this claim she provided testimony from her family members. Her brother, Gerald Welty, claimed that their mother was hospitalised for prolonged periods of time with tuberculosis and as a result of that illness had died when Buenoano was only three or four years old. He went on to state that their father was hospitalised with injuries sustained during World War II. As a result of those factors, Judy Buenoano was separated from her siblings and moved around among families during her childhood.

Her father, Jessie Welty, declared that he was constantly ill during her childhood. He went on to explain how the family were very poor, and that his daughter never enjoyed a 'real' family life.

Judy's cousin, Jean Eaton, claimed that her (Judy's) childhood was terrible. She said that she had once overheard her parents discussing how Judy had been sexually abused as a child. Judy herself claimed that once her family split up, she was sent to live with a series of different families. At one time she lived with the Cross family in Temple, Texas. That family she insisted, paid her father $500 to allow her to live with them. There, she was frequently beaten with a rubber hose. She added that another family who adopted her, the Purselys, sexually and mentally abused her.

She believed she should have been psychiatrically evaluated before trial, but that never happened. Her petition asserts that her lawyer knew she had grandiose delusions. She argued that mental health mitigating factors was confirmed by several psychiatrists. Dr. Pat Fleming performed a psychological evaluation on her but was not allowed to testify during the district court's evidentiary hearing. It was her belief that Dr. Fleming would have testified that she exhibited signs of paranoid schizophrenia, and organic brain damage; that her background and childhood caused psychological problems which when combined with her cerebral dysfunction significantly disrupted her thought processes; and that she met the criteria for Organic Personality Syndrome evidenced by persistent personality disturbance, recurrent outbursts of aggression or rage, impaired social judgment, and paranoia. Another specialist, Dr. Robert Phillips, raised the possibility that severe head trauma during her childhood could have caused brain damage.

"I don't know that I did any of the things they say I have. I was a good mother and wife. My son, that was a terrible accident, it broke my heart when he passed away. I'm not frightened of dying, but I hope that someone will understand that the circumstances of my life were not normal. I was sexually abused as a child, not by one family but by many, that leaves mental health problems that are insurmountable. You wouldn't understand, but as a child or even as an adult you never get over those things. It makes you permanently angry, upset, you want revenge."

At this point I had confirmation that she was not being honest with me. Unbeknown to her, I have that childhood experience behind me, yet, not once have I sought revenge or felt permanently angry. I also know that the problems are not insurmountable. Assessing her claims from that perspective left me in no doubt of her guilt. I found it reprehensible that she was trying to use childhood sexual abuse as an excuse for her behaviour.

"I have been maligned for taking out exaggerated life insurance on my family and people close to me. Is that not normal behaviour, we need to be able to feel comfortable in the thought that others are provided for in the case of early death. I bet you're insured?"

I confess, the irony of the last comment almost caused me to laugh out loud.

"The one thing I am looking forward to is seeing the face of our Lord. I'm ready to go home now. I've had enough of this hell. Imagine feeling the warmth and love that he projects to all, even to those who have sinned. I believe it will be a

joyous occasion when I'm entering heaven. I will feel a sense of fulfillment and the knowledge that this physical life was little more than a rehearsal for the eternal life and happiness that awaits."

Throughout her life she displayed classic psychopathic and narcissistic tendencies, a lack of any real emotion or understanding of the repercussions of her actions. As an adult, everything was about her, Judy. Growing up in a poor and dysfunctional family environment, she must have felt abandoned when she was fostered out to different families. Her stays were brief and she received little parental love or attention. It is likely that she yearned for security through financial wellbeing. In her own mind, love and emotional wellbeing would possibly accompany financial security. It never did, and so family and her partners became expendable, nothing but objects from which she could attain wealth.

There can be little doubt when one looks at her court appeal document that she was intelligent with an understanding of manipulation, since she seeks compassion from the courts by raising childhood trauma she may or may not have suffered. From my own perspective, I feel this was used simply as a ruse to escape the death penalty. I found it difficult to comprehend that she could be so dismissive of her son's death, gradually poisoning him. Then to speed up the process without raising suspicion, she drowns him in such an awful manner. It is truly cold, calculating and shows premeditation. It's despicable that a mother could do this.

Despite her best efforts, Judy Buenoanos' appeals failed, and her final days were spent crocheting blankets and baby clothes. She was one third through the crime novel 'Remember Me' by Mary Higgins Clark when she died. She was executed by the electric chair at Florida State Prison in 1998. Few will mourn her passing. Her body was cremated after the execution.

SEVEN
Smooth Operators

"If I was to be honest with you, then I'd say we all have the capacity to be serial killers. My world is complete when I'm in that kind of mood." - *Ted Bundy*

Every so often, a serial killer emerges that causes us to take stock of our shallow understanding of the phenomenon. These are killers who are far removed from the media invented monster, individuals who are charming, pleasant company and have an incredible way of disguising their manipulation of others. Over the years, hundreds of criminals, serial killers, murderers and felons of all types have tried to manipulate my communications with them. They will resort to every means possible to gain control, using flattery to win over the subject of their attention. I recall one offender informing me:

"You know more about murderers than anyone I know. I've heard killers say that about you. Respect, nobody inside will fuck with you. The real deal, the guy who gets inside our heads."

Whilst I enjoyed hearing such praise, I knew it was delivered for a number of reasons, primarily to win me over and therefore make me like the offender. It enables the offender to manipulate the conversation, particularly when discussing their crimes. They also over used my Christian name (Paul), in an attempt to make the discussion more personal. To an extent it works, however, try to flatter them and you are initially rebuffed. They trust no one, especially cops or ex-cops until they get to know them to a degree they feel comfortable with. When you meet a serial killer who shakes your hand firmly, looks you straight in the eye and asks what he can do for you, it forms a very different introduction to those conversations.

"My name is Theodore, but most folks around here call me, Ted. You can call me Ted, I'm fine with that. How's your day been so far, how you liking this great country of ours, America, it's full of life isn't it? Oh, it's full of death too."

Theodore Robert Cowell was born in Burlington, Vermont on 24th November, 1947, to a single mother, Eleanor Louise Cowell. To avoid a family scandal, Ted was raised by his grandparents as their own child. His grandfather wasn't the best role model for little Ted, and regularly abused him. During his formative years he was lied to by his family who told him that his mother was actually his sister. Eventually, when Ted was five years old, Eleanor had taken enough of the deception and the abuse and ran away with her son to live with cousins in Tacoma, Washington. There, Eleanor met and married cook John Bundy, who formally adopted the young boy giving him the Bundy surname.

Ted had a lifelong dislike of his step-father and later described him to a girlfriend saying he wasn't very bright and didn't make anywhere near enough money.

Years later, before his execution, Ted Bundy came across as the average type of person you'd bump into in any street in any place across the world. His eyes were focused, and he had an air of superiority about him, someone who cared about his appearance and took care in grooming himself. Appearance meant a lot to Ted. His good looks served him well in selecting and taking control of his victims before he killed them. Innocent women who were in the wrong place at the wrong time. I am unable to get that thought out of my mind, this man killed at least 30 poor souls, potentially many more. His charm offensive was nothing but a facade, beneath that sham of a veneer lay a sadistic necrophile killer. A man who was an expert liar.

In 1965, he graduated from High School in Tacoma, Washington, and entered the University of Washington (Seattle). Within a period of two years he amassed 190 credit hours and a degree in psychology. This was a bright young man with a great future ahead of him. By 1972 he was working for Kings County Law and Justice Planning Office in Washington, tracking down missing, habitual criminals. The following year, in September he entered Law School at the University of Puget Sound in Tacoma, nine months later he abandoned his education to work in the Emergency Services Department in Olympia.

The first known attack attributable to him occurred in January, 1974, an assault on eighteen year-old Karen Sparks, a student and dancer at the University of Washington. Bundy broke into her apartment, where he bludgeoned her to a state of unconsciousness using a metal pole from her bed frame. He then sexually assaulted her with the same object. Such was the severity of the attack that it left her in a coma for ten days and with lifelong physical disabilities. Let alone the mental scarring she was permanently forced to live with.

His murder spree began, when a month later he killed Lynda Ann Healy. It was the same modus operandi as in the Sparks attack, Bundy broke into the young woman's apartment in the early hours of the morning. Once inside, he knocked her unconscious, then dressed her body before carrying it out to his car. Lynda Healy was never seen again, though part of her skull was discovered years later at one of Bundy's body deposition sites.

Changing tactics, he began to pick up young female student hitchhikers and offer them a lift, or to watch car parks for lone women, who he would approach wearing a fake cast and ask if they would help him put something in his car.

He would bludgeon his victims unconscious, before binding, raping, and killing them. Finally, he would drive their bodies to remote woodland where he would dump them. His sadistic ways didn't stop there, very often Bundy would revisit the deposition sites and have sex with the decaying corpses. In a number of instances, he decapitated his victims and kept their skulls in his apartment, occasionally, through his own admission, sleeping with them.

"The ultimate possession was, in fact, the taking of the life, And then ... the physical possession of the remains. Murder is not just a crime of lust or violence. It becomes possession. They are part of you ... [the victim] becomes a part of you, and you are forever one ... and the grounds where you kill them or leave them become sacred to you, and you will always be drawn back..."

The lust for killing overwhelmed him and the murders become more frequent, and he was killing at a rate of about one victim a month. The investigating bodies saw patterns emerging, certainly in the victim type. His predilection was for young, slender women, with dark brown hair with a centre parting. The women bore a similarity to his ex-fiancée, Stephanie Brooks. In January 1975, Bundy was on his travels again, this time to Colorado where he abducted and murdered Caryn Campbell in her hotel in Aspen.

On the night of 18th August, 1975, he was seen driving around suspiciously at 2.30 a.m. by a Police officer in Utah, who demanded he stop. He drove off at speed but was quickly caught and arrested for evading a Police officer. Among his possessions that night were a ski mask, a pair of handcuffs and pantyhose with eye holes cut out. Less than eight months later on 1st March, 1976, he was convicted of kidnapping Carol DaRonch in Utah. He was found guilty and sentenced to prison.

The same year he was charged with the murder of Caryn Campbell and was remanded in custody. Before the trial he somehow managed to escape from Pitkin County Courthouse and went on the run for ten days before the Police caught him.

After being imprisoned for murder, he again managed to escape, this time from Glenwood Springs jail and sought temporary sanctuary in Denver, Chicago, then Michigan. Arriving in Tallahassee, Florida in January, 1978, where he rented a room in a boarding house posing as a student. Just a week later, two students, Margaret Bowman and Lisa Levy were killed in Chi Omega sorority house in Tallahassee. Escaping from the college campus Bundy then killed Cheryl Thomas in her home.

The following month, 12 year-old Kimberly Leach, was reported missing from her junior high school in Lake City, Florida.

The Police eventually caught up with him in February, 1978, after he was stopped while driving a stolen Volkswagon Beetle in Pensacola, Florida. Evidence linking him to the Chi Omega murders was found, resulting in him being charged and tried for those crimes. During his trial for the murders of Lisa Levy and Margaret Bowman, he elected to represent himself, despite having five different attorneys capable of doing so. Filled with arrogance, Bundy was insistent that he could defend himself better than they could. Ultimately, he failed, and was found guilty of those two murders and received the death sentence plus 196 years as punishment. He was later found guilty of the Kimberley Leach murder and given a further death sentence. Before his death he confessed to thirty murders in total but continued to deny others where evidence clearly linked him to the crime. This was a man who wanted to maintain some level of control even in death, taking secrets with him to the grave.

"There are some people who are just born bad, others learn it like a trade. I'm probably a bit of both, I'm your daughter's worst nightmare but at the same time I can be a caring attentive lover. Something just snaps in me, the feeling, the euphoria of a kill can't be reproduced, you have to do it again. The next time

you make it more exciting, you think of different ways to take control not only of yourself but of them. Take full ownership of your actions, enjoy them, then enjoy your victim's emotions, they're totally different to what the sensation you are feeling. You feel their pain, you see it, you smell it. That's a powerful way to possess someone.

I love young women, fresh and sparkling, they made wonderful companions. I like the pretty ones the best, dark haired, slim and intelligent, smart. I don't think any of them suffered, not in my mind anyway, when I took control, it was over very quickly. I was good at it, that's why the cops couldn't catch me. I guess I got sloppy, too casual in the end. I have no issue with the Feds, I know I'm different from other people, I'm articulate and I read people very well. You aren't phased by me at all. I know how killers operate, I understand what goes through their mind. I'm glad If I can help the Feds and you to understand my type. But you'll never stop us from existing. We are everywhere around you, breathing the same air as you, walking the streets, buying in the same grocery store, listening and enjoying the same music. We don't look different, but we sure as hell are different in the way we think.

The next time you're rude to someone, think twice, because that person might be internalising anger, pain and your comments could be the tipping point and you could be the next victim. You need to take a close look at everyone, not just men, women too, they're as evil as any man I know. Then there are their children, innocent at birth, cheeky in infancy, rude and temperamental as a school kid, fighting and a trouble maker, they get to know pain, and the best way to physically or verbally stop someone in their tracks. They've learned about and sampled sex and enjoy it. It might well drive them on. Before you know it by the time they're a teenager, they might well be a killer. After that, it becomes a process that turns into a habit. Because we can all kill, each of us has it in them. Check out your daughter's boyfriend, interrogate him find out what you can about him, because for all you know, he could be the next me. If there's anything you don't like or feel uneasy with, give him no room, get rid of him.

I'm scared of dying, I don't know what it'll feel like, there's no one can tell you. So it's a new experience for me. I won't give anyone the satisfaction of seeing me suffer, should it hurt, I'll go out smiling."

By 1989, he received a further death warrant and was placed on death row at Florida's Raiford Prison. It has since been claimed that he suffered greatly during his time in prison, with talk of abuse by fellow prisoners and a gang rape by four fellow inmates. No official documents I've seen support those allegations, however, but that isn't to say they didn't happen.

He was executed in the electric chair (Old Smokey) in Florida State Prison on 24th January, 1989. Outside, a crowd of several hundred had gathered including family members of some of his thirty-plus victims. They rightly celebrated when confirmation of his execution and death was posted, with loud cheers and applause. In his own words,

"I know they hate me, everyone will when they know more about me and what I have done, my entire life was a lie, I deceived people every day of my adulthood, it came easy to me, I had fun."

From one smiling assassin to another. The evening television show The Dating Game of Wednesday 13th September, 1978 was no different from any other. Crass and superficial, it threw couples together after a process of various matchmaking questions and answers. Shown in front of a live audience it was seen as light entertainment and attractive to a certain age group. Cheryl Bradshaw selected from a number of eligible bachelors, the man she believed would be her ideal date. A confident smiling Rodney Alcala, a smooth talker with an attitude won the night and the date. No one on that show or watching could at the stage ever have known that he was a sadistic serial killer in the middle of his murder spree. After the show, the publicly acquainted couple met up for a chat. Alcala promised her the date of a lifetime, a date she'd never forget.

"I started to feel ill, he was acting really creepy. I turned down his offer. I didn't want to see him again," she told the Sydney Telegraph in 2012. A fellow contestant on the show recalled how Alcala was kind of good looking, yet creepy. He never made eye contact with anyone and looked down whenever he was talking. The show producers failed to carry out thorough background checks on Alcala, had they done so it would have been revealed that he had spent three years in prison for beating and raping an eight-year-old girl. He was guilty of a similar act on a thirteen-year-old girl too, showing a predilection for paedophilia and abuse of young children. Most definitely not the kind of television game show contestant producers would have hoped for.

The sad fact of the case is, no matter how many background checks had been carried out on Alcala, none would show that he was at least four murders into a series of killings that rocked a nation. In interviews after arrest, Rodney Alcala himself claimed to have killed between fifty to a hundred people.

"I guess if you believe them, they say I may have killed plenty more, I can't remember' he is said to have told one officer. 'They're statistics now, as am I, it seems."

Alcala was born Rodrigo Jacques Alcala Buquor, in San Antonio, Texas in 1943. His father, Raoul Alcala Buquor relocated the family to Mexico when Rodney was eight years old, with his parents and sister, to Mexico. The family never really settled and when his father moved out and effectively abandoned them there, three years later, his mother Anna Maria Gutierrez, and his sisters, Christine and Marie, moved to suburban Los Angeles. An intelligent young man he did well at school despite being unsettled and being moved around by his family. At the age of seventeen he joined the Army as a clerk but was medically discharged after he suffered a nervous breakdown and had mental health issues. He took up a place at University College Los Angeles and with an IQ of 135 was a bright student. However, the introduction to a new social life and the discipline of the army long forgotten, he began to make bad choices. We can never be certain when his first criminal acts occurred, what we can be certain of is that in 1968 he groomed eight-year-old Tali Shapiro sufficiently for her to come to his Hollywood apartment.

The little girl was raped and beaten, and it could have been worse had it not been for the actions of a neighbour who suspected something was wrong when he saw the girl going into Alcala's apartment, and reported it to the Police. The Police forced entry and found the child barely alive. Meanwhile, Alacala had fled out of another exit and became a fugitive. He changed his identity to John Berger and moved to New York. At New York University he enrolled into film school and for a time studied under Roman Polanski. Polanski was himself to understand what it was like being a victim of a killer, when, the following year, the Manson family cruelly murdered his wife, Sharon Tate, and her unborn child along with a number of friends at their family home.

A perverted sadist, part of Alacala's modus operandi was to torture and strangle his victims to the point of unconsciousness. He'd then revive them and start again. One can only imagine the terror these young children endured.

Alcala meanwhile had made it onto the FBI's most wanted list. He was viewed as a dangerous and predatory paedophile. After a poster campaign to find him, Alcala was identified and arrested for the rape and attempted murder of Tali Shapiro. Unfortunately, the parents of the child refused to allow her to testify against him, believing it would be too traumatic, so he was tried on assault charges only. After spending three years behind bars, he was released and again attacked a girl - he was soon back in prison, this time for two years.

Eligible for parole, the authorities deemed him rehabilitated and allowed him to visit family relatives in New York. Within a week of being there he had killed a student called Elaine Hover, the daughter of a familiar and well-liked Hollywood nightclub owner. Elaine was also the goddaughter of Sammy Davis Jr. and Dean Martin.

Through self-confidence and more deceit, he was now using his own name again, and managed to get a job at the Los Angeles Times as a typesetter. Working in the print office he heard news stories before they broke and learning about the newspaper industry he took a liking to photography. Soon he was plotting a new way to connect with young victims. As part of his professional photography portfolio he encouraged girls wishing to enter the modelling industry to pose for him. The ideal scenario and cover for someone like Alcala. Keen and easily manipulated young men and women desperate to be top models or television stars lined up for the Alcala photo shoots.

The year following his television appearance on the Dating Game, seventeen-year-old Liane Leedom went to a photo shoot in Alcala's studio. There, he showed her his portfolio. The teenager was shocked to see dozens of images of naked teenage boys in amongst those of young girls.

The disappearance of twelve-year-old Robin Samso, a little girl on her way to ballet classes from Huntingdon Beach, California in June 1979, caused a local sensation. Her friends told how they had been sat on the beach when a stranger approached them and asked if they'd want to do a photo shoot. They turned the man's offer down, and Samsoe left, borrowing a friend's bike to get to ballet. At some point between the beach and her class, Robin Samsoe disappeared. Her remains were eventually found twelve days later by a park ranger in a heavily wooded area close to the Pasadena foothills of the Sierra Madre.

The Police spoke to the girl's friends, and soon had a composite artist sketch of the man they wanted to speak to. It was a former parole officer who recognised the face of Rodney Alcala. He was arrested, and searches carried out of all premises under his control, including his mother's house. There they found a receipt for a storage locker, where the authorities found a pair of Samsoe's earrings and hundreds of photographs of children and young women in various poses and stages of undress.

The authorities knew they had caught their man, but there was still a lot to prove. His trial began in 1980 and the evidence provided was straight forward and damning. The jury found Alcala guilty of first-degree murder and he received the death penalty. Later, the California Supreme court overturned this verdict due to the jury being prejudiced. It was felt that Alcala's criminal antecedents including his past sex crimes discriminated against him. With legal arguments it took a further six years to get him back on trial.

The second murder trial took place in 1986, and again, a different jury found him guilty and sentenced him to death. Unfortunately, five years later, a Ninth Circuit Court of Appeals panel overturned it. This was partially due to the claim that the second trial judge prevented a witness from supporting the defence's claim, that the park ranger who found the body of Robin Samsoe, had been hypnotized by Police investigators.

Finally, in 2010, 31 years after the murder, a third trial was held. In one of the most bizarre trials in criminal history, Alcala acted as his own lawyer. Rodney Alcala,would ask himself questions, always referring to himself as Mr. Alcala in a deep voice. As the defendant he would then answer his own questions. This charade continued for five hours, as he explained how he had an alibi for the Samsoe murder; he claimed to have been at Knott's Berry Farm. At one point he said to himself, *"Okay, Mr. Alcala, let's move on, let's talk about earrings"*. With regard to the other charges, he pleaded his innocence and ignorance. A psychologist claimed that he suffered from memory lapse which supported his claim of borderline personality disorder.

It had been thirty-one years since the Robin Samsoe murder and investigators now had concrete evidence against him on four different murders from the previous decade. Prison DNA swabs linked him to the crimes. The prosecution was able to combine these new murder charges alongside that of Robin Samsoe. He was found guilty of all charges and the death penalty sentence was handed down for the third time. At the sentencing hearing, one particular witness looked relieved to hear the verdict and sentence. It was Tali Shapiro, the child that Rodney Alcala had raped and beaten some forty years before.

"People make wild accusatory claims about my life, I'm a nobody who's become a somebody. Much of what is in the public domain is rubbish, sensationalistic nonsense that sells newspapers or books. It's all designed to make me look bad. Seriously do I look like a killer, I'm a good guy. I have a good brain and my mind

is as sharp as ever, I recall everything, every part of my life. It's locked away now for good, no one will ever get me to talk about things I don't wish to. Of course I have a conscience, we all have."

The Police have continued to link Alcala to other cold case murders, two of which took place in New York in 2013. When confronted with the evidence of these, he later pleaded guilty to both. He is currently on death row in Corcoran State Prison, California, planning further appeals.

Narcissistic, arrogant and easily disliked, Alcala today is not the man who appeared on the Dating Show back in the 1970s. A scruffy and weedy looking old man, he has little of any interest to say to the public. A pathological liar, his word cannot be trusted on any matter. The day of his execution cannot come quick enough for his victims, all one hundred plus of them.

EIGHT
The Devil Walks Among Us!

"The devil, who's he? He's scared of me!" - *Carl Watts*

The most feared serial killers are those who hunt down their victims, who stalk them and get to know their every movement. This serial killer tracked women, monitored evert part of their life, so that one day, he could confront them, look into their eyes and see evil. This individual never raped or sought sexual satisfaction from his victims. No, he enjoyed hunting down his quarry then the kill. Throughout his killing career, he stabbed, strangled, drowned and hanged his female victims. We don't know how many, perhaps up to 100 unfortunate women lost their lives to this man.

His past life is a shadowy, somewhat mundane and at times, seemingly very normal. There are only the odd glimpses of violence or deviant behaviour, this is a man who retreated inside himself and refused to talk to anyone once his true nature had been revealed. He had few confidants.

His parents were Appalachian blacks from McDowell County in the southern tip of West Virginia. In 1952, Dorothy Mae Young, a teenager still in high school, met and married soldier Richard Watts. He was older than her and it wasn't a relationship that was blessed by her mother. Dorothy was her youngest daughter and maternal bond recognised that no matter how much she protested, her daughter was going ahead with the relationship, she couldn't stop it.

The newlyweds moved to Killeen, a central Texas Army town where Richard Watts was stationed at Fort Hood, A year later, they had a son, Carl Eugene Watts born on 7th November 1953. The following year, a daughter, Sharon Yvonne Watts was born. Perhaps the age difference caused issues, but the marriage didn't last much longer, and the couple divorced in 1955. Dorothy Mae seeking a better life moved with her two children to Inkster, Michigan. In 1962 Dorothy married a mechanic's assistant, Norman Ceaser, and the couple had two more children. Keen to maintain the family roots and bond, she would regularly return to Coalwood to visit her mother. There, young Carl enjoyed time being spoilt by his grandmother and cousins. It was during this stage of his life that he adopted the nickname Coral, the accent and drawl led to the pronunciation of his first name to sound like Coral.

He learned many boyhood skills that came naturally to him, such as hunting. He learned how to kill and skin rabbits, a chore he appeared to take great satisfaction from. His grandmother said of him:

"He was always a good little boy, he always stayed around me or his mother. Even when the children got older and some of the boys would be goin' out at night, maybe drinkin' or chasin' women and gettin' in trouble, he stayed right up here with me. He wasn't interested in that sort of thing."

Academically, he was a slow learner and struggled in the classroom environment, yet at home he felt relaxed enough to study, and each evening, conscientiously did his homework, attaining reasonable grades as a result. When he was 8 years old he developed meningitis, resulting in an extended stay in hospital. As a result, he lost out academically as he missed a year of schooling. Doctors advised his mother that brain damage was possible as a result of the illness.

Returning to school, his grades fell back and he was unable to keep up with his peers in lessons. He excelled outdoors and in athletics, a powerful runner, football player and a Golden Gloves boxer, yet his brain struggled to keep pace with his studies. On the 24th June, 1969, he was delivering newspapers in an apartment block when he called at the home of Joan Gave, a young woman he knew by sight, and liked. He knocked on the door and Joan answered it. She was surprised to see the boy who normally tossed her the paper. She barely had time to say hello, when Watts drew back his fist and hit her full in the face. He continued to batter her before she was able to scream for help. Watts fled from the scene only to return a few minutes later and continue with his paper round. Afterwards, he returned home as usual and said nothing about it to his parents. When the Police called the next evening, he said little as they took him into custody. He appeared devoid of any emotional understanding of his situation.

It was clear something was psychologically wrong, and he was sent to the Lafayette Clinic, a forensic psychiatry centre in Detroit. Clinicians there found him unresponsive. The only explanation he would provide was *"I just felt like beating her up"*. On getting him to talk further, he told them he had dreams of beating women and killing them. He had been 12 when they had started, he'd punch their evil spirits and kick the women in his dream. They weren't nightmares, just dreams. The psychiatrists asked if the dreams disturbed him. *"No, I feel better after I have one,"* he replied.

"This patient is a paranoid young man who is struggling for control of strong homicidal impulses. This individual is considered dangerous," said the Lafayette report. Nobody took any notice. Over the six years that followed Coral Watts would execute his crimes with impunity.

He graduated at the age of 19 and moved for a few months to Lain College in Jackson, Tennessee, as part of a football scholarship. A leg injury ended that episode and he returned home where he found employment working at a wheel company in Detroit. In 1974, he enrolled in Western Michigan University in Kalamazoo under the Martin Luther King programme for minority students. By this time, he later confessed, *"I was committing an attack every two weeks or so"*.

The attacks soon began around the student campus. In an eighteen-day spell between 25th October and 12th November, two young women were attacked and severely beaten and a third, Gloria Steele, was murdered.

Witnesses put Watts in the frame and he was arrested and questioned over the assaults and was later convicted and sentenced to a year's imprisonment. In prison, the Police visited him and questioned him about the Steele murder. Watts shut down and refused to answer any of their questions, demanding a lawyer. After a consultation with his legal advisor he began to complain about depression, resulting in him being sent to Kalamazoo State Hospital. While there, he attempted to take his own life, by hanging himself with the cord from a laundry bag. The attempt failed and he suffered only minor injuries as a result of the incident.

The Psychiatric team who monitored him during his stay at the hospital reported that his temperament was 'moody and negative'. Other documentary records indicate that he spent part of his convalescence playing ping-pong and basketball and seemed cheerful around other patients and staff. During those periods of talkativeness, he told counselling staff that he had recently attacked a number of women and believed he had killed at least two of them.

Once he realised that these records might be subpoenaed by a court he refuted the suggestion claiming confusion. A few months later, in 1975, Watts was released from the hospital and returned to his home in Detroit. Here he found work as a mechanic and lived with his mother.

For two years he avoided arrest, his attention turning to more positive ventures, he was in a relationship with Delores Howard, a girlfriend from childhood and together they had a child. The relationship ended and by 1978 he had met someone else in a Detroit nightclub, Valeria Goodwill. It was what can only be described as a whirlwind romance and Watts was very much besotted by the girl. The couple married in August, 1979. Six months later they went their separate ways. Valerie Goodwill was to later tell Police of her husband's behaviour:

"One thing that bothered me, he would go to sleep at night and either have nightmares or something, I don't know what it was, but he would wake up suddenly and start fighting in his sleep...with his fists or something, like he was fighting somebody in his sleep. He wouldn't say anything. Sometimes he would fall out of the bed. One night I woke up and he was on the floor.

He was still asleep. One night I woke up and he was kneeling outside the bed with his arms up on the bed and him kneeling down on the floor. I've seen him fall asleep on the couch and fall off of the couch asleep and get back up on the couch and never wake up. I'd have to be very careful waking him up. If I would touch him waking him up, he would jump and almost jump out of the bed. I had to get out of the way.

He said he was nervous over his job, but I knew there was something the matter. Nobody sleeps like that."

He continually lied, telling her he couldn't read or write. Then later she saw him filling out job applications. He lost his job and, alone at home he would constantly rearrange furniture. There were unexplained absences when he would leave the house for hours on end, often returning in a disheveled state with his clothes dirty and torn. She must have had her suspicions about where he was going and what he was up to, as twice she had bailed him out of jail when he was arrested for prowling in Southfield.

On one occasion he decided he was an atheist and complained at her for purchasing a Christmas tree. He was vehemently opposed to her wearing any makeup and once attempted to flush her wig down the toilet so she couldn't wear it.

Then there was his behaviour after sex. After the couple had enjoyed intercourse, he would get up and go.

"He would get up and leave the house, he would just get in the car and go. He'd be gone hours and hours."

The Police held their own suspicions. At least fourteen women had been attacked in the region, eight of those fatally, between October 1979 and November 1980. The modus operandi was similar across the Detroit area, in Windsor, Ontario, and in nearby Ann Arbor.

The attacker would strangle or stab his victims. There was no sign of sexual assault or robbery. The survivors appeared to be describing the same individual, a muscular black man, wearing a blue, hooded sweat shirt.

An early victim killed in Detroit was Jeanne Clyne, who had been stabbed to death on Halloween in the suburb of Grosse Point Farms. Watts later described the attack:

"I was out driving, when I saw her walking on the sidewalk. I parked, got out and crossed the street walking toward her, I passed a group of children in trick-or-treat costumes. I came at her from the front, pulled out a screwdriver from beneath my sweat shirt and stabbed her over and over in the chest. She kept saying something like, 'OK, OK', and she fell back on the grass. I just walked back to my car and drove away."

His murders were getting more clinical in their execution.

After his divorce from Goodwill, he moved back to his mother's home in Inkster where the attacks continued and were relentless in their frequency. They tended to happen in the early hours of Sunday mornings, creating panic among the communities where they occurred. The town of Ann Arbor was rocked by a sadistic crime on 20th April, 1980, when 17-year-old Shirley Small, who had been seen arguing with her boyfriend at a local skating rink, had stormed off and decided to walk home. The following morning her body was found close to her front door. She had been stabbed twice in the heart.

Just two months later another attack occurred on a young woman, 26-year-old Glenda Richmond, she too was stabbed outside her home. Then a third attack and death occurred. Rebecca Huff was a 20-year-old student who died under almost identical circumstances. The Police knew they had a serial killer on their hands and they had no suspects.

The press dubbed the killer the 'Sunday Morning Slasher'.

On the night of 15th November, 1980 two patrolling Police officers saw Watts stalking a young woman walking along the sidewalk. He was driving in his car, and continually pulling up in front of her, causing her to change direction and turn into another street. The Police monitored the incident which continued over nine blocks before the woman ducked into a doorway and lost her stalker.

Watts saw the Police watching him, and in panic tried to drive away. He was stopped and when the officers carried out a background check on him, he was arrested for driving with a suspended license and for having expired license plates. A search of his car produced unexpected evidence. They found a box containing small, rectangular wood files and in the back seat was a large, collegiate dictionary. Why would an out of work mechanic have one of these? Scratched on its cover, as though by the force of a pen nib being heavily forced through from a separate surface were the words, 'Rebecca is a lover'.

The detectives finally had a suspect, and painstakingly double checked every detail regarding the recent murders, and the movements of Carl Watts. A cursory enquiry into the Kalamazoo assaults and the Gloria Steele murder reaped rewards. Through his ex-attorney, Watts informed detectives that they had no need look any further for a suspect in those cases.

The Police needed more evidence to prove his guilt, since he hadn't yet made any kind of confession. Bailed and released, he was followed night and day, he was aware it was happening and for two months no attacks or murders occurred. The detectives working the case decided to bring him in for further questioning. In the space of those eight hours, the case began to unravel beyond the detectives' wildest imagination. One of those officers later said:

"He was nice. He was polite. If you can forget about what he does, he seems like a soft-spoken, timid but personable, pleasant person. I think I got close once. We knew the women had been attacked from behind. The killer had wrapped his left arm around their throat, then reached over their right shoulder and stabbed them. The blouses were pulled up at the front, and marks on the throat of one, just under the chin, came from a man's wristwatch on a left arm.

Finally, toward the end of the session, I said to him, I not only know you did these, I know 'how' you did them. I got up and walked behind him and said,

you grabbed them like this. Then you pulled their heads back like this, and you
reached over with your right arm and stabbed them like this!

And he started crying. Just broke down and started crying. It was the first real
emotion we'd seen from him. I thought he might break for a minute, but he didn't.
He wanted to talk to his mother and we let him - that was probably a mistake -
and, after that, he wouldn't say a word. It was all over."

He still hadn't made a full confession and was again released on bail. In March
1981, he left Michigan briefly stopping off in Coalwood, where he visited his
grandmother. He then drove thousands of miles to Columbus, where he was able
to find work as a diesel mechanic.

This was the first time Watts had made a major life decision without first
consulting with his mother, who later said.

"He didn't even tell her where he was going. He'd never done that before. He'd
always lived at home with his mother or stayed with me except when he was in
college. She didn't know what to think. He'd just gone off and left his whole family.
He was on his own and we were worried for him."

A Police detective tracked him down to his work place in Columbus, but little
else was done to further the investigation. It was a time of political unrest in the
Houston Police Department. With complaints of understaffed Police resources
within the division, and no funds for overtime, or time for investigations. They
were busy with day to day cases, so old crimes tended to be put on hold.

In Columbus, Watts returned to his old habits; eleven further female victims
were to die at his hands. Somewhat sadistically, he had taken to breaking into
properties and watching his victims from within their own homes. During a
further nine month period he attacked at least 18 women and killed half of them.
Then finally he was caught. He killed in the early morning hours of 23rd May,
1982. Having followed Michelle Maday to her home, he launched into an attack
and dragged her inside where he changed his modus operandi and drowned her
in a bathtub of hot water. That act didn't satiate his appetite to kill and he went in
search of a further victim.

He had trawled this neighbourhood already and had identified a potential
future victim, Lori Lister. Aware of her movements and timings, he lay in wait and
surprised her as she began to climb the stairs to her apartment. Placing his hands

round her throat he began to throttle her, not sufficient to kill her, but enough to leave her dazed and semi-conscious. Dragging her up the stairs, he took her door keys from her hand and opened the door.

He received the shock of his life as Lori's roommate, Melinda Aguilar, was in the apartment. Snapping back to his senses, he dropped Lister to the floor and forced Aguilar into her bedroom, where he bound her using metal coat hangers. Leaving her trussed up, he filled the bathtub with water, returned to Lister who was still dazed and confused and lay where he had dropped her. Picking her up in his arms, he carried her to the bathroom where he began to force her under the water.

A neighbour had earlier seen Watts loitering and later saw him stood over the body of Lori Lister by the stairs. He had called the Police. Aguilar, meanwhile, managed to free herself and escaped by jumping from a balcony onto the lawn below. It was almost coordinated, as at the same time the Police arrived on the scene. Watts tried to escape and ran down the stairs but was caught in the courtyard and arrested.

Held in custody, he later appointed an experienced lawyer, Zinetta Burney, who was shocked by her new client:

"I thought I'd find a young, black man who happened to be at the wrong place at the wrong time and got arrested. When I got there, when I started talking to him and he started telling me the things he'd done, I thought he was lying or crazy."

As a result of his odd and sinister behaviour, for her own protection she began to wear a crucifix during her visits with him

"He's the only client I ever had who made me feel that way. There's something evil in the man. He never threatened me. He was always quiet and polite to me, but he scared me more than anyone I've ever dealt with."

The statement of confession began, it was devoid of emotion and delivered in a staccato monotonous rambling tone. Watts confessed to 13 murders but gave interviewers nothing about himself or his motive. Below are some of the statements he made to investigating detectives.

"She had evil eyes...I could see her eyes and they were evil...I had to release the spirit. I just felt like beating her up. I figured that would kill the spirit.

She wasn't dead. I didn't have no real reason, but I took the elastic strap and hung her up off a branch and left her sort of sitting that way. She was a pretty big woman. Her feet were moving, still moving. I took her socks off and took them with me and I burned them to release the spirit. She was evil. I saw it in her eyes.

I grabbed her. Choked her. Then I took her inside the apartment and took her dress off. Then I put her in the bathtub and ran hot water on her, covered her with it, then I let the water out. I took the dress, but I didn't burn it. I just threw it away. I didn't have to burn it because I had put her in the bathtub with the water. The water wouldn't let her spirit get out. I can't identify her picture. I can't identify none of them."

Carl Coral Watts died of prostate cancer on 21st September 2007 in hospital in Jackson. It is said that authorities still consider him a suspect in at least 100 unsolved murders. As a killer he was power oriented and enjoyed seeing his victims suffer. Like many serial killers he took trophies from the crime scene though in his case, he wouldn't keep them but burnt them, since he believed this would help dissipate the evil that possessed each of his victims. As an individual he was able to lead an unsuspecting life among those who knew nothing of his darker side. Even his wife was unsuspecting of his murders.

His family would recall the opinions of psychologists and psychiatric staff in Lafayette many years earlier, who commented that he may have mental health issues as a result of suffering meningitis and severe head trauma in his adolescent years. They believed this was the cause, the trigger behind his deviant behaviour.

The crimes were not sexually driven, since he never committed rape or sexual assault, yet he clearly enjoyed looking at the naked bodies, and on occasions cleansed them by drowning or submerging them in water, again because he believed it drove out the evil within. Some of his crime scenes were best described as carnage, disorganised and extremely messy. Few forensic clues were found at these scenes therefore some care must have been taken during the attack to prevent this. Yet, we have witnesses and survivors describing him as black and wearing a blue-coloured hoodie so there was an air of recklessness about him.

Like so many of his peers, Watts was afraid of dying and in particular of the electric chair.

"Will it hurt do you think? I don't want to die that way, I will get my lawyers to appeal each of the death sentences, until no more appeals are open to me. I've

heard so many tales about executions and the electric chair, it's a barbarian way to kill a human being. No one deserves to die like that. I have rights, I know I have, and I will fight for them. I'm sick, I have something inside me that tells me bad things, not a voice, it's something I can feel, I know that, I'm very sick, they can't do this to me. I didn't know what I was doing, they were evil, all of them. I was doing what I was told, I'm not evil or anything of that kind, just bad. They can't blame me, I was driven to do these things. They knew why I had to do what I did, they tried to disguise their eyes, they wouldn't look at me, but I could see it in their eyes, the evil. I couldn't let them go after that."

NINE
Nasty!

"Bothersome." - *Donald 'Pee Wee' Gaskins*

To say that our next profile had a difficult start in life would be an understatement. His mother, Molly, came from a poor background in Florence County, South Carolina, and at the age of 12 she quit school to join her family who picked cotton and plant tobacco for local land and plantation owners. One of these was an older man called Gaskins who was a paedophile and would pay Molly $1 for sex several times a week.

When she was 14 she fell pregnant to Gaskins and on 13th March, 1933, she gave birth to a tiny baby boy, who weighed in at just four pounds. He was given the name Donald Henry, however, he was always referred to as 'Pee Wee' due to his size. Gaskins allowed the mother of his child to live in a three bedroomed shack on his land and paid her $10 a month. When he was just one year old, 'Pee Wee' drank a bottle of kerosene which caused him to have convulsions that repeated themselves until he was three years old.

It's a sad indictment of their lives that 'Pee Wee' would watch as Molly and Gaskins had sex in front of him. When he tried to intervene, they would push him away and laugh at him. Molly wasn't the most morally appropriate mother ever, and throughout his childhood took on many lovers, mainly for financial reward. The type of client she was attracting cared little about the boy being present; drunks, down and outs and generally the dregs of society. Naturally, it wasn't long before some clients sexually engaged with 'Pee Wee' while his mother looked on.

At school his life was thoroughly miserable. Mainly because of his size and appearance he was relentlessly bullied and teased. It was a further failure of the system that saw him beaten by some teachers who blamed him for being a trouble maker and not getting along with his peers. This treatment and the neglect he suffered at home, saw him turn into a loner and by the age of eight he was playing truant and hiding out in local woods, making dens and hides and hunting animals for fun.

In 1943, Molly married a field hand called Hinnant Hanna, an unpleasant and arrogant man, he believed he had the right to do as he pleased in the family home. Soon he was physically and sexually abusing 'Pee Wee' and continually telling him he was the child no one liked or wanted. He treated 'Pee Wee' like his personal slave, beating and kicking him and demanding sexual favours while his mother looked on and did nothing to protect her son. As a result of the marriage, four further children were born, two boys and two girls; 'Pee Wee' now had half brothers and sisters.

By the time he was 12, he was working as a mechanic in a garage. His time spent in the woods had seen him fix abandoned rubbish and industrial items dumped there because they were broken, and he would then sell these on for a small profit. Earning a decent wage for his age in the garage, and doing okay for himself, his step-father soon became jealous of his status, and intervened. He didn't want 'Pee Wee' to be more successful and respected then he was, so pulled him from the garage work and forced him to work in the fields. Resilient 'Pee Wee' did as he was told but would often sneak off back to the garage and help with repairs, thus secretly earning extra money for himself.

When he was 13, he, along with two of his friends, Danny Smith and Henry Marsh, found an abandoned shack in the woodland where they had been playing. They fixed it up and made it their gang headquarters. Calling themselves the 'Trouble Trio' they lived up to their name and would steal from cigarette vending machines and pinch from local stores and sneak back to gang headquarters and smoke, drink and eat their illegally-gotten gains. Their reputation soon spread and whenever they were seen together, storekeepers and householders would close their doors to keep them out. Other kids around the same age group tended to avoid them like the plague as crossing them would invariably result in a severe beating.

Their behaviour became more sexually extreme when they deliberately drilled spy holes and used to peep through them in the women's outhouse at the local church. There they'd get sexual kicks from watching the women undress and take a break of nature. They were caught red-handed by the church Minister and taken home to their parents. 'Pee Wee' was savagely beaten black and blue and told to publicly apologise in church. This incident provides us with our first real insight into his psyche, as when asked to say sorry, he said the only thing he was sorry about was that they got caught, but he was not sorry they did it!

His friend Danny had a father who was anything but a good role model, he was into crime of all kinds. Soon he had the 'Trouble Trio' working for him, breaking into houses and stores and stealing. Splitting the proceeds from the sale of the stolen goods, the boys soon earned sufficient money to buy a car - a big, black hearse - between the three of them. With transport, new fields of opportunity arose, and the boys were soon engaging in sexual activity in the vehicle with local street sex workers. Two would watch while the other one participated in sex.

Eventually this kind of activity failed to satisfy them, they now wanted to know what it was like to have sex with a virgin. The three boys raped Henry's 13-year-old sister, Julie multiple times and in every way imaginable. They then threatened her with further sexual attacks should she ever tell anyone. As an adult, 'Pee Wee' spoke of this rape:

"When we had sex with Henry's sister, it was exciting, fulfilling, rewarding. I learned a lot from that experience, we all did. It spiralled from an exploration, into a frenzied attack as we all wanted to be involved at the same time. It was extremely violent, but I somehow enjoyed it and I think she did too, she learned from it that's for sure. It seemed quite natural to all of us. I wasn't sorry, children do these sorts of things don't they? It was a learning exercise, a fulfilling memory that I will never forget."

The devastated girl returned home and instantly told her mother what had happened. Again, 'Pee Wee' and his cohorts suffered parental beatings. Not long after this, and wholly because of it, and blaming 'Pee Wee' for being a bad influence on their sons, his friends moved away with their respective families, leaving him to his own devices. He wasn't a loner for long as he met with another boy, Walt, and soon they too were planning criminal acts. House burglaries were the most obvious route towards wealth. So the pair began a spree of this type. On one occasion, they broke into a house and were confronted by a 16-year-old girl, who lunged at 'Pee Wee' with a hatchet. Snatching it from her, he then hit her over the head with it, causing the girl to fall to the ground, unconscious. His partner in crime fled the scene. Shortly after the attack, 'Pee Wee' was arrested and charged with assault with a deadly weapon and intent to kill.

"When the court called me Donald Henry Gaskins I hadn't a clue who they meant, then it suddenly struck me, it was me. My real name wasn't 'Pee Wee' it was Donald. I had a proper identity. No one, my mother or anyone had told me that before."

Found guilty of the crimes, he was sent to The South Carolina Industrial School for Boys in Florence, South Carolina.

At reform school in 1950, on his first night there a boy called 'Boss Poss' approached him and instructed him that he was now his sweetheart, and each night he was to come to his bed, otherwise he would suffer. Pee Wee ignored the instruction and the following night, was gangraped and sodomised by Boss Poss and twenty of his followers for several hours. For over a year, Boss Poss raped Pee Wee each night and pimped him out to other students in exchange for money. Eventually, 'Pee Wee' and four other abused boys escaped from the school and went into hiding. They were found in nearby woodland, however Pee Wee escaped again and took sanctuary in his old gang headquarters.

The Police discovered his hideout and returned him to the school. The punishment was severe, lashes for thirty consecutive days, three months hard labour, and three months in solitary confinement which must have seemed like a blessing to him.

The same day his punishment ended, Boss Poss was back onto him, and the gangrape continued. Degraded, he was often asked to run around the dormitory in girl's underwear. Again he ran away. This time he avoided capture for several months, by staying with an aunt who protected him and for the first time in his life, he had a feeling of being cared for. Ultimately, he had to return to reform school, so his aunt persuaded him to do that. Again, the punishment was lashes, solitary confinement and hard labour.

One prison guard took a dislike to Pee Wee and sought to punish him on every occasion possible. The animosity worked both ways until Pee Wee snapped, punched the guard in the face and the testicles. This behaviour was sufficient for the school to refer him for mental evaluation. Within a day of being admitted into the asylum, he suffered a burst appendix and was sent to hospital.

It was a viscous circle, the cycle of abuse continued when he was returned to the reform school. Continually gang raped, beaten and abused, he ran away again. This time he was free for around two years, during which time, in his desperate attempt at normality, he married. The day after, he turned himself in to the reform school to conclude his penalty.

He was released a short time later, and now married, he briefly worked on a tobacco plantation but then started setting fire to outbuildings and barns where the tobacco was often stored. The plantation owner's daughter confronted him and told him they knew he was responsible for the fires and they would turn him in. He attacked the teenage girl with a hammer leaving her for dead. She survived and told the authorities what he had done and of the fire starting. As a result, he was sentenced to six years imprisonment at the Central Correctional Institution.

Prison life was abysmal for Pee Wee. It wasn't long before another prisoner took ownership of him. 'Author Boy' raped and sodomised him continually for six months. Then Pee Wee hatched a plan to earn some respect, he killed the most feared man in the prison, Hazel Brazell. Making it look like he was defending himself, he received a lighter sentence, and in doing the act, gained some kudos from his fellow inmates. His lack of respect for figures of authority was amply displayed when he called the Judge during the hearing, a 'son of a bitch'. He was sentenced to an extra three years in prison. It was a turning point in his life, as no longer was he the insipid victim, he was now the aggressor. He managed to escape from prison in 1955 and fled to Florida, where he found employment with a travelling carnival. Two years later, he was again arrested, remanded in custody, and later in August 1961 given parole.

A life of crime and bad decision making followed, including two further failed marriages. He was desperate to be loved and seen as an equal. Two years after his parole he was arrested for raping a 12-year-old girl, he absconded while awaiting sentence. This time he took off to Georgia but was soon arrested and later sentenced to eight years imprisonment. Paroled in November 1968, he moved to Sumterand and took employment there working for a roofing company.

In September 1969, cruising around in a car, he met with and picked up a female hitchhiker, who he quickly overpowered, raped, tortured and murdered before sinking her body into a swamp. This murder was the start of a spree, as he went on to pick up and murder many more, while cruising the coastal highways of the American South. Incredibly he classified such crimes as his 'coastal kills', with his victims being both male and female. The executions were carried out for pleasure, and as his kill count increased he claimed to average a kill approximately once every six weeks, hunting for victims to satiate his 'bothersome' feelings. Each victim was tortured and mutilated whilst still alive, and he took pleasure in seeing them suffer. It made him feel powerful. The killings themselves escalated in the suffering he forced onto the victim. His mindset was all about showing the world that he was strong and yielded power and authority. Essentially everything he wasn't. He stabbed, suffocated, mutilated, allowed them to bleed to death, and claimed to cannibalise some of them. He went on to confess to the murder of 'eighty to ninety' such victims,

What he referred to as the 'serious murders' began in November, 1970. The victims were his own niece, Janice Kirby, aged fifteen, and her friend Patricia Ann Alsbrook, aged seventeen. These young girls were savagely beaten to death when they challenged him after he tried sexually engaging with them. Their refusal and undignified name-calling prompted his anger, so he killed them both.

Over the following four years, a variety of victims were selected for the most obscure of reasons; they had perhaps mocked him, some had attempted to blackmail him, others owed him money, some looked at him the wrong way, and some, he claimed, had stolen from him. In 1973, he broke into the home of two of his neighbours and raped and murdered two of their family. Doreen Dempsey was 23-years-old and eight months pregnant, and her daughter only aged two when they were savagely attacked and killed by Gaskins.

On another occasion he killed for reward. Silas Yates was executed because a woman paid him to kill the man. The commission of these murders was simple, they were more clinical, typical hitman, execution style. He'd surprise the victim, then shoot them, and bury their remains in the coastal region of South Carolina.

The murderous activity of 'Pee Wee' Gaskins looked to have drawn to a close when on 14th November, 1975, he was arrested after a fellow criminal, Walter Neeley, confessed to Police that he had witnessed Gaskins kill Dennis Bellamy. He confirmed in his written statement that Gaskins had confessed to killing many others during the previous five years and he had described where he'd hidden the bodies.

He was arrested and held in custody where he openly began speaking about his crimes. Eventually on 4th December, 1975, heavily manacled and surrounded, he led Police to an area of land that he owned in Prospect. One by one he pointed out the deposition sites for eight of his victims.

The following year, on 24th May, he was tried on eight charges of murder. In a trial that lasted just four days he was found guilty on all eight counts and was later handed the death sentence.

I mentioned earlier, that his murderous activity looked to have drawn to a close in November 1975. 'Pee Wee' Gaskins enjoyed the taste of the kill far too much to simply stop, even in prison. On 2nd September, 1982, he committed a further murder inside the high security block at the South Carolina Correctional Institution. A death row inmate named Rudolph Tyner was his last victim. This man had received the death sentence as a result of the murder of an elderly couple during a bungled armed robbery of a store they owned.

Word got out that the victims' son, Tony, was prepared to pay for a clinical hit on Tyner. Wanting to be seen as powerful, Pee Wee offered to do the kill and was hired. After several unsuccessful attempts to kill the man by lacing his food and drink with poison, he opted for an altogether more powerful option. He had always been good at repairs, so had a rudimentary knowledge of many things, including how to construct bombs. He managed to rig an electronic speaker-like device in Tyner's cell. As part of the manipulation Gaskins convinced Tyner that he was his friend, and that the rigging of this contraption would allow them to secretly communicate with each other at night during lockdown.

The death row prisoner listened intently to what Gaskins told him and followed his instructions to the letter. At an agreed time, he was to hold the plastic speaker to his ear when Gaskins asked him to; he had no idea that it was packed with C-4 plastic explosive. Gaskins gave him the instruction to listen to the speaker, and moments later he detonated the device from his cell, killing Tyner instantly. He later explained to me:

"The funniest thing is, the last thing that guy heard was the sound of me laughing. I thought that was really funny because he trusted me, then right at the death, when it was too late, he realised I was going to kill him. Once a killer, always a killer, that's my motto and it's true. Killers like me don't stop for anything or anyone."

He was tried and found guilty then sentenced to death for this last vicious act of murder.

After a last ditch failed attempt to commit suicide by slashing his wrists with a razor, it took twenty stitches to keep him alive for a few hours until he kept his appointment with the electric chair. 'Pee Wee' Gaskins was executed at Broad River Correctional Institution at 1.10 a.m., on 6th September, 1991.

We will never truly know how many people Gaskins killed, he was undoubtedly a man used to making grandiose claims, mainly because of his stature. His childhood was traumatic to say the least, and his aunt aside, there was no one who displayed any genuine care towards him during his life. Even in prison, the guards would regularly beat him, mainly because of his attitude.

There are many key stages to his life where issues went unresolved and turned him into the killer he was. The lack of respect for human life came about as a result of his mother's behaviour in front of him, allowing others to abuse him and not protecting him. This must have made him feel unwanted, unloved and unsafe. The feeling of security for a child is paramount. Undoubtedly Pee Wee had insecurity issues and trusted no one. As he grew older, he was punished by a step-father who showed him no compassion and was jealous of his mechanical skills. This man would continually beat and abuse him, destroying any chance of a relationship.

His peer group mocked, bullied and intimidated him. Girls he approached laughed at him; essentially he was ostracised by this group. The only childhood friends he made were active criminals and the father of one of those encouraged his nefarious activities. When caught and placed into the care of the authorities, they too beat and abused him, and allowed others to sadistically torture him. By the time he was an adolescent, there was little hope of recovery and no one there to guide him or explain societal rules.

His behaviour deteriorated and turned sexual, first as a peeping tom, then turning to physical intercourse with street sex workers, and finally to the raping of a young girl who he knew. All the time hitting back at a society who he felt laughed at him because of his size.

The escalation in violence continued as he sought greater euphoria from each criminal act, leading to murder, then different murder types. The desire to be seen as someone strong and powerful drove him on as he rebelled against the world. Finally, he committed the ultimate act of power and control over the establishment by murdering within its own walls.

This was a boy who had a bad start to life, accepting the role of the victim rather too well. To the point where others saw his vulnerability as a child and abused it to satiate their own desires. Those people didn't see him as a child, but as an object. I believe the Gaskins is potentially one of the most prolific killers of modern times. His cold and calculating manner when discussing the murders with investigating Police officers, was bone chilling. Later in interviews he lacked emotion and showed no remorse for what he had done:

"I can't recall how many people I have killed, I lost count. I can't remember their names either. We were ships that passed in the night, acquaintances who I enjoyed some fun with. I'm not saying I killed thousands, I let more people go than I killed. I could have been killing every day if I had wanted to. I just did the bothersome ones, you know the ones you take an instant dislike to. It would have been too tiring to kill every day. It takes a lot to kill someone, mentally and physically it takes it out of you. Then there's dumping the body. What do you do with a dead body? You can't just dump it on the highway. You have to be clever, ingenious because you don't want the cops sniffing around.

I didn't really have a preferred method of killing, they all gave me an experience of some kind. I felt like a giant when I killed, I took control of their lives. Who'd have thought it, 'Pee Wee' Gaskins killing all those people all on his own. I'd like to guess I could take you out to some other body dump sites, but I don't know if I can remember them. That's if I could be bothered. Most days I don't give a damn.

When I look back at my life, I had some okay times, I had some fun. The one thing I'll never truly understand is why me, why did all those things happen to me. Who picked that life for me? Someone with a sick sense of humour that's for sure."

I'm often asked if I have any empathy for the serial killers I work with, study and research. There are just two who evoke any kind of emotion within me, the first being Aileen Wuornos. The other is Robert John Maudsley, who is currently incarcerated in Wakefield High Security Prison, in Yorkshire. I can fully understand what drove those two people to kill; however, I don't agree with the actions they took, nor do they deserve any sympathy. For me, it's my opinion that they are products of a society that failed them. That does not give them a license to kill nor is it any excuse for doing so, yet undoubtedly, the system failed them both at critical times in their lives, when potentially, further lives could have been saved.

Robert Maudsley was born and raised in Liverpool, and at a young age (prior to his second birthday), along with his brothers Paul and Kevin and sister Brenda, was removed from what neighbours described as a 'hostile and abusive' family home and placed in care. He was sent to Nazareth House foster home, where he was raised by the Catholic nuns. In the home he was viewed as a good little boy who did as he was told. However, life in a religiously strict Roman Catholic orphanage is not conducive to a loving nurturing environment, Robert was of a number of boys there, so received little or no personal care or attention. He did form a closer family bond with his siblings while there, but it was a false environment, no love or nurture was present. In those early formative years of his life, he was shown little compassion by his blood line parents, the regular violent fighting scenes and screaming bouts, were permanent memories etched into his brain. He too suffered regular beatings at home, with no respite. Neighbours would hear him crying, sobbing and pleading with dad to stop it. Unfortunately, dad couldn't stop it, he believed child beating was the best way to instil discipline into such a young life. Eventually, the neighbours could stand no more and reported the matter to the authorities, who removed him for his own safety, to what they believed to be a safer environment.

It's important to note that Robert was given no voice at home, or later in the orphanage. Nobody listened to him, as he was taught the improper age-old mantra that children should be seen and not heard, and speak only when spoken to. Effectively he was alienated, living his life with no one listening to him. The spectre of depression soon enveloped him in his teenage years, with no one truly caring for him he attempted to take his own life on a number of occasions, a cry for help perhaps? Whatever, he never received the correct care that would perhaps have helped trained medical staff understand the reasons behind the attempts.

Instead he was fed prescribed drugs as part of his rehabilitation, leading to him becoming a drug addict. For some inexplicable reason, the orphanage allowed the Maudsley family to return home to mum and dad, who by now had eight further children. The beatings and the abuse continued behind closed doors causing any positive feelings he held towards his parents to dissipate.

"I remember the beatings my father gave out. On one occasion I was locked in a room for months, he'd only open the door to come in to beat me, four or six times a day. He once broke a .22 air rifle over my back. I hated that bastard part of my life."

Now a teenager, life in Liverpool offered him nothing, he hated his home life and wanted to get as far away from the horrific memories as he could. So he headed for London in the hope of employment and a better future. It was another false dawn and he soon found himself a hopeless drug addict, doing whatever it took to earn him some money for his next fix. The years that followed saw him drift in and out of psychiatric hospitals as the suicide attempts increased. His life was empty and he felt alone and worthless. In hospitals he told doctors that he constantly heard voices in his head telling him to kill his parents.

It was while working as a rent boy in 1973, that he committed his first killing. Labourer, John Farrell proudly produced a number of images of young children who he claimed to have sexually abused and showed them to Robert who in his own words, said:

"I lost it, I felt angry that he seemed proud of what he was doing, getting a child to commit sex acts with him. Would he do it to his own children? No, so why me? In him, I saw my own parents, so I killed him. I garroted him and handed myself in to the Police."

It was clear that he was suffering from serious mental health problems, and after independent examinations by qualified psychiatrists, was declared unfit to stand trial, and sent to Broadmoor hospital for the criminally insane, where he remained for three years. It was here in 1977 that he committed his second murder. Along with a fellow patient, a psychopath, they kidnapped a fellow patient, a convicted paedophile and held him hostage barricading themselves into a cell. Inside, they systematically tortured their victim for nine hours. He was then garroted. To show the prison guards that their threat wasn't empty, they held the dead man's body in the air so it could be seen through the spy hole in the closed cell door. A witness recalled:

"The patient was clearly dead. It was a shocking sight, seeing a man's head cracked open like you take the top off a boiled egg. There was spoon or a fork or something like that sticking out of the brain, like they had tried to eat it. It predated the Hannibal the Cannibal films by several years. It sent serious reverberations through the system, we were told not to discuss it with anyone outside the work environment. If we were caught mentioning it inside work, then we would face disciplinary action. This was embarrassing for the powers that be, he'd made them look bad, as though the situation was out of control. I remember some journalists were sniffing about for a time, looking to find out what had happened and offering decent money for a story too. I don't think anyone spoke out about it. We daren't, it was our livelihoods that were at risk."

This time, Robert was found fit to stand trial, and was later convicted of manslaughter on the grounds of diminished responsibility. He was sentenced to life imprisonment, not at Broadmoor, but at Wakefield Prison, better known as

'Monster Mansion' due to the amount of killers it houses within its high brick walls. Details of the Broadmoor killing quickly filtered through the prison system from prison to prison, earning Maudsley an unwanted reputation ahead of his arrival at Wakefield, where the inmates nicknamed him the 'cannibal' and the 'brain-eater'. Mentally unwell, he continually requested medical help but was denied this by a system that cynically assumed he was attempting to get a fast-track back to Broadmoor. Again, no one listened to Robert. Throughout his life he had been ignored, now in prison, that treatment continued.

Within weeks, the voices in his head were beginning to take control of his actions. There are those who claim he deliberately set out to kill several people on that fateful day, we can't say for certain. Others say that he had the look of crazed madness in his eyes and that no one generally wanted to engage with him, but with the look he had about him that day, they were even more reticent, which apparently made him more angry.

The first prisoner to die that day was imprisoned for murdering his wife. Maudsley was able to lure him to his cell, where he slit his throat and hid the body under his bed. He then hunted down a second victim, who was lying on the bunk in his cell. Using a makeshift knife made from a fork handle he had stolen from the prison kitchen, he hacked at his victim's head and face area, before repeatedly smashing his head against the brick wall of the cell.

With that, and seemingly in complete control of his actions, he walked calmly to the guards' office on the wing, and placed the makeshift knife on the table before them, advising, *'you'll be two prisoners down on roll call this evening'*.

He pleaded guilty to the double murder and was sentenced to life in prison. Unbelievably, he was returned to Wakefield Prison and moved into solitary confinement for the safety of other prisoners, and one suspects his own. He is held there in a glass cell, specifically built for him in 1983. It measures around 5.5m by 4.5m and is one of two glass cells in the basement area of the prison. It has large bulletproof windows allowing the inmates to be monitored day and night. The only furnishings, out of necessity, are a compressed cardboard table and chair. The bed is a concrete slab and the toilet and sink are firmly secured to the floor by heavy duty bolts. Access is gained by a solid steel door which opens into a cage slightly smaller than the cell, it is encased in thick Perspex and has a small slot low down, through which Maudsley receives his meals. There is no change to the routine and it has been like that for decades. He is kept locked up in the cell for 23 hours a day. During his one hour of exercise, he is not allowed contact with other prisoners; the six guards given this duty, are instructed not to speak to, or enter into conversation with him. This is isolation in the extreme, time alone that he uses well. He studies and has the IQ level of a genius. Much of his time is spent writing to key decision makers in the establishment, highlighting his situation:

"The prison authorities basically ignore me, they see me as a problem, the only solution they have is to put me into solitary confinement and to literally throw away the key, to bury me alive in a concrete coffin. It doesn't matter to them whether I am mad or bad, they don't care. It's like I don't exist. No one ever replies to my requests. They do not know the answer and they do not care just so long as I am kept out of sight and out of mind.

I am left to stagnate, vegetate and to regress; left to confront my solitary head-on with people who have eyes but don't see and who have ears but don't hear, who have mouths but don't speak. My life in solitary is one long period of unbroken depression.

If I had killed my parents in 1970, none of those people need have died. If I had killed them, then I would be walking around as a free man without a care in the world."

Maudsley enjoys classical music, reading and writing poetry, and art. For a short time, he was moved to HMP Woodhill, where he was allowed social interaction with inmates, access to books and could listen to music. Then, suddenly he was moved to the glass cell in Wakefield Prison.

When studying the case one thing leaps out from each page; the prison system appears to have made illogical decisions in the case of Robert Maudsley. It seems clear that being locked away in his bedroom for six months on end, with no domestic or social interaction, except the beatings from his father, psychologically traumatised young Robert. So keeping him locked away in the basement, with no natural light and starved of conversation, takes him back to those early years which undoubtedly mentally scarred him.

At his 1979 trial, his legal team argued the murders happened as a result of pent-up aggression resulting from a childhood of near-constant abuse. Another psychiatrist worked with him for a short spell and saw an improvement in his mental condition, helping him work through his anger that was present as a result of his childhood difficulties. The treatment was suddenly withdrawn for no apparent reason, or one that the prison system deems inappropriate to share with anyone.

It's as though Robert Maudsley is a bad smell, a nightmare the prison system wishes to forget. A human being languishing alone in the very depths of that prison. I accept he took the lives of four men who he believed were paedophiles or child abusers. In killing them he was killing his own parents each time. Quite rightly he has been convicted for those deaths and punished appropriately, though in my opinion, the level of punishment does seem archaic and is almost torture by starvation of social interaction. That in itself can only lead to greater mental health issues. How long can this term of solitary continue? It would take a strong Lord Chief Justice to go against the system and revoke that decision. As wrong as it sounds, in certain quarters it's far easier not to be reminded of this case, best forgotten. There will be those who believe that Maudsley prevented four male victims from having any social interaction, so his punishment is karma. That being so, there are far more dangerous and violent killers held in Wakefield Prison, who interact and lead normal prison inmate lives. Yet, Robert Maudsley has been denied that for several decades.

The first killing in Broadmoor, as deplorable as it was, undoubtedly caused huge embarrassment to the criminal justice system, and has been perpetuated ever since in stories told by one-time fellow inmates and loose-tongued prison staff. Exaggerating the story each time to almost mythical levels. One can only feel sympathy for the victim's family in this nightmare scenario.

The murders that followed elevated his crimes to serial killer status. A serial killer on the loose, seemingly murdering at will while held in prison doesn't make pleasant reading for the authorities. It shows a lack of control and awareness. It humiliated certain authorities in the system, causing a devastating blow to their careers. That, for me is an important aspect of this case. It's been taken personally, and Robert is continually being punished for their failures, and not his own.

I felt so moved by his situation (the solitary confinement) that I decided to write to people in authority, making them aware of this case. From the Lord Chief Justice, Prime Minister, Members of Parliament, Home Secretaries, right through to Prison Governors across the UK. Like Robert Maudsley, I suddenly became invisible; where this case was concerned, I had no voice. I received not one acknowledgement or response of any kind. This truly is the case of a man the system has denied. There is no such thing as coincidence, mention his name and the system literally clams up and goes into lock down.

"All I have to look forward to is further mental breakdown and possible suicide. In many ways, I think this is what the authorities hope for. That way the problem of Robert John Maudsley can be easily and swiftly resolved."

TEN
A Leopard Doesn't Change Its Spots

"There are two ways to get money. You earn it or you just take it." - *Donald Neilson*

The leopard is one of the most adaptable creatures in the world, varying its diet according to the environment and terrain. Occasionally it scavenges from the outskirts of towns and villages. Such is its level of cunning and strength, it surprises its prey through unexpected attack before dragging them up the bough of a tree, safely consuming the meal away from its hunting competitors. One form of leopard is melanistic - the black panther.

When I first met Donald Neilson it was in a crime writing capacity; I had gone to interview him at his request about his life story which he wanted recorded for posterity. Not unnaturally my interest was piqued at the thought of holding conversations with him for the sake of profiling and understanding what drove him to kill. It was a difficult task, since I had not expected such an insipid character to be sat in front of me. Despite this, he had an arrogant and completely defiant side that made him difficult to listen to. I found myself loathing his obnoxious attitude and was close to walking away from him. Each time I made to get up, he would ask me to reconsider staying if he behaved himself (classic manipulation tactics employed by serial killers, that I had witnessed hundreds of times previously) and stopped his continued denigration of the Criminal Justice System and certain Police officers in particular.

His main issue was his belief that due to press coverage he received an unfair trial as jury members had read of his crimes. The media had dubbed him The Black Panther, giving him a monster like persona. A curious juxtaposition then arose as he explained:

"I like The Black Panther moniker, it gives me an identity which is something I've never really had. I hated the whole Nappey thing, my original surname. That wasn't me at all, and it made me act differently, defensive to the point when I became the aggressor I suppose. It was such a terrible name. At school, if anyone made fun of me because of it, I'd give them a good hiding. People would take a look at me, and take it as read because I was smaller than them, that they could pick on me, bully me. That name just added to the anger I felt inside at being picked on. So every so often I lashed out to spread the message that I wasn't someone to mess with.

Even when I left school, it continued, the bullying and abuse. In my service days it was a daily thing, name calling and having a go at Nappey man. Just like a rerun of my schooldays, I'd take it until I snapped then I'd go beserk and fly off the handle. Those people, they deserved to be taught a lesson, I can't stand bullies. It's the same in here (prison); there's a pecking order, you have to stand up to the bullies from day one, never back away from a confrontation.

Most of them know who I am, The Black Panther, so they want to have a go at me. Wasters, low life scum, paedophiles and nonces trying to tell me what to do. They try once, then never again, I make sure of that. It's all about egos in here, who's the hardest, who's the worst killer, that sort of thing. All shit stuff but it matters if you want to survive."

Donald Nappey was born in August 1936. Later when he joined the armed forces during a period of National Service, he was posted to Kenya, Cyprus and Aden. The forces gave him training in firearms, something that stayed with him throughout his life. In 1955 he married Irene and moved to Bradford to settle down. Five years later, in 1960, their daughter Kathryn was born, and it was at this time that he changed his surname to Neilson. He took employment as a carpenter, but struggled to make a success of this, further failures occurred with a taxi business and after that a security firm flopped.

Distressed because he was unable to provide for his family, he took out his failures on his wife and daughter, who he dominated and dictated to.

He took up another career in 1965, that of property burglary, this time with some success. It is estimated he committed around 400 such crimes without ever being caught. Because the returns from such acts offered little in the way of financial profit, he took to robbing rural sub-post offices. Between 1967 and 1974 he carried out nineteen robberies around Yorkshire and Lancashire. The cash rewards were much improved, but Neilson wanted more and so his actions became much more ruthless as his mercenary greed took over.

He had been watching a sub-post office in Heywood, Lancashire in February 1972, working out the best day to commit the robbery to maximise takings. In the middle of the night he broke in, awakening the postmaster, Leslie Richardson, who lived upstairs. When Richardson came downstairs he was confronted by a hooded intruder and immediately lunged at the individual. Neilson was brandishing a shotgun and fired it at the postmaster who fell to the floor. Neilson then fled.

Leslie Richardson survived the attack and was able to give the Police a full description of the offender. A photo-fit was subsequently composed, but it looked nothing like Neilson!

Then on 15th February, 1974 Neilson broke into a sub-post office in Harrogate, North Yorkshire, where he shot dead postmaster Donald Skepper during a confrontation. Another postmaster murder occurred seven months later in Higher Baxenden, near Accrington, Lancashire. Victim, Derek Astin was shot dead during a night time raid. A few months later, a third postmaster was killed on 11th November 1974. Sidney Grayland was just 55 when Neilson broke into his sub-post office on Oldbury, West Midlands and shot him dead before running off with £800 in cash and postal orders.

By now, the local media were connecting the murders, and dubbed the killer 'The Black Panther' because he dressed all in black and only operated during night time hours. Conversations between the different Police forces formally connected the crimes and a mini taskforce was formed to investigate. Despite lots of potential witnesses, very few provided anything insightful or clues that might open up leads towards catching the killer.

Neilson meanwhile had gone to ground. With increased awareness around sub-post office security, and additional Police patrols being carried out on all such premises, it was getting too risky, so he stopped. He needed a new way of getting rich the easy way.

A couple of months later, he turned to kidnap. In the early hours of 14th January, 1975, he broke into Lesley's home in Highley, Shropshire, and abducted her from her bedroom, allowing her just enough time to grab a dressing gown. From there, he took her to a drainage shaft in Bathpool Park, Kidsgrove, Staffordshire. She would never walk in the sunlight again as that was where she was killed.

At the Whittle family home in Highley, Neilson had left detailed instructions on Dymo tape messages in the lounge of their house, which the family were to follow to the letter. Worryingly for the Police and the family, he stated that Lesley would be killed if the Police got involved or he suspected their involvement. The Police were made aware and all press releases and comments on the case was shut down, only a select number of officers knew what was taking place. Neilson then shot and fatally wounded a security guard, Gerald Smith, after he had challenged him in a railway yard in Dudley. Smith, who died a year later, saw Neilson and gave the Police a full description of the wanted man, including the make, model and colour of the car he was driving.

After a bungled pay out, Neilson never received his ransom, and a week later, the naked body of Lesley Whittle was discovered hanging in the cold damp shaft. Despite everything, Neilson avoided arrest for a further nine months. I recall many years later carrying out investigations into locating motor vehicles he once owned.

With greed returning, he resumed raids on sub-post offices. One December evening in 1975, two uniformed patrol officers driving a panda car spotted a man acting suspiciously near such premises in Nottinghamshire. They pulled over and got out of the Police car to talk to the man. Neilson produced a sawn-off shotgun from his bag, and pointed it at the two shocked officers, threatening to blow their heads off if they tried to escape or use their Police radios. He forced them back into the car, and sat in the back, constantly waving the weapon between both officers.

Fearing they were going to die, the driver dramatically swerved the car, causing the occupants to be thrown around. The shotgun went off injuring one of the officers. The Police car ground to a sudden stop smashing into the kerb outside a fish and chip shop. As the officers were frantically trying to overpower Neilson, a passer-by stopped to assist and helped them handcuff him to a set of railings. Witnesses described Neilson as fighting like a wild animal during his arrest.

"I never set out to deliberately harm or kill anyone, it was always about the money for me. The shotgun was for my own protection, not for the kill. They were going to hurt me, they were the ones who forced the issue not me. I tried talking to them where I could, getting them to open the safe and hand over cash and postal orders and I told them, all of them, no one would be hurt if they did what I said. It couldn't have been simpler for them, but no, they had to be heroes, brave, giving up their lives for the post office.

Why would anyone do that? I mean if you are in armed combat in the forces, then fighting for your country is the right thing to do, you do it with pride. Those men worked for the post office, it's not like it was a position of power or anything.

Would shop employees give up their lives so easily for the sake of a few measly quid? I doubt it.

I'm not sure why I lost my way in life, though I've never really been me at any point in time. I love my family and wanted to provide for them, give them everything they wanted. I'd see people raking the money in, doing nothing, sat on their big fat arses while unfortunate people like me used to work long hard hours for next to nothing. I could see myself being rich, I wanted to be powerful and financial wealth gives you that power. I'd read in magazines about people getting away with burglaries and crime, so I thought with my services background, discipline and training, I could be the best. I was, I did hundreds of burglaries and the Police were nowhere near catching me on any of them. Stealth, cunning and no fingerprints or clues left behind. I was good, the best.

I stand by my statement, I didn't kill the one in the drainage shaft. That one fell, slipped probably off the ledge. I told her she must not wander about, but she ignored it. I was trying to help her, not hurt her. I'd never have killed her if she hadn't hanged herself. It was sheer coincidence that it happened after the family messed up the drop off in the car park. The Police car wasn't supposed to be there, I thought it was a set up. Next thing I know, she's dead so I left her there.

You know, the post office and that family, they had plenty of money, it's not like they couldn't afford it, they could. They had it, I wanted it, no, I needed it, so I took it. You've asked me if I feel any remorse or anything like that, my only remorse is getting caught. I should never have got into the Police car, but I panicked. It was funny how two coppers couldn't take me down, they needed help. The last person you'd want beside you in the trenches during a war would be a copper. Cowardly useless bunch. If I hadn't made that mistake, they would never have caught me, I was a superior sort of criminal. Not even Sherlock Holmes could have caught me, I was that sophisticated in covering up my crimes.

It's as I say, those men who gave up their lives for the post office, so senseless, a pointless loss of life. If they had done what I asked they'd still be pottering about now. So whose fault is that? Mine, or theirs? Ask yourself that one, I hadn't gone out with intent to kill. As brutal as it sounds, they are dead, it was their choice, not mine. I was only defending myself."

Within hours of his arrest, his Bradford home was subjected to a thorough Police search, revealing an arsenal of weapons and ammunition, and burglary kits, ski masks, full face balaclavas, ropes, knives, cable ties, and a variety of camouflaged clothing. There was even a model of a black panther on display in the upstairs room.

He refused to cooperate with investigating officers for several days, then made a full confession, claiming Lesley Whittle died as a result of accidentally slipping from the tiny ledge in the damp miserable shaft where she was being kept.

In June and July 1976, he went on trial at Oxford Crown Court, was convicted and given five life sentences.

Over the years that followed Neilson lodged various appeals to get his sentence reduced, claiming an infringement of his human rights with such a lengthy tariff. Successive Home Secretaries upheld his whole life tariff. In November 2002, the whole legal landscape surrounding Donald Neilson changed dramatically when the Home Secretary's power to set minimum terms of imprisonment was removed by the European Court. This meant that Neilson might well have been eligible for release in 2006, having served a 30-year term.

It was case closed in 2008 when High Court Judge Mr Justice Teare, ruled that he should never be released, and that he should die in prison. Neilson passed away in hospital on 18th December 2011, after being transferred there from Norwich Prison whilst suffering from breathing difficulties, later dying as a result of contracting pneumonia.

I was fortunate enough to meet one of Neilson's silent victims many years later - Dorothy Whittle, the mother of murdered teenager, Lesley Whittle. That encounter changed my entire outlook on my Police career. At the time I was writing a book titled 'Shropshire Murder Casebook' (Countryside Books 1994) and one of the cases I was to cover was that of The Black Panther and in particular, the kidnapping in Highley. I wanted to portray Lesley accurately and not sensationlise or glamourise Neilson in any way. I wanted the story to be about Lesley Whittle, and not him.

Whilst I've communicated with and held hundreds of conversations with serial killers and deviants of all types, I have also sat with thousands of victims, and the families left behind as a result of a selfish act of fatal violence. It's a good way to balance out a profile, keeping the focus on the victim allows you to understand and feel the damage crime and murder in particular creates.

Dorothy was a lovely lady, I instantly liked her, though I could see the all too familiar haunted look in her eyes, a sadness and emptiness. For a few hours we sat and talked; she was wonderful, kind, caring and considerate, in explaining how it had affected her and the family. I chose not to use any of the material from our meeting, as for me, it was a very personal experience. This lady was open and honest, and when the tears streamed down my cheeks she was there offering a tissue asking if I was okay. At one point she even asked if what she was saying was too upsetting for me.

In the end, I was weeping inconsolably, not only at the tragedy of the murder but of the impact the senseless loss of life creates. I felt no shame, or weakness, this lady caused me think about the victims I walked away from once a case was closed post-prosecution. I use the term walked away, because I rarely considered back then the continuing trauma people might have felt. We often forget these human beings as we move onto our next case or investigation. It's a sad indictment that as officers of the law, we often rely on agencies like Victim Support to sweep up those most in need. Rarely do we get the time or opportunity to do more, to revisit and show that we do care, that we have remembered them. Sadly, today, due to political measures and austerity, a high percentage of victims of crime don't even get to see a Police officer, a sad indictment of how policing has gone awry, in some places losing touch with certain groups of people.

Dorothy Whittle taught me so much that day, she opened my eyes to fundamental weaknesses in our Police system, in that we don't take time to show we care about our victims or in the case of loss of life, the families left behind. Despite the obvious failures by the authorities to find Lesley alive, she remained positive about the Police and the Criminal Justice System:

"When he was sentenced to life imprisonment, it seemed like the interest ended there. Until that point, the press were camped on the green opposite the house, the Police kept us up to date as best they could, then there was nothing. I didn't like any of it. How do you cope afterwards?

Of course, the Police might have been able to do more, but then so could everyone else involved. It's no good apportioning blame, it's about making sure it doesn't happen again, learning from our mistakes. The sadness lives with us (the family) every day, we get through it because we are a family and we are there for each other. Bob (Booth - the Police senior investigating officer) has been good, he's a kind caring man. I think they made him a scapegoat for their own failings."

When news broke about Donald Neilson's death, I was apathetic. I can generally find some positive feature in the criminals I encounter, whether it's a good childhood memory they share, or a glimpse of remorse for their actions. Donald Neilson was not one of those killers. I found him and his actions totally deplorable. From a profiling perspective, we can see a dysfunctional environment in his background, low self-esteem, alienation from his peer group and anger. Undoubtedly once in National Service and wearing a military uniform he enjoyed the power that the badge and being part of something created, it's about feeling wanted. He desperately wanted to be respected, and the uniform provided that.

In his own mind, wealth provided power, and would allow him to make his own decisions, as opposed to being subjected to workplace rules. This is probably why his businesses failed, because they were ill thought out - to him, they were get rich quick business ventures. Like so many killers, there is an escalation in violence until it accompanied most of his later crimes. Now, he was experiencing the ultimate power, that of life and death. Perhaps he wanted more, the need to instill fear into someone, watching and knowing they are suffering and having the power to stop it.

Neilson was very much more than just another serial killer, this was a man yet to find his true darker destiny. Would he have gone on to kill other victims? In my opinion, without doubt. Thankfully, before he did, he was imprisoned for life, and therefore of no further threat to innocent people. His appeals were little more than an effort to show he still yielded some level of power, keeping him in the minds of the press and the public. I don't think he ever recognised the level of negativity felt towards him by the public. His crimes were cowardly, and unwittingly a portrayal of the 'real him' that he claimed he never got to be.

MIND GAMES

ELEVEN
Hell On Earth

> "I'm ready to be released. Release me, you have no cause for worry!"
> *Kenneth McDuff*

Judges and Parole Board officials take note. The first and last question on your list of criteria that you should ask yourselves before sentencing, or granting parole is: Knowing of their crimes, would I genuinely trust this person if he or she lived next door to me? That's the acid-test of course, could you ever trust a convicted criminal around your loved ones? The Judiciary come from privileged backgrounds, they don't live among the masses, nor, from personal experience, do they often understand the reality of everyday life. The stresses and pressures of paying bills, clothing the kids and generally making ends meet while living in an area that may well have been neglected. Judges, in their defence, are led by prescribed rules and sentencing tariffs that in today's society often aren't fit for purpose.

Human rights are more prevalent today than ever before, even rapists and serial killers, by law, have rights. It's a moral dilemma, as when someone repeatedly commits the most heinous crimes against another person, do they deserve rights? What of the rights of their victims or their families? Then we have the prison system. Is prison a punishment, or a place of rehabilitation? It clearly does not work as a deterrent, as global reoffending is greater than it has ever been which, in its current state, tends to rule out rehabilitation.

Most of us thankfully don't have to consider too much any of these issues, until they physically affect us, perhaps as victims of crime, or our own neighbourhood being targeted for criminal activity. Every so often a case pricks our social consciousness and causes national debate. Improper sentencing of serious felons, or parole being granted to someone who is clearly still, in the eyes of the public, a threat. Forgotten in the midst of these, often farcical, decisions, is the victim or victims. Focusing attention on the offender does not aid the victims one little bit. Through my own experiences within the Criminal Justice System, I am able to say with some confidence that in my opinion, the worst deviant offenders cannot be rehabilitated. Trying to justify this through claims that they can be educated to manage their own behaviour is little more than a whitewash to appease courts and influence sentencing.

Serial killers continue to do what gives them the greatest level of euphoria - kill. Even during their incarceration, they can never truly be trusted, hence the manacles and cells to house them. There are claims that some simply stopped because they outgrew their passion or compulsion for killing. In debates around this topic, the case of Denis Rader (BTK) is often quoted. From what we know, he killed five people in 1974, a further two in 1977, one person in 1985, another in 1986 then, according to him, he didn't kill again until 1991. Eventually he resurfaced in 2004, and the Police caught him. He tried to explain to the Police that the reason he resurfaced in 2004 was that his kids had grown up(and left home) and he was bored!

The big question here has to be, do we (or why should we) believe him? We are suddenly taking his word as being truthful. I, more than anyone, know that serial killers manipulate the facts and the truth to fit their own story. They are deceitful, and one has to delve deep into their psyche and gain their trust to get some understanding of their odd reality. For decades we have been fed inaccurate information that serial killers don't change their method of killing. Yet they frequently do. In the United Kingdom we have incarcerated serial killers who have undoubtedly killed more victims than we currently know about. Cold case reviews unearth new evidence that links them to the crimes. When confronted with this evidence they often confess - what they don't do is volunteer it. Only when faced with facts will they admit the crime. So, while the murderous activities might appear to have stopped, they haven't; they possibly changed location, victim type, or modus operandi for a time, all in search of increased excitement to fulfill their own needs. I don't believe Rader did stop. The one thing all incarcerated serial killers have in common, is secrets. They don't confess to every misdemeanour, as it gives them a sense of power and control over the authorities to withhold certain information.

One case where the system got it very wrong began on the evening of 6th August, 1966. Kenneth Allen McDuff was born at 201 Linden Street in the central Texas town of Rosebud. He was the fifth child of six children born to John and

Addie McDuff. His father ran a successful concrete business and as he grew older Kenneth often worked for the firm. From a young age he had been flirting with crime, stealing from stores and other kids. Due to his above average height and build, he was also a bully. Raised in a religious family environment, his behaviour was often covered up by parents refusing to accept or acknowledge their son's ill-disciplined behaviour. When the law did get involved with Kenneth, lawyers would be employed by his parents to challenge any allegations. Addie McDuff, herself had a reputation. She once fired a gun at a school bus driver because he had kicked her son off the bus and refused to allow him back on.

The rules of life were not being correctly enforced within the family home and as a result, socially at least, his behaviour deteriorated as he grew older. Evidence of the family's denial of their childrens' inappropriate behaviour can be found when one looks at Kenneth's older brother, Lonnie. He was regarded by all who knew him as a troublemaker with a reputation. On one occasion he had pulled a knife on the Rosebud school principal, D. L. Mayo. The principle defended himself and threw Lonnie down the stairs. Lonnie was also a bully and undoubtedly, during his formative years, Kenneth learned some of his more desperate life skills from his older brother. Lonnie courted trouble and was ultimately shot to death by the ex-husband of a woman he was seeing.

The bullying continued as Kenneth targeted vulnerable people. Sexually active, his crimes began to take a deviant nature. A number of attacks on young girls went unreported, even though the Police were aware; the victims were too frightened, in fear of reprisals, to make a complaint. The Police finally got the result an entire town desperately wanted, when McDuff was jailed on a series of burglary charges in 1965. McDuff's initial assessment saw penalties that should have seen him imprisoned for 52 years. However, he was just eighteen, and so the sentencing tariff was reduced to run concurrently instead of consecutively. Because of good behaviour and the fact his rehabilitation was deemed to be successful, McDuff was released after 10 months, and immediately returned to the town he terrorised. As a reward for his release, his mother treated him to a surprise gift: a new Dodge Charger car.

We now move to the night of Saturday 6th August 1966. Having spent the morning pouring concrete at a construction site in nearby Temple, along with his friend Roy Dale Green, the pair smartened themselves up, before driving out to Fort Worth. Showing off in his new car, McDuff insisted that they cruise around the region, after meeting up with some old acquaintances and drinking. They continued their drive around the area. It was then that McDuff's eye was caught by a teenage girl talking to two boys who were sitting in a 1955 Ford. The teenage girl, 16-year-old Edna Sullivan, looked pretty dressed in a red-and-white-striped blouse and wearing cut-off jeans. The two boys were her boyfriend, 17-year-old Robert Brand, and his cousin, 15-year-old Mark Dunnan.

Parking up, McDuff slid a .38 pistol from beneath his car seat and walked over to the group. Pointing the pistol at them, he took money off them, then forced all three of them to climb into the boot of the Ford, slamming it shut behind them. He then walked back to Green who was sat in the Charger. *"Those kids got a good look at my face, I'll have to kill them. Follow me in the Dodge."*

McDuff returned to the Ford and drove off with the three teenagers locked in the boot, followed by Green driving the Dodge. He turned down a remote track, before pulling up in a field. He was ready to do harm and opened the boot, grabbing the girl by her arm and forcibly pulling her out of the vehicle. Green was instructed to take her and lock her in the trunk of the Dodge, which he did.

McDuff looked on as the terrified girl begged them to let her go. He then turned back towards the Ford which had its boot lid open. Inside, the two boys were crying and pleading for mercy. McDuff told them get to their knees, they acquiesced to his every command in the hope he wouldn't hurt them. It was over in seconds. From point blank range McDuff shot them both in the face, Brand twice and Dunnam three times. Looking at the bodies, he pulled Dunnam up by the hair, and fired a further shot in him. Unable to close the boot, McDuff was forced to reverse the Ford against a fence so the bodies wouldn't be openly on display from the field. McDuff and Green then drove off in the Dodge, with Edna Sullivan still locked in the boot.

Driving into Johnson County, McDuff brought the Dodge to a halt down a deserted dirt track. Dragging Sullivan from the boot, he made her undress, then raped her in the back seat of his car. Twice he defiled the poor girl before making Green do the same. He then raped her again. His mind in overdrive he then drove to another location where he parked up. Sex was no longer the intent, he now had murder on his mind. Screaming, Sullivan was again dragged from the car and made to sit naked in the road in front of the vehicle. Green looked on as McDuff pushed the girl's head to the ground and using a broomstick, began choking her. Green later told law enforcement officers:

"He mashed down hard on the girl's head. She was panicking and started to struggle, waving her arms and kicking her legs. McDuff told me to grab her legs. I was frightened, so I did what I was told."

McDuff finished the girl off, crushing her throat until every ounce of life was extinct. He then tossed her body over a nearby fence and drove home. He had the sense to tell Green they needed to remove their bloodstained underwear and bury it, which they did.

Green was mortified and the following afternoon, as news of the murders was broadcast on the radio of a car he was travelling in, he blurted out "My God, I have to tell someone". Thereafter he became the prosecution's star witness. He was to later serve five years for his part in the crimes.

Typically, McDuff's mother, Addie, refused to accept the allegations, and hired a good lawyer. Kenneth McDuff denied all knowledge of the crimes and any involvement in the brutal killings. It was his claim that the murders were probably committed by Green and that he was being victimised by the Falls County Sheriff who saw only bad in him. His claims were unsubstantiated as the evidence stacked up against him.

At one point, his desperate mother spoke to reporters covering the trial and told them that Kenneth had confessed to being with a girl he knew from church at the time of the murders, so had an alibi. However, to protect that girl's reputation he was willing to face the electric chair. *"He's too good for his own good"* she claimed!

Found guilty, the jury passed him the death sentence, and that should have been the end of it. In 1972 a Supreme Court decision overturned all the death sentences in the United States and Kenneth McDuff was one of a number of prisoners who had their sentence commuted to life imprisonment. Shockingly, in 1976, just ten years after the triple murders, McDuff had served sufficient time in prison for eligibility for parole. He applied for parole, and when the board turned him down, he continued to submit applications until he was deemed capable of leading a life back in society, and in 1989 his application for parole was approved. He was released on 11th October 1989.

Few people in that area could fathom out why McDuff had received parole having committed the most ghastly crime in living memory in the region. The reality was that parole boards were keen to empty overflowing prisons, so if someone met the criteria, then they would be released. One local Sheriff who knew McDuff well, on hearing the news of his release, made a shocking claim:

"I don't know if it'll be next week or next month or next year, but one of these days, dead girls are gonna start turning up, and when that happens, the man you need to look for is Kenneth McDuff."

It was like a self-fulfilling prophecy, and where murder is concerned, there is no such thing as coincidence. Just three days later, the naked body of 29-year-old Sarafia Parker was found, beaten and strangled in a field of weeds in southeast Temple. The very town where McDuff was ordered to sign in on parole. Unable to connect him to the crime, he remained at large.

A man such as McDuff cannot simply stop doing what he enjoys most, criminality. In the summer of 1990, he was charged with making a terroristic threat, sufficient, because he was on parole at the time, to see him back behind bars for life. McDuff had yelled racist comments towards a group of black teenagers, and chased one down an alleyway, producing a knife and threatening to kill him. In prison, his lawyer fought to get his client released on parole.

After legal contestations, McDuff was again granted parole without any hearing or consultation. A decision was made by an anonymous official who saw no reason to keep him imprisoned. On 6th December, 1990, Kenneth McDuff walked out of prison, a free man.

He remained under the Police radar by constantly moving address; for a time he lived in Temple, Cameron, Rockdale, Bellmead, Tyler and Dallas. His mother continued to support him and despite being unemployed he was seen driving new cars, wearing nice clothes and with plenty of money at his disposal. In the early months of 1991, street sex workers around the Waco area were reported missing. At this time, McDuff had enrolled in the Texas State Technical College in Waco and lived on campus.

When he ran through a Police checkpoint driving his red pick-up, a woman recognised by officers to be Regenia Moore, was seen thrashing about and screaming in the cab. The Police failed to follow up this incident for several days and nothing further came of it. Other matters went unreported on campus, as he turned to violence and robbery, threatening his victims with serious reprisals if they spoke out.

He was again escalating his violence towards murder, and when the body of missing 22-year-old Melissa Northup was found, bound and floating in a local gravel pit, no one suspected McDuff. A few weeks later, another body was discovered. Naked and badly decomposed, the remains of Valencia Kay Joshua were found buried in a shallow grave. Joshua had been reported missing in February of that year. New witnesses had come forward recalling seeing her on campus looking for McDuff's dormitory room. Realising he was again a wanted man, he fled.

The authorities were onto him, and a task force was assembled in Waco. Working eighteen hour shifts, the law enforcement officers tirelessly pushed on, realising that a dangerous criminal was loose and needed to be apprehended. A report from Capitol City noted that a young woman, Colleen Reed, had been abducted from a car wash. The witnesses described the vehicle into which she had been forced, it was a Thunderbird. Kenneth McDuff owned a Thunderbird.

It wasn't long before one of the two men seen abducting Reed was located and arrested. He told a gruesome story of what happened to the woman. McDuff had parked up a few miles out of Austin and told his partner in crime to drive. As he drove the Thunderbird along I-35, McDuff forced Colleen to strip naked. He was abusing her and at one point stubbed out a cigarette between her legs and raped her. For the hours that followed, this poor woman was to suffer rape and torture by both her abductors. He claimed that McDuff locked the woman in the trunk and dropped him off at his home. He believed her remains were buried near to the home of McDuff's mother.

The statement was released to the media in the hope of attaining some kind of public response and sightings. At the beginning of May, America's Most Wanted programme featured the Police search for Kenneth McDuff. The public response opened many new leads of inquiry, as fresh sightings of the wanted man came in. One in particular struck a chord. It came from Kansas City, Missouri, where the Police there received a call from a viewer who recognised a fast-talking garbage truck worker, with an eye for women and suggested it might be the wanted man. He was calling himself Richard Fowler. Within hours, at the city dump, Kenneth McDuff was surrounded by armed Police officers; he was submissive and was arrested without a struggle.

On 18th February, 1993, the jury, in a special punishment hearing, sentenced him to death. The execution date was set for 17th November, 1998. Before he died, he is said to have given up the burial site of Colleen Reed.

"There are times in a man's life that he needs to take stock of what he's achieved. I was a pain in the butt for the authorities, so take something from that. I can't blame anyone else for what I did, not any of my family. I got in with the wrong crowd, earned a reputation, once you've got that in a small town, you're marked for life. Cops in small towns have small minds, they don't ever forget. Each time something shit happened there, the first name they called out was Kenneth McDuff, it was unfair and wrong.

I don't want to talk about murder or death or any of that stuff. This is all about me yeah? If I'm able to say this, I don't believe I was born to be bad, it just happened, circumstances weren't right for me and things developed. I got streetwise at a young age, and it went from there. People dare you to do things, and you think it's big to carry them out, but it isn't good, it's stupid.

Do I hold grudges? Yeah, I guess I do, there's a few people crossed me over the years, tried to set me up for things I didn't do, or lied about me. I don't forgive or forget those bastards. In church, we were told to turn the other cheek. I did that and it got punched even harder the second time. I resented some of the stuff that happened to me and Lonnie (brother). People saw us evil, we were kids having fun that's all, Rosebud was a boring insular place, I think I lived up its reputation. I hear people visit there just to see where I lived and committed some of my crimes. That's weird but it makes me famous, infamous so I did achieve something I think.

My mother was super protective of us all, she was as good a mother as anyone could hope for. Whatever I needed, I asked her and I got it. You need someone watching your back when you are a bit of a rogue. That's how I see myself, a rogue, not a serial killer. The medics in here often ask me all sorts of things about my life, I think they're looking for something to pin my behaviour on, there's nothing out the ordinary to tell anyone. It never sat comfortably that I was picked on by teaching staff ahead of anyone else. That's because I was such a well-built lad, they saw me as a challenge I think.

The one thing that sticks out from my schooldays is the confrontation with another kid, he is so insignificant that I cannot recall his name. Whatever his name was, he had a problem with me because I got more respect than he did, I was a better fighter, he was the school creep, a sporting sort. We somehow ended up in a fight, and he caught me unawares, took me down. I wasn't ready, so it was unfair. I remember being laughed at by some of the other kids, girls included; they called me weak and stupid. I admit I wasn't great at school, I hated the classroom work, it was boring as shit.

I guess I became angry after the school experience, I can't say. I do know that after that unfair fight, I vowed never to let anyone walk all over me again or humiliate me in public through name calling or in any other way. I was always a bit of a loner, I preferred my own company and I think that caused problems for me too, as other kids saw me as different, and people in Rosebud didn't do different. You were either in the right group, those in power, or you weren't, no individuals were accepted.

That's probably the reason I rebelled and fought back at the world. I hate this serial killer tag, that's not what I am, I'm Kenneth McDuff, a human being, I'm not a label, I have a personality, I breathe, I get happy and I feel sadness. Will I ever conform? Of course not. I'm me and I like being me.

The whole matter of parole is down to officials who make assessments, they judge you on your behaviour and how you conduct yourself during discussions with them and others in the prison system. I knew I wasn't right and should never be released, but the opportunity was there for me, so I took it. It wasn't hard duping the officials that I was a reformed character, a good, a God-fearing guy. Having a good lawyer fighting my corner for me helped too.

It felt like a black cloud of doom and gloom surrounded me when I went into one of my rages, there was no stopping me from doing what I wanted. I think I shocked some people when they saw me lose it. I've been told it was depression, but I don't think so. I had everything, fast cars, ladies, quality clothes and money in my pocket. I blew all of that, for what?"

From my conversations with McDuff, there can be no doubting that his mother's attitude towards him blurred the lines between right and wrong, morality and immorality. Though she can hardly be blamed for caring about her family and protecting and spoiling them whenever she could. Her denial is not unique, and like any mother, she would defend her children always. What stands out from conversations with McDuff, are his childhood feelings about being viewed differently because of his appearance, and attitude. His behaviour alienated him from others and he was targeted as a problem child by the authorities who saw his level of anti-social behaviour escalate. It's fundamentally important for children to understand right from wrong, it seems that Kenneth McDuff never quite grasped that, he never learned from his experiences, instead he repeated them twofold, punishing those who tried to stop his behaviour.

The initial three murders he committed should have been sufficient for any professional body to see this was a dangerous man, with a dark and sinister personality. The manner of his killings - the two boys were executed, the girl raped and horribly tortured before being killed - show his desire to be viewed as powerful and having a need for control. Hiding their underwear displays not an unsound mind, but one forensically aware, it also shows that he knew what he had done was wrong, further excluding serious mental health issues.

His refusal to discuss the crimes is typical of a killer in denial. He did not want to be reminded of the vile things he'd done, his own mindset had moved on from that, they were now a distant memory. The victims weren't viewed as human beings, but objects, pawns from which he derived a sense of satisfaction. There was not a glimmer of remorse in his conversations, and as he initially, narcissistically pointed out, *"this is all about me, not them"* (the victims).

McDuff struck an imposing figure in prison, he was not someone I'd ever contemplate crossing or upsetting. Despite his so-called good childhood, he had no happy recollections of family bonding or life. Whenever questions were asked of his family morals and principles, it was easy to sense simmering animosity building within him. When his own daughter was mentioned, he refused to talk about the child or any of his bloodline relatives: *"As my own mother protected me, now I protect my own too."*

It's a pity he didn't give his victims the same courtesy or consideration. In all my years of doing this work, Kenneth McDuff sits among the group of killers I would describe as entirely emotionally detached. His own reality was not that of the average human being, there existed an unsettling undercurrent about his personality. It's a real possibility that there are many more victims of Kenneth McDuff out there, both dead and alive.

Paroled three times and judged to be safe for reintegration back into society, I ask again, do you think any member of a parole board would feel safe living next door to someone with McDuff's antecedents?

TWELVE
Guilty As Charged

"Enjoy a witchy kind of day." - *Charlie Manson*

Like most people reading this book, I had preconceived ideas about some of the killers I had dealings with over the years. Those whom I expected to be genuinely fearsome individuals turned out to be anything but. Those whom I expected little of were often shocking and vile by their very nature. Individuals like Metheny, Gaskins, Watts were truly disgusting, McDuff was overbearing and if I was so inclined to allow it, a little intimidating. None are what you could ever call an average human being. There is something different about each of them and quite rightly so, they are all individuals with their own drivers and dealing with their own emotional traumas in very different ways.

That's what this journey has shown me, we cannot put these people in a box and give an overarching explanation for their collective behaviour. It doesn't exist, no matter how much we analyse or assess the phenomenon, people are all different. We cannot predict how serial killers of the future will commit their crimes, or who they might be. All we can do is identify potential causes and try to prevent them in future generations.

When reading and profiling a crime scene, we must do so with care and not rely solely on scientific evidence to help us catch perpetrators. Assessing it and walking in the shoes of the offender, may provide qualified conclusions to work with. Take nothing for granted and believe in what we perceive until evidence dictates otherwise. It's about looking closely with our eyes, listening to witnesses and asking the right questions of those people as well as using sense and intuition. It's about thinking outside the box and not accepting anything as fact until it's categorically proven to be so.

One question that regularly crops up at my talks is, who's the most famous serial killer you know? My answer is always the same: I never sensationalise or 'big up' serial killers. They are not and should never be considered as celebrities. They are dangerous individuals, who, if you met them, you'd probably be sickened by their attitude. Some have personalities, charm and wit, and all of them are prone to deep, dark moods. Years of incarceration has institutionalised many of them, they are often childish or act in a pathetic outrageous manner. At no point should we consider them friends, and for the untrained, toying with them in TV interviews often makes for a harrowing or pointless engagement. They are not performing artists, they are seriously disturbed people with a propensity for killing.

This leads me nicely onto my next profile, a much-maligned individual who, in my opinion, receives more television and online media air time than any other serial killer across the globe. Even Jack the Ripper's spotlight pales into insignificance when it comes to this man. His name is Charles Milles Manson. A person whose character and actions divide opinion - a crazy manipulator or a cunning mastermind? If anyone played to an audience, it was Manson, online media sites are full of his performances in front of camera. News media companies line up interviews with him, each one with an agenda to get Manson to play up for their audience and to enhance their own status. Again, this brings me back to victims; what thought really went into those interviews, other than to enhance viewing figures? Did anyone consider the victims? In those clips I have seen, each one has been heavily focused on Manson and getting some controversial quotes and/or behaviour out of him. Don't get me wrong, he loved playing the eccentric fool, the angry bitter man with a grudge against civilisation. The innocent victim. The "I never killed no one" quote is regularly regurgitated by him like some kind of mantra. In my opinion, none of those clips show the real Charles Manson.

Born in Cincinnati, Ohio, on 12th November, 1934, his mother, Kathleen Maddox was just 16 when she gave birth to him. His father, who he never met, was Colonel Scott from Ashland, Kentucky. Kathleen later married William Manson, but the marriage failed; Kathleen's violent temper and her abhorrent behaviour soon had William packing his bags. Unable to cope financially, Kathleen commenced a life of petty crime. For a while she got away with stealing from grocery stores, until in 1939, desperate, brandishing a firearm, she held up a petrol station demanding cash from the till. As a result, she was caught by the Police and sentenced to prison.

Before sentencing, she had no option but to send Charles to a foster school for boys. As a child he was desperately unhappy and yearned for his mother's love. Finally, the court stepped in and ordered him to be sent to Gibault School for Boys in Terre Haute, Indiana. Later, after his mother's release from prison, he ran away from the school and returned to his mother, and each time she sent him back. The sad truth was, Kathleen enjoyed her freedom without him in her life, she wanted nothing to do with him. With his school days over, Charles had no home to go to, and spent his life living on the streets. Like his mother, he survived by committing petty crime. At the age of just 13 he was caught by the Police after a string of burglaries and armed robberies led to his arrest. Not eligible for jail time, he was convicted of the crimes and sent to a juvenile detention centre. From there, he escaped once again and while free commited a further two armed robberies. By now he was gaining an unwanted reputation as a law breaker and someone who didn't abide by rules or laws. Anti-establishment, he began to feel that the system was preventing him from being looked after and loved by his mother. He wasn't at large for long and was quickly arrested, and this time sent by the courts to the Indiana School for Boys in Plainfield.

In a period of three years there, the length of his sentence, he escaped from the school no less than eighteen times. On one occasion he stole a car and drove West, burgling and robbing up to twenty petrol stations during the trip. With excellent personal descriptions of him and the car he was driving provided by witnesses, he was caught in Utah and charged with the new crimes. Convicted on each count, the courts sent him to the National Training School for Boys in Washington, D. C. By now, Charles was identified as a boy with problems, and underwent psychiatric assessment. One such professional described him as being "slick, yet extremely sensitive".

"All I wanted was my mom, I needed to know she cared for and loved me. I never got the chance to show her how I felt about her and let her see I could be a good boy; instead, those rotten apples in the establishment kept me from her. The sent her to prison so we couldn't be together, then they picked on me because I was young and an easy target I guess. Those were important years of my life they stole from me. They wanted to turn me into some kind of dangerous criminal, the way they talked about me in the courts and to each other, it was like I didn't exist and I had no way of talking to them. Whenever I spoke out, I'd be beaten, so I talked louder and used bad language to get their attention. They just beat me

some and told to shut the fuck up. So I became the rebel they wanted me to be. I thought, fuck it, I can be who I want and I don't want to be part of this system, I'll do my own thing. I had no idea what the hell I was going to do back then, it just happened thereafter."

By 1952, because of his behaviour and attempts at escaping, he was moved to the secure reformatory at Chillicothe, Ohio.

"They couldn't find anywhere secure enough to hold me. I was agile and small so could hide away in tiny spaces, then sneak out when the coast was clear. It was fun, like a game of hide and catch me. I showed them that no one could hold Charlie Manson."

Eventually, time served and still on probation, he was released. The discipline forced on him during his incarceration saw Manson adopt a slightly more responsible attitude. It wasn't long before for the first time in his life, he found himself in a real relationship. Rosalie Jean Willis was a waitress in a hospital. As a result of the relationship they married, and Charles Manson Junior was born. With the need to provide for his family, Manson reverted to type and returned to what he knew best, breaking the law. While working as a parking lot attendant and a bus boy, he started stealing customers' cars and using them in crime and later tried to sell some of them on. He was sent to prison at San Pedro, California for breaching the orders of his probation and for auto theft charges.

Imprisonment effectively ended his relationship with Rosalie who divorced him in 1958, retaining custody of their child. His behaviour in prison was exemplary and he managed to win parole. On release he moved to Southern California where he connected with a number of street sex workers, acting as their pimp. Spending so much time in prison mixing with other criminals taught him the rules of survival on the street, where life is cheap, and no one gives a damn about authority. This is a place where life is lived day by day, with no future or career prospects, other than in a life of crime.

The following year, after forging a treasury cheque, he was again arrested and charged with the crime. In court, his criminal antecedents worked against him as he was given a ten-year suspended sentence. Ten years is a long time for someone like Manson to stay out of trouble and the authorities undoubtedly recognised that he would be returning to prison sooner, as opposed to later.

Still operating among street sex workers, Manson fell in love with one woman, a 19-year-old called Leona 'Candy' Stevens. Together, they had a child, Charles Luther Manson junior. The relationship was fraught with tension and the couple struggled financially to survive. Again, Manson reverted to crime in an attempt to provide for his family. It wasn't long before he is caught, in Laredo, and indicted on Federal charges. He was brought back to California where he was sentenced to serve his outstanding ten-year suspended sentence. It goes without saying, that his wife took the only action open to her with her husband imprisoned for ten years and divorced him.

"It upset me how quickly these relationships turned when things were getting bad. I worked hard to try to make them work, I wanted someone to care about me, but each time I gave my everything, they threw it back in my face. They were fine when the money was coming, never asked questions where it had come from, its right what they say, when the money goes out of door, so does the relationship. I learned tough lessons from those relationships, you can't trust no one."

In prison, with few visitors, he focused on his love of music and became obsessed with the Beatles. In prison education he learnt to play the steel guitar and began to write his own music, often playing and singing for fellow inmates.

"It didn't feel like I was in prison back then, I was doing exactly what I liked, listening to and playing music. I wrote my own songs. When I listened to the lyrics of some of the Beatles tracks, it was as if they were sending subliminal messages to me, speaking to me. I could listen to them all day. The other inmates and the guards, they said I was a gifted musician and I should pursue a career in it when I got released. For the first time in my life, I felt I had a purpose, I wanted to write music and songs."

In 1967, Charles Manson was released from prison. He is said to have pleaded with prison authorities not to release him. In his own mind, again no one listened or cared what he thought. This plea has been made to sound sinister, when the truth is it wasn't.

"I didn't want to leave prison, why would I? It was the fondest part of my life, learning music, playing the guitar, being fed and watered. I knew no one wanted

me outside, so I was better off inside, no temptation. Yes, I was probably scared. It wasn't a threat."

In April 1967, he was on the streets of San Francisco, California. Now he had a plan, he wanted to be a musician and he wanted to teach the authorities a lesson. He believed he could create a life where rules didn't exist, where music, sex and drugs ruled, where people were free to do as they wished. When he met librarian Mary Brunner, he explained his life plan to her and she believed in it. They entered into a relationship, and again, Manson fathered a child, Valentine Michael. Soon, he was preaching his mantra to friends of Brunner and his following grew; he was given guru like status by eighteen or so men and women.

In the summer of 1968, realising he needed seclusion to build and rule the perfect world he believed he could create, he moved his followers, who he now called 'The Family', into an abandoned town known as Spahn Ranch in southern California.

Living in a bubble of LSD and other hallucinogenic drugs, Manson began to believe he was special, different and gifted. Obsessed with the Beatles' 'White Album' - and in particular, the song Helter Skelter - he interpreted the lyrics as being significant and inferring the beginning of a race war between black and white people. He began to believe in the notion of Armageddon and regularly quoted from the Book of Revelations. Whether he realised it or not, he had formed his own cult, so his interest in Scientology and the Church of the Final Judgement seemed relevant to his understanding. He formed an idea through his teaching that he was Jesus Christ and soon had the 'Family' believing this too.

Still heavily influenced by music, he wrote several songs and would play them on his guitar around a camp fire. He introduced himself to a musician, Gary Hinman, and let him hear tapes of his music. Hinman said he liked the music and would introduce him to Dennis Wilson of the Beach Boys and their producer, Terry Melcher (who was also the son of Doris Day and lived nearby). Armed with that information, Manson went in search of both men.

In July 1969, Hinman was found stabbed to death. Daubed on a wall close to his body, in his own blood, were the words 'political piggy'. It was later revealed that one of Manson's followers, Bobby Beausoleil, had carried out the attack, though whether he was acting independently is unknown.

Looking to meet with Melcher and let him listen to his music, Manson identified his home, 10050 Cielo Drive, which at the time was lived in by film producer, Roman Polanski and his actress/model wife, Sharon Tate. They were renting the property from Melcher. Knocking on the door, Manson was greeted by Tate's personal photographer who told him to leave the property by the back alley.

Manson and his Family also targeted Dennis Wilson's home and contrived to have him pick up family members who were hitchhiking and take them back to his house. Once inside, they were able to manipulate Wilson, through sex and drugs, into an association with Manson. The stay with Wilson was short-lived and they were quickly sent packing, with no record contract and no future in music. Manson was devastated and angry, he felt cheated by a group of people who looked after themselves and used others. In this instance, stealing their music. It should be said that some of Manson's doctored tunes did feature in an album with no credit given to him.

Manson's angst refused to subside, and he wanted to teach the music and showbusiness world a lesson. In August 1969, after a serious session of preaching and LSD, Manson told members of the Family, *"Now is the time for Helter Skelter"*.

That evening Patricia Krenwinkel, Susan Atkins, Tex Watson, and Linda Kasabian were instructed to get knives and a change of clothing. From there, they were sent to the Tate residence and told to leave a sign - something witchy. Shortly after midnight on 9th August 1969, the attack began. It was a defiant show of inexplicable violence and torture. Five people lost their lives that fateful night, four of them suffering a total of over one hundred stab wounds; a fifth victim was shot dead in his car. Cruelly murdered, were Sharon Tate, Jay Sebring, Voytek Frykowski, Abigail Folger, and Steven Parent. Tate, who was with child, was left dead on the living room floor. Her unborn baby died too. It was a scene of pure carnage. The court later heard how Sharon Tate had pleaded with her killer, Susan Atkins, not to kill her as she was having a baby. The cold killer responded: *"Look bitch, I have no mercy for you. You're going to die and you'd better get used to it."*

The word 'PIG' was scrawled onto the front door of the property, in Tate's own blood. The four killers returned to Spahn Ranch and described to Manson what they had done. He chastised them for being so messy. Later, that same night, Manson, accompanied by Patricia Krenwinkel, Tex Watson, Leslie Van Houten, and Linda Kasabian, cruised around the Los Feliz district, looking for further potential victims. They pulled up outside the home of supermarket executive, Leno LaBianca and his wife, Rosemary. This time, Manson was involved. After breaking in he tied the elderly couple up, then left the house. He walked back to the car and told Charles 'Tex' Watson, Patricia Krenwinkel and Leslie Van Houten to go inside and to kill them. In another brutal attack the couple were killed, repeatedly stabbed to death in separate rooms. The words 'Death to Pigs' and 'Healter [sic] Skelter' were scrawled in the victims' blood on a wall and a refrigerator door.

Putting it mildly, the Police botched the initial investigation, searches of the area provided no evidence or clues. Then, on 1st September, 1969 a 10-year-old boy found, beneath a bush close to his home, the gun used in the Tate murders. The gun was immediately handed over to the LAPD.

Charles Manson and his followers were arrested at Barker Ranch in Death Valley where they had moved to, on the entirely unconnected charge of grand theft auto and held in jail in the town of Independence. Everything began to unravel when Susan Atkins revealed to another inmate that she knew more about the Sharon Tate murders than she could mention and went on to say she was involved. The inmate informed the Police and soon the murder investigation began to pick up pace. Another witness came forward to claim that Manson had bragged about "knocking of five pigs the other night".

In July 1970, Charles Manson, Susan Atkins, Patricia Krenwinkel and Leslie Van Houten, went on trial in Los Angeles, charged with murder. In a bizarre trial, Manson was provided with a captive audience and showed off, briefing the other defendants to act strangely, and to pose in certain ways as though controlled by him through mind power. He, in the meantime, jumped on a table and called the Judge names while he pulled peculiar faces. Drama it was, but more farcical than compelling. At one point, Manson produced a newspaper headline from that day, which quoted President Richard Nixon unbelievably stating that Manson was guilty. Manson declared the trial unfair, though his claim was thrown out by the Judge.

It was a mess and when the State rested its case the court was stunned when defence attorney, Ronald Hughes, revealed that the Defence also rested its case, without any evidence being heard. Manson was livid and verbally threatened Hughes, dismissing him. Hughes was never seen alive again, and speculation that he was killed by other Family members circulated.

Manson was then allowed to testify, making his well quoted statement:

"The children that come at you with knives are your children. You taught them. I didn't teach them. I just tried to help them stand up."

With cases presented, the jury convicted all three defendants on the charges of first-degree murder and the death penalty was fixed. Charles Manson was sent to death row in San Quentin. Later, tried separately, Charles "Tex" Watson was convicted on all seven counts of first degree murder.

The California Supreme Court was to declare the death penalty unconstitutional, therefore Charles Manson's death sentence was automatically reduced to that of life in prison. He was soon transferred to Folsom prison, then later to Vacaville prison, where he was held for nine years.

"Some crazy stuff happened during that trial and later, to me in prison. The Judge was scared of me, he was frightened to look me in the eye in case I got inside his head. The prison guards were told not to speak to me or engage me in conversation, in case I brainwashed them. What was that all about? I'm human not a magician, I don't read minds but them officials, they believed the shit they were reading and hearing from the media and through reporters. They made me into some kind of freak.

Inside, I was getting death threats every day, they all wanted to take Charlie Manson down, it got so I couldn't trust anyone, and I didn't want to speak with no one. Everyone, and I mean everyone was making things up about, saying I said this, I said that, none of it was true."

In one serious attack on his life, an inmate, claimed "God told me to kill Manson". He proceeded to set him on fire, causing serious burns to parts of his target's body. Manson was in shock and frightened.

The courtroom farce continued when in March 1997 Manson, for the ninth time, was denied parole. The hearing was broadcast live to millions of viewers on Court TV. On being denied, Manson commented, *"That's cool. I'm not saying I wasn't involved in Helter Skelter. I'm just saying that I did not break God's law. Thank you."*

By 2012, Manson was denied parole a further three times. However, his cause was hardly helped when he told a psychologist assessing him that he was a "very dangerous man". Despite this and his ridiculous public outburst, during his years of incarceration he was always described by the authorities as a model prisoner.

"I'm not certain where it all went wrong for me, I did my best to help people, to offer them better lives. That's all I wanted, a better life than the shit lies the system preaches to you. They feed you bull shit and then tell you how you must believe it. Them people out there, you know those in power, they lie, cheat, steal and kill; yes, they kill people who dare cross them. Them people, they don't look you in the eye,

they stand on podiums and preach, you look at them, they talk above the people's heads, they can't look them straight in the face.

What's it all about? It's greed, money, avarice whatever you want to call it. That's what makes the world go round, money and power. That power, it causes war, death and destruction of whole civilisations. They're the psychopaths, the state leaders, not Charlie Manson. No one gives a fuck about me, I'm nothing. So why do you suppose they give me so much attention and air time? It's because they are distracting attention onto me, so everyone hates me meanwhile they are stealing through their taxes, killing innocent people, and destroying whole countries.

I may not be Jesus Christ, but if he was around to see this, he'd be angry, upset. This isn't the world he wanted, this isn't the world any of us want, it's full of treachery. I didn't kill anyone, I may not have liked what those people did, but I wouldn't have killed them, any of them. It was the whole package that pissed me off, none of what happened was personal. So here I sit, a serial killer who hasn't killed anyone.

The problem I have with all of this is, no one really listens or cares. All my life, the only people who listened to me was my family, I'm talking about my Manson family, not my blood family. They understood, they saw my vision and liked it. As a kid I told the damn Judge I wanted to be with my mom, he didn't listen. When the cops caught me doing things, they didn't listen, it was all about setting me up to be condemned in court. In prison, no one cares they don't want to hear what I got to say. How do you think it feels going through life with no voice? It's inhumane not to give someone a voice. Once you're in the Police system then everything is taken away from you, no one believes a thing you say, you are guilty once you're arrested, end of. Is that right, is that fair?

I have my secrets, yes, and I'll be taking them with me, to my death, because no one ever wanted to hear me, or gave me any chance to explain. Maybe you, but it's too late for any of that now. I look back at my mother, maybe if she'd been straight with me, and she hadn't suffered herself, she might have been able to teach me right from wrong. I can't tell, no one can. My life might have been different, this madness, anger whatever it's called, that wasn't created by my mother, this was created by them, by the system. They are the ones who should be looking at themselves if they want answers about why I turned into what I am. I don't think I'm crazy, it's the rest of you. Little Charlie Manson,is still inside me, we are all the children we once were, we all have those memories. I needed two parents who cared, took time to listen and to look out for me. It's hard when as a kid you've got no one who wants you, not even the system. Where do you keep running to? You've got to stop some time. In prison, I could stop and be me, Charlie the guitar player, Charlie the music man they would call me. That's who Charlie Manson is, not that crazy guy they wanted to see."

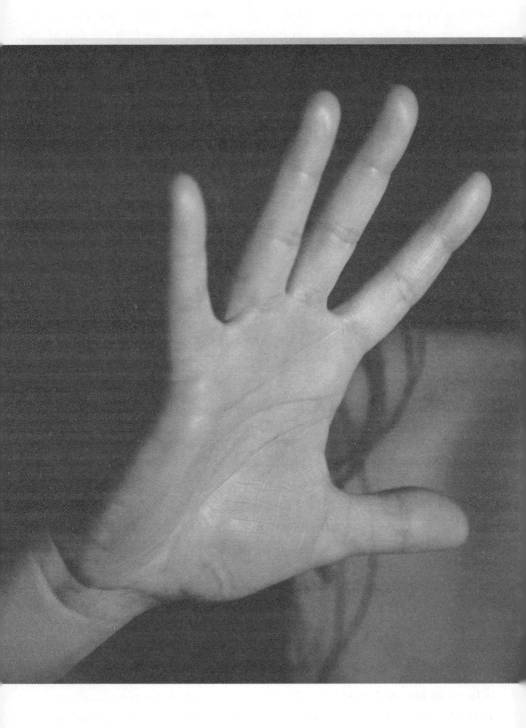

THIRTEEN
Help, I Need Somebody!

> "Why did I do it? Because being close to someone made me feel better about me." - *Jeffrey Dahmer*

"I love him, I can't help myself, I could have saved him, made him feel better about himself and understand that he was someone very special indeed. I have photographs of him around my flat, it's those eyes, they are filled with sadness. He just wanted someone to love him, that's all."

"To me, he's a fascinating human being, someone I feel sadness for, yet someone I feel so much love for. Not in a sexual way, but maternally. I've done the Dahmer walking tours, collected all the books, walked the very streets he walked. It's so sad, tragic that no one spotted the signs and tried to help him. I often think if I would have been able to rehabilitate him? I honestly think I might have been able to do so."

"He's such a cutie, handsome, intelligent and with those drop-dead gorgeous eyes, who couldn't fancy him? As a psychic medium, I have a special connection with him, he's with me all the time. Always looking out for me, he's a kind caring spirit that I love."

"I'm a gay man, I can't tell you what my professional position is. I adore Jeffrey Dahmer, really adore him. The first time I saw a photograph of him I fell in love with him, he looked hopelessly lost, and in need of someone to hold him and cuddle him. I don't care that he did those things to those people, he had his

reasons. Maybe he was misunderstood, I'm also sure that a load of what has been said about him is made up fiction. I used to write to him in prison, two or three times a week. He replied and thanked me for my support. How cool is that?"

"I don't think there is anything wrong with fantasising over a serial killer. Next time you're on the highway and there's a smash on the other side, note how many people slow down to peer at the wreckage. It's a morbid curiosity we all have in us. Serial killers are another aspect of that, and Jeffrey Dahmer is the superstar of them all. My friends rave about Ted Bundy, he's old school, Dahmer is the new idol. I hate it when he gets misrepresented in the media, made out to be some evil monster from a slasher movie. Beneath that surface, he was little lost child, a boy who wanted attention."

The above is a very small selection of communications I have received from people who openly flaunt their devotion to a man whose crimes were so diabolical that they could never be accurately reproduced in a book. A necrophile, cannibal and sexual deviant, Dahmer hunted down vulnerable prey, and lured them to his private rooms; be it in a hotel, his grandmother's home or his apartment. There he drugged them, tortured them, then killed them. Dahmer, long since dead, remains a commercial industry in his own right, with walking tours, merchandise, a fan club and forums dedicated to his name and life. It seems the appeal of taming, or at least trying to unravel what many of his followers feel is the misrepresented beast, is fundamental to this obsession.

When he was alive and incarcerated in prison, Dahmer would receive hundreds of letters a week from adoring fans, male and female, each one swearing their allegiance to helping him and understanding his plight. Some revealed their own private fantasies and desires, no doubt hoping for some kind of positive response from the vilest of serial killers. I was privately told by one prison authority that Dahmer rarely read the letters, some because of their content never made it to him and were destroyed. I was told:

"Serial killers are complex beings, we can't have correspondence that contains potential triggers passed to them. It might tip them over the edge, it's not fair on them or the staff and other inmates. People don't realise what they are playing with when they engage with a serial killer. It's someone's emotions they are toying with, and that as you well know can be dangerous."

There is a term for people who engage in a more sexually-oriented manner towards violent criminals or killers - Hybristophilia. This term was defined by the sexologist, Professor John Money, as *"a sexual paraphilia in which an individual derives sexual arousal and pleasure from having a sexual partner who is known to have committed an outrage or crime, such as rape, murder, or armed robbery"*.

I don't for one minute profess that all those people who contacted Dahmer held such a deep-rooted passion. Many undoubtedly fell for his lost little boy look and his handsome appearance, and despite knowledge of what he'd done to other human beings, wanted to help him in some way. Yet other communications I have seen, are much more sexual in their tone and language. Some proposed marriage to him.

Dahmer himself couldn't understand the fascination with his life.

"I don't know whether to feel honoured or shocked by the adulation; that's the word, adulation of my fans. Most of them are women, and they know I'm gay. That's not by mistake or through accident by the way, I'm gay because I honestly prefer men. So I'm a little curious about some women's fascination with me."

It's a sad indictment of society today that the victims are largely forgotten in this case. Yet, that's why Dahmer selected them, because they were vulnerable, vagrants, down and outs, transients and therefore less likely to be missed. His crimes were carefully planned, his victims randomly selected from those groups previously mentioned. He found them in shopping malls, gay bars, clubs and even hitchhiking along the highway. This was a master manipulator, charming and kind, which appealed to his victims and clearly allayed their suspicions.

Jeffrey Lionel Dahmer was born on Saturday 21st May, 1960 to Joyce Annette and Lionel Herbert Dahmer in West Allis, Wisconsin. His parents led two separate professional lives, his mother being a teletype machine instructor, and his father, a student of chemistry at the Marquette University. The relationship between the pair was not as close as it could have been, with Lionel spending much time away from home due to his work. His relationship with his father was much stronger than that with his mother. Dahmer though, seemed a content child, and teachers at his school referred to him as intelligent and friendly. It was at the of age of four that things began to change. He required a double hernia operation, which was successful, and around the same time, a younger brother, David, was born into the family. He was no longer the centre of attention; added to this, the family moved to Doylestown, Ohio, due his father's new work role as an analytical chemist. Everything in his life changed from that moment on as he became insular and quiet; preferring his own company he had few friends. Playing alone he would spend hours with the family cat and dog.

He had a fascination with animal anatomy and was often seen by neighbours collecting butterflies and insects in jars and analysing them. This curiosity grew, morphing into larger animals. Road kill would be collected, dissected, studied and deposited around the garden of the family home. It appears that his family were unaware of this habit, and every so often his father would clear the animal bones from the ground.

It should be said, that Jeffrey Dahmer seems to be have been starved of spending quality time with both parents. His mother was anything but a stable influence in his life, demanding and needy, she was often ill and expected attention. His father was keen to excel in his new role and worked long hours to succeed. Meanwhile, Dahmer was left to his own devices, his passion for anatomy being his main interest. On one occasion he asked his father about the bleaching process used on chicken bones. Lionel was thrilled that his boy was showing such an interest and continued to explain and show him how to bleach and preserve animal bones. This was useful information that Jeffrey Dahmer stored away for future reference.

By the time he was 14 and reaching puberty, he recognised that he was sexually attracted to other boys. Scared to divulge his homosexuality to his parents he hid it from them. For a brief time he had a relationship with another local youth; however, apart from touching and exploring each other, no physical intercourse took place.

"Nothing of any note happened in my early teen years. I had a close friend and we kissed and touched each other, it went no further than that. I would masturbate in my bedroom thinking about being with other boys and men. I had a few pornographic books hidden and I would look at those and get excited. As I grew older, I would daydream about having them as my sex slaves, totally submissive to my every need, their only role in life would be to sexually satisfy me or allow me to dominate them."

At high school, his peers regarded him as a loner and a bit strange. His behaviour was clown-like and full of childish daftness, face pulling at teachers, moving around on the ground pretending to have an epileptic fit, or cerebral palsy, dribbling from his mouth, walking with a limp as though he was disabled. In grocery stores, he would feign illness and collapse onto shop floor displays, sending them crashing to the ground, causing damage to stock. He enjoyed the attention this behaviour brought him, and the more he received, the more constant it became. Eventually, his childish behaviour became known among his peer group as 'Doing a Dahmer'.

Alcohol began to take over his life. His own mother drank in front of him, so it seemed natural for him to try it. With a taste for it, his life began to fall apart, his grades dropped and his anti-social behaviour grew worse. Now, no one wanted to know him, he was being excluded by a peer group who didn't like him as a person but thought his behaviour funny. Early in 1978, Lionel Dahmer, after years of issues with his wife, moved out of the home, and despite his differences with Jeffrey's mum, remained a constant in his eldest son's life. Joyce was awarded custody of the younger child, David. Jeffrey, since he was eighteen and judged to be an adult, required no such legal decision.

It was in 1978 that he committed his first murder, that of hitchhiker, Steven Hicks. Picking him up, he took him home, then having made him a drink, smashed him over the head with a barbell. Afterwards, he dismembered the body, before storing it in plastic bags and later disposing of it. Being a transient, Hicks' disappearance went unnoticed for some time and as in so many cases of this kind, there was no evidence to help the Police establish a crime of murder, accidental death, or just list him as missing.

In 1978, in an attempt to instill some discipline into his son's life and to get him off the alcohol, Dahmer's father persuaded him to sign up for the Army. Enlisted, he was posted out to Germany where he worked as a medic, a position which no doubt appealed to his anatomical interests. Despite this new challenge and career, he couldn't stop himself drinking, and after a series of allegations about his sexual and foolhardy behaviour, he was discharged from the forces in 1981. It was later claimed by some of his service colleagues that he would get drunk then talk about how he was responsible for killing the hitchhiker in Ohio. No one believed him and put it down to his attention seeking.

Returning home to live with his father, his inappropriate behavior deteriorated and allegations of sexual assaults on minors and drunkenness charges saw him serve prison time. His father had had enough of his attitude and sent him to live with his grandmother in Wisconsin. His attitude never altered. By now he was so deep thinking that he rarely spoke to her, on his mind much of this time was sex and murder. Not everyone he met and brought home was killed, some left without any challenge from him. This in itself might be symptomatic of future murders. The feeling of abandonment from childhood, then a stream of lovers coming and going without a care, undoubtedly left him feeling alone.

His second victim, Steven Toumi, was murdered in a hotel room. Dahmer admitted drugging him. He then claimed he had fallen asleep and when he awoke, Toumi's body was lying in the bed next to him, dead with bruising to the chest. He dismembered him before going out and purchasing a suitcase, in which he placed Toumi's remains. He then hired a taxi, and took it to his grandmother's house, where he disposed of it.

By now, he was sexually aroused by all aspects of his lustful crimes. The body count began to rise, as did his level of violence before, during and after the murders. Desperate to have sexual companions who would never leave him, he experimented on his victims. First he drugged them, then bound them. While they were still alive he would drill holes into their skull and pour boiling water into the holes. He effectively wanted to create living zombies who he could completely control by placing them in a vegetative state. The water did little, so he changed to hydrochloric acid, which naturally killed them.

Each of his victims was sexually abused after death, and he would often return to the body before he dismembered it and masturbate over it. Some victims he posed and then photographed in unusual positions. He had a predilection for keeping some of the body parts; the genitals and penis would be carefully cut off then stored in jars as trophies. Bleached skulls, hands and other organs were also kept in a freezer and refrigerator in his apartment.

One can only imagine the stench that emanated from his apartment, and it comes as no surprise that a local resident complained to the authorities of the foul smell and strange sounds coming from his home. Each time someone visited, he was able to convince them that it was not him, nor anything sinister. He claimed the locals didn't like him and were trying to force him to move out.

On one occasion, a young boy below the age of sexual consent, and a potential victim, was lured back to his apartment. There he was drugged, stripped naked and handcuffed, in readiness for torture and sex. He had been beaten by Dahmer. Somehow, he managed to escape and get out of the apartment. Confused and dazed he was running around in the street outside Dahmer's home. Neighbours called the Police, who were quickly on the scene and stopped the boy. Dahmer appeared and calmly approached the officers and the boy. He explained that the naked individual was his gay 18-year-old lover, and as he was drunk and confused, it would be better if he was to return with him. The officers agreed, ignoring the slurred appeals of the heavily drugged boy. Returning to the apartment, the officer made a cursory check inside, before bidding an apologetic Dahmer, goodnight. Just a few hours later, the boy was murdered, butchered and partly eaten by the serial killer.

Dahmer continued to rape torture and mutilate victims for almost thirteen years. His victims were generally African - American men or boys. Some were known criminals, so again a vulnerable group whose disappearance wouldn't seem out of place. Cunning and careful in the premeditation, Dahmer had mastered his craft. Such arrogance often leads to complacency and mistakes. This serial killer was no different.

His desires made him take risks. For example, he took satisfaction in taking polaroid photographs during various stages of each murder or mutilation, a record of his evil deeds and something he could look back over in the future to gain sexual excitement. He made a shrine from his victims remains, bones, skulls, hands, and would sit in front of it, satisfied and content that they were physically - in some form - still with him. In essence, they never left him, which provided feelings of being wanted and needed.

On 22nd July 1991, Dahmer picked up his next chosen victim, a man called Tracy Edwards. Back at Dahmer's apartment, he was drugged, stripped naked and bound with handcuffs. Together, they sat on the end of Dahmer's bed and watched TV. Sensing danger, Edwards managed to knock Dahmer to the floor and escape, running outside. He wandered the streets in search of help and shouting for the Police. Patrol officers found him and listened to his confusing story, but decided to check it out, as Edwards was talking about some dark and sinister acts. He described a bloodstained knife in a bedroom. The officers went directly to Dahmer's apartment and explained what they had been told. Dahmer allowed them access since the officer had said he needed to quickly check the bedroom for a knife. In the bedroom an officer found not only the knife but dozens of polaroid photographs of dead bodies in various positions and stages of dismemberment. Looking elsewhere, heads, skulls, various parts of dismembered bodies, and preserved genitals in jars were found. Under violent protest, Dahmer was restrained and arrested. The authorities found the remains of eleven different men in his apartment.

At trial, he later confessed to his crimes, using as his defence a plea of insanity. The jury did not believe him. He was found guilty but sane and sentenced to 15 consecutive life terms or 957 years of imprisonment. In prison, he was placed in solitary confinement, but appealed against this and demanded to be allowed to mix and socialise with other inmates. At a hearing this was permitted and so he joined the mainstream prison population.

His childish behaviour returned as he attempted to win fellow prisoners over by pulling silly faces, feigning illness and acting the fool. Prison is no place for random behaviour like that. Soon he found himself the brunt of their ire, and to wind them up further, at meal times in the prison canteen, he would mould human forms from his food. Then calmly and sadistically cut into it as though savouring it. This was done to shock and remind them of his past deeds. Not only attention seeking but a symbol of his power over human life.

Permission was granted by the Columbia Correctional Institution to allow him to be baptized by a local preacher. Like so many other killers before him, he was turning to religion as a comfort for his sins. Whether this was genuine atonement we can only guess.

"Look at me, I'm just a guy who lost his way maybe? The more I think about it, I feel something dark took over my thoughts, Satan perhaps? I was a good kid, who, when you read the history books, they'll say turned evil, rotten to the core. That's not the case, I'm not sure what happened, or my reasons or motives, if there were any at all.

I'm not the type who puts blame elsewhere, the things I have done, they are all down to me. I don't blame my parents, the cops or anyone else. I did it because I wanted to. The more I look at it, and I do, each night in my cell, think about my life, it's because I'm different. I was always a scared kid, no one really wanted to be around me, so I had to entertain myself. It's a hard place to be, by yourself as a kid, pretty soon, other kids are laughing at you, because you don't fit in, you aren't like them. It leaves scars, pain. I knew my behaviour was bad, but it got people to talk to me, and to kind of like me.

I was always fascinated by the dark side, blood and guts, death, morbidity. It manifested itself in me because I didn't really want to die, I wanted some kind of immortality. When I went into hospital as a kid, I thought I was going to die. It changed the way I looked at things, life. When you are being operated on, you are wholly reliant on the surgeon not to slip, your life is in their hands. That's power, real power. So maybe that's what I wanted, who knows?

The whole sex thing, well let's talk facts, sex is a driver for all of us. We feel aroused by different things, fetishes like bondage, sadomasochism, torture, cannibalism, as long as it happens in your own home, no one cares. I believe

I needed control over part of my life as for so long I had none at all. I wanted companionship without the burden of conversation. Someone said to me I would have been better off purchasing a sex doll. That's not funny at all.

My victims? I try not to think about them, if I did it would take me to a place I don't want to go. I know I did wrong and I will suffer for it, for the rest of my life."

In late November 1994, Jeffrey Dahmer was murdered (alongside fellow inmate and murderer, Jesse Anderson) by Christopher Scarver, who crushed his head with a metal bar. Scarver confessed to the crime and years later revealed his motive as not only being Dahmer's criminal antecedents but also his provocative and annoying behaviour in front of other inmates.

Looking at Jeffrey Dahmer's formative years, we can now see a dysfunctional family environment, alienation, a feeling of being different and a desire to be liked and wanted - needs which remained with him throughout his life. Hence his childish behaviour in his teenage years and in prison. Insecurities borne through disharmony in the family home, in school and through his own sexuality, caused his addictive behaviour (alcohol, cigarettes), and for him to further withdraw from his peer group.

No one could have foreseen the sinister path he was walking, since he premeditated and thought through his crimes. From the drugged drink that he prepared before he went out, to the butchering and hiding of the body and the careful selection of his victims, it all ensured he was able to kill at will. Until his arrogance saw him take his behaviour for granted.

Cunning and intelligent, Dahmer, like all the criminals discussed here, epitomizes the classic profile of a serial killer. We still have so much to learn about their behaviours and motivations, but rest assured we are always finding new and more effective ways to prevent such horrific crimes in the future.

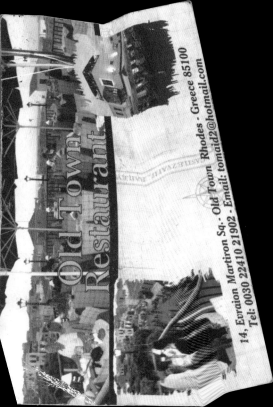

Old Town Restaurant

14, Evraion Martiron Sq.- Old Town Rhodes - Greece 85100
Tel: 0030 22410 21902 - Email: tomaid2@hotmail.com

OLD TOWN RESTAURANT "This restaurant has the most beautiful large view across the old fortress town and port of Rhodes. A good meal offers you a pleasant experience, with the best seasonal and fresh available food. The menu consists mainly of fresh fish and seafood, along with local specialties. If you are looking for seafood, you're in the right place. We are looking forward for your visit. Please do not forget your camera. Bon appétit!

APPENDIX

Below is a list of the most well-known 'media monikers' applied to serial killers:

THE DOODLER - Unknown

THE BRICK MORON - Robert Nixon

THE GIGGLER - Kenneth Harrison

THE HUMAN DRACULA - Tsutomu Miyazaki

THE BEAST - Luis Garavito

THE SORCERER - Ahmad Suradji

THE CRAZY NECROPHILE - Ted Bundy

THE HITCHHIKER KILLER - Donald Henry Gaskins

THE DAMSEL OF DEATH - Aileen Wuornos

THE BIKE PATH RAPIST - Altemio Sanchez

THE HILLSIDE STRANGLERS - Kenneth Bianchi/Angelo Buono Jr

THE RAILROAD KILLER - Angel Maturino Resendiz

THE TOURNIQUET KILLER - Anthony Allen Shore

THE GENESEE RIVER KILLER - Arthur Shawcross

THE WOODYARD CORRIDOR KILLER - Benjamin Atkins

THE CLASSIFIED ADS RAPIST - Bobby Joe Long

THE KENTUCKY CANNIBAL - Boone Helm

THE SUNDAY MORNING SLASHER - Carl Eugene Watts

THE SUNSET STRIP KILLERS - Douglas Clark/Carol Bundy

THE EYEBALL KILLER - Charles Albright

THE PIED PIPER OF TUSCON - Charles Schmid

THE OPERATION MIRANDA KILLERS - Charles Ng/Leonard Lake

THE SHOTGUN KILLER - Christopher Peterson

THE BEAUTY QUEEN KILLER - Christopher Wilder

THE CLAIREMONT KILLER - Cleophus Prince Jr

THE SON OF SAM - David Berkowitz

THE BROOMSTICK KILLER - Kenneth McDuff

THE TRAILSIDE KILLER - David Carpenter

BTK (Bind Torture Kill) - Denis Rader

ANGEL OF DEATH - Beverley Allitt

THE BATON ROUGE SERIAL KILLER - Derrick Todd Lee

THE GORILLA MAN - Earle Nelson

THE CO-ED KILLER - Edmund Kemper

THE GENIUS KILLER - Edward H Rullof

THE FLINT SERIAL SLASHER - Elias Abuelazam

THE GREEN RIVER KILLER - Gary Ridgway

THE BEDROOM BASHER - Gerald Parker

THE WEST VIRGINIA BLUEBEARD - Harry Powers

THE WANT-AD KILLER - Harvey Carignan

THE LONELY HEARTS KILLER - Harvey Glatman

THE TACO BELL STRANGLER - Henry Louis Wallace

THE POSTCARD KILLER - J Frank Hickey

THE WEREWOLF BUTCHER - Jack Owen Spillman

THE ANCHORAGE SERIAL KILLER - James Dale Ritchie

THE SHOTGUN STALKER - James Swann

THE SHOE FETISH SLAYER - Jerry Brudos

THE BOY TORTURER - Jesse Pomeroy

THE ALLIGATOR MAN - Joe Ball

THE STOCKYARD BLUEBEARD - Johann Otto Hoch

LONG ISLAND SERIAL KILLER - John Bittrolff

THE SOUTHLAND STRANGLER/WESTSIDE RAPIST - John Floyd Thomas Jr

LIVER EATING JOHNSON - John Johnson

THE NEBRASKA BOY SNATCHER - John Joubert

THE KILLER CLOWN - John Wayne Gacy

THE ARYAN BEAUTY KILLER - Jonathan Preston Haynes

THE MIDTOWN SLASHER - Joseph Christopher

THE CANNIBAL - Joseph Roy Metheny

THE ALPHABET MURDERS - Joseph Naso

THE HAPPY FACE KILLER - Keith Hunter Jesperson

THE INTERSTATE KILLER - Larry Eyler

THE TOOL BOX KILLER - Lawrence Bittaker

THE GAFFNEY STRANGLER - Lee Roy Martin

THE GRIM SLEEPER - Lonnie David Franklin Jr

THE KANSAS CITY STRANGLER - Lorenzo Gilyard

FLYPAPER LYDA - Lyda Southard

THE BASELINE KILLER - Mark Goudeau

THE SEX BEAST - Melvin Rees

THE SOUTHSIDE SLAYER - Michael Hughes

THE SACRAMENTO SLAYER - Morris Solomon Jr

THE GIGGLING GRANNY - Nannie Doss

THE FAST FOOD KILLER - Paul Dennis Reid

THE CASANOVA KILLER - Paul John Knowles

THE WEEPY VOICED KILLER - Paul Michael Stephani

I-5 KILLER - Randall Woodfield

THE SCORECARD KILLER - Randy Steven Kraft

THE LONELY HEARTS KILLERS - Raymond Fernandez/Martha Beck

THE VAMPIRE OF SACRAMENTO - Richard Chase

THE BUTCHER OF TIMES SQUARE - Richard Cottingham

THE ICEMAN - Richard Kuklinski

THE NIGHT STALKER - Richard Ramirez

THE TRUCK STOP KILLER - Robert Ben Rhoades

THE BUTCHER BAKER - Robert Hanson

THE BOXCAR KILLER - Robert Joseph Silveria Jr

THE DATING GAME KILLER - Rodney Alcala

THE I-5 STRANGLER - Roger Kibbe

THE TAMIAMI TRAIL STRANGLER - Rory Enrique Conde

THE NEBRASKA FIEND - Stephen Richards

ROUTE 40 KILLER - Steven Brian Pennell

THE DEMON OF BELFRY - Theodore Durrant

THE SOUTHSIDE STRANGLER - Timothy Wilson Spencer

THE SKID ROW SLASHER - Vaughn Greenwood

THE BROOKLYN STRANGLER - Vincent Johnson

THE MILWAUKEE NORTH SIDE STRANGLER - Walter E Ellis

THE LIPSTICK KILLER - William Heirens

THE SPEED FREAK KILLERS - Wesley Shermantine/Loren Herzog

THE FREEWAY KILLER - William Bonin

FORCES OF EVIL - William Henry Hance

THE RIVERSIDE PROSTITUTE KILLER - William Suff

THE ARGENTINE VAMPIRE - Florencio Fernandez

THE BIG EARED MIDGET - Cayatano Santos Godino

THE SATYR OF SAN ISIDRO - Francisco Antonio Laureana

THE DEATH ANGEL - Robledo Puch

AUSTRALIA - THE MOORHOUSE MURDERS - David & Catherine Birnie

THE SNOWTOWN MURDERS - John Bunting/Robert Wagner/James Viassakis

THE NIGHT CALLER - Eric Edgar Cooke

THE FRANKSTON KILLER - Paul Denyer

THE ROCKHAMPTON RAPIST - Leonard Fraser

THE GRANNY KILLER - John Wayne Glover

THE BABY FARMING MURDERESS - Frances Knorr

THE BROWNOUT STRANGLER - Eddie Leonski

THE BERRIMA AXE MURDERER - John Lynch

THE MUTILATOR - William MacDonald

THE BACKPACKER MURDERS - Ivan Milat

THE BLACK WIDOW OF RICHMOND - Martha Needle

THE MURCHISON MURDERS - Snowy Rowles

THE SCHOOL GIRL STRANGLER - Arnold Sodeman

THE BEAST OF SEARNING - Alfred Engleder

THE VIENNESE HOUSEMAID KILLER - Hugo Schenk

THE LAINZ ANGELS OF DEATH - Mark Gruber/Irene Leidolf/Stephanija Mayer/Waltraud Wagner

THE SVIETLAHORSK NIGHTMARE - Igor Mirenkov

FATHER BLUEBEARD - Andras Pandy

THE CHILD SNATCHER- Marc Dutroux

THE PARK MANIAC - Francisco de Assis Pereira

THE VAMPIRE OF NITEROI - Marcelo Costa de Andrade

THE PEDRINHO MATADOR - Pedro Rodriques Filho

THE INDUSTRIAL MANIAC - Marcos Antunes Trigueiro

THE LONDON CHAMBERMAID SLAYER - Gerald Thomas Archer

THE SCARBOROUGH RAPIST - Paul Bernardo

THE VAMPIRE RAPIST - Wayne Boden

THE MONSTER OF PONT-ROUGE - Leopold Dion

THE BEDROOM STRANGLER - Russell Morris Johnson

THE BOOZING BARBER - Gilbert Paul Jordan

THE MONSTER OF MIRAMICHI - Allan Legere

THE MAD BUMPER - Yves Trudeau

THE CHILEAN ROBIN HOOD - Emile Dubois

THE PSYCHOPATH OF ALTO HOSPICIO - Julio Perez Silvio

CHINESE JACK THE RIPPER - Gao Chengyong

ER WANG - Wang Zongfang Wang Zongwei

THE MONSTER KILLER - Yang Xinhai

THE SADIST OF EL CHARQUITO - Daniel Camargo Barbosa

THE BEAST - Luis Garavito

THE MONSTER OF THE ANDES - Pedro Lopez

THE MONSTER OF THE CANE FIELDS - Manuel Octavio Bermudez

THE MONSTER OF MACHALA - Gilberto Chamba

THE OGRE OF ARDENNES - Michael Fourniret

THE BEAST OF BASTILLE - Guy Georges

THE CRIMINAL BACKPACKER - Francis Heaulme

THE BOAR OF THE MOORS - Albert Millet

LA VOISIN - Catherine Monvoisin

THE KILLER OF ESSONNE - Yoni Palmer

THE BEAST OF MONMARTRE - Thierry Paulin

THE WATCHMAKER OF MONTREUIL - Albert Pel

RAMBO - Louis Poirson

THE KILLER OF THE TRAINS - Sid Ahmed Rezala

THE CUTTER OF THE CANAL - Nadiri Sedrati

THE FRENCH RIPPER - Joseph Vacher

THE CARNIVAL KILLER - Jurgen Bartsch

THE GRANNY KILLER - Olaf Dater

THE RHINE RUHR RIPPER - Frank Gust

THE BUTCHER OF HANOVER - Fritz Haarmann

THE RUHR CANNIBAL - Joachim Kroll

THE S-BAHN MURDERER - Paul Ogorzow

THE DEAD MAKER - Rudolf Pleil

THE GHOST OF KEHL - Jacques Plumain

THE HAMMER KILLER - Norbert Poehlke

THE BEAST OF BEELITZ - Wolfgang Schmidt

THE TERROR OF FALKENHAGEN LAKE - Friedrich Schumann

THE ANGEL MAKER OF ST PAUL - Elisabeth Wiese

THE WEREWOLF - Peter Stumpp

THE ACCRA STRANGLER - Charles Quansah

THE ATHENS RIPPER - Antoni Daglis

THE PSYCHO SHANKAR - M Jaishankar

CYANIDE MOHAN - Mohan Kumar

DOCTOR DEATH - Santosh Pol

PSYCHO RAMAN - Ramon Raghav

THE SINGING SERIAL KILLER - Ripper Jayananden

THE BAHADURGARH BABY KILLER - Satich

THE CASGHAR MURDERER - Ali Asghar Borujerdi

THE TEHRAN DESERT VAMPIRE - Mohammed Bijet

THE SPIDER KILLER - Saeed Hanaei

THE WITCH OF KILKENNY - Alice Kyteler

THE TEL AVIV STRANGLER - Muhammad Halabi

THE MONSTER OF LIGURIA - Donato Bilancia

THE MONSTER OF ROME - Ralph Brydges

THE MONSTER OF FOLIGNO - - Luigi Chiatti

THE SOAP MAKER OF CORREGGIO - Leonarda Cianciulli

THE MONSTER OF MERANO - Ferdinand Gamper

THE MONSTER OF NEROLA - Ernest Picchioni

THE SUICIDE WEBSITE MURDERER - Hisroshi Maeue

HOUSE OF HORROR - Futoshi Matsunaga/Junko Ogata

THE LITTLE GIRL MURDERER - Tsutomu Miyazaki

THE HAMAMATSU DEAF KILLER - Seisaku Nakamura

METAL FANG - Nikolai Dzhumsgliev

MEXICAN JACK - Macario Alcala Canchola

THE HAMBURGER - David Avendano Ballina

THE OLD LADY KILLER - Juana Barraza

THE STRANGLER OF TACUBA - Gregorio Cardenas Hernandez

THE MARRAKESH ARCH KILLER - Hadj Mohammed Mesfewi

THE BEAST OF HARKSTEDE - Willem van Eijk

THE NEWLANDS BABY FARMER - Daniel Cooper

THE BRICK KILLER - Amir Qayyum

WILD BILL - William Dathan Holbert

THE APOSTLE OF DEATH - Pedro Pablo Nakadu Ludena

THE BUTCHER OF NIEBUSZEWO - Jozef Cyppek

THE MONSTER OF CHORZOW - Henryk Kukula

THE GENTLEMAN KILLER - Wladyslaw Mazurkiewicz

SCORPION - Pawel Tuchlin

THE STAFANKOWICE VAMPIRE - Mariusz Sowinski

FANTOMAS - Mieczyslaw Zub

THE BUTCHER OF IASI - Vasile Tcaciuc

THE NECROPHILE REBEL - Mikhail Novosyolov

THE WOLF OF MOSCOW - Vasili Komaroff

SATAN IN A SKIRT - Irina Gaidamachuk

THE ROSTOV RIPPER - Andrei Chikatilo

THE NOVOSIBIRSK MANIAC - Yevgeny Chuplinsky

THE HUNTER OF BABIES - Anatoly Biryukov

THE HIPPOPOTAMUS - Sergei Ryakhovsky

THE GRANNY RIPPER - Tamara Samsonova

THE FUR COATS HUNTER - Alexander Tchayka

JESUS KILLER - Jimmy Maketta

THE AXE KILLER - Elifasi Msomi

THE STATION STRANGLER - Norman Afzal Somins

THE PANGAMAN - Elias Xitavhudzi

THE SUGAR CANE KILLER - Thozamile Taki

THE ABC KILLER - Moses Sithole

THE PLAYING CARD KILLER - Alfredo Galan

THE WARLOCK - Damaso Rodriguez Martin

THE OLD LADY KILLER - Jose Antonio Rodriguez Vega

THE ANGEL MAKER OF BRUKS STREET - Hilda Nilsson

DEATH KEEPER OF LUCERNE - Roger Andermatt

THE NAILING KILLER - Suleyman Aktas

THE BEAST OF ARTVIN - Adnan Colak

THE BABY FACE KILLER - Ali Kaya

THE SCREWDRIVER KILLER - Yavus Yapicioglu

THE TERMINATOR - Anatoly Onoprienko

THE BALASHIKA RIPPER - Oleg Kuznetsov

THE BLACKOUT RIPPER - Gordon Cummins

THE MOORS MURDERERS - Ian Brady/Myra Hindley

THE LAMBETH POISONER - Thomas Neill Cream

THE SUNDERLAND STRANGLER - Steven Grieveson

THE CROSSBOW CANNIBAL - Stephen Griffiths

THE ACID BATH MURDERER - John George Haigh

THE STOCKWELL STRANGLER - Kenneth Erskine

THE BEAST OF MANCHESTER - Thomas Hardy

THE GAY SLAYER - Colin Ireland

THE WOLF MAN - Michael Lupo

THE A34 KILLER - Raymond Morris

THE YORKSHIRE RIPPER - Peter Sutcliffe

BIBLE JOHN - Unknown

THE MONSTER BUTLER - Archibald Hall

THE BEAST OF BIRKENSHAW - Peter Manuel

THE WORLDS END MURDERS - Angus Sinclair

THE BULLSEYE KILLER - John Cooper

THE MAN IN BLACK - Peter Moore

SELECT BIBLIOGRAPHY

Signature Killer - Robert D. Keppel (Arrow Books, 1998)

Psychology of Serial Killer Investigations - Robert. D. Keppel (Academic Press, 2003)

The Riverman - Robert D. Keppel (Constable Books, 1995)

Serial Violence - Robert D. Keppel/William J. Birnes (CRC Press, 2009)

I Have Lived In The Monster - Robert. K. Ressler (Thomas Dunne Books, 1997)

Sexual Homicide Patterns & Motives - Ressler/Douglas/Burgess (Free Press, 2008)

Crime Classification Manual - Ressler/Douglas/Burgess (John Wiley & Sons, 2013)

Mindhunter - John E. Douglas (Arrow, 2017)

The Pretender - Marc Ruskin (Thomas Dunne Books, 2017)

Jack The Ripper - The Mystery Solved - Paul Harrison (Robert Hale, 1991)

Shropshire Murder Casebook - Paul Harrison (Countryside Books, 1995)

South Wales Murder Casebook - Paul Harrison (Countryside Books, 1994)

Yorkshire Murders - Paul Harrison (Countryside Books, 1993)

Northamptonshire Murders - Paul Harrison (Countryside Books, 1992)

Dancing With The Devil - Paul Harrison (Vertical Editions, 2014)

Deviant - Paul Harrison (Vertical Editions, 2015)

Chasing Monsters (A Novel) - Paul Harrison (Urbane Publications, 2018)

Matador of Murder - Patrick J. Mullany (Create Space, 2015)

Introduction to Forensic and Criminal Psychology - Dr. Dennis Howitt (Pearson, 2015)

The Stranger Beside Me - Ann Rule (Sphere, 1994)

The Like Switch: An ex FBI Agents Guide to Influencing, Attracting and Winning People Over - Jack Shafer Ph.D./Marvin Karlins Ph.D. (Touchstone, 2015)

In the Name of the Children - Jeffrey L. Rinek/Marilee Strong (BenBella Books, 2018)

Helter Skelter - Vincent Bugliosi (Arrow, 2015)

Serial Killers - David Wilson (Waterside Press, 2007)

Casebook of a Crime Psychiatrist - James A. Brussel (Mayflower, 1970)

Incendiary - Michael Cannell (Minotaur Books, 2017)

Dangerous Personalities - Joe Navarro (Rodale, 2014)

Author Unknown - Don Foster (McMillan, 2001)

Serial Killers - Peter Vronsky (Berkley, 2004)

Serial Killers - Joel Norris (Arrow, 1990)

Journey Into Darkness - John Douglas/Mark Olshaker (Arrow, 1998)

Forensic Psychologists Casebook - Laurence Alison (Willan, 2005)

Offender Profiling & Crime Analysis - Peter B. Ainsworth (Willan, 2001)

The Jigsaw Man - Paul Britton (Corgi, 1998)

Picking Up The Pieces - Paul Britton (Corgi, 2001)

Inside The Minds of Serial Killers - Katherine Ramsland (Praeger, 2006)

The Mind of a Murderer - Katherine Ramsland (Praeger, 2011)

Forensic Psychology - Crime Justice, Law, Interventions - Graham M. Davies/
Anthony R. Beech (Wiley/Blackwell 2017)

Psychopathology - Graham Davey (John Wiley & Sons, 2014)

Inside the Criminal Mind - Stanton Samenow (Broadway Books, 2014)

Blue - A Memoir - John Sutherland (W&N, 2018)

Investigative Psychology - David Canter (Wiley, 2009)

Criminal Shadows - David Canter (Harper Collins, 1995)

Mapping Murder - David Canter (Virgin, 2007)

Serial Murders - Contemporary Perspective on (Ronald M. Holmes/Stephen T.
Holmes (Sage, 1998)

The Art of Profiling - Dan Korem (International Focus Press, 2012)

The Capture of the Black Panther - Harry Hawkes (Harrap, 1978)

Man Into Wolf - Robert Eisler (Ross-Erikson Publishers Inc, 1978)

Meaning of Murder - John Brophy (New York Crowell, 1967)

The Last Victim - Jason Moss (Virgin, 1999)

Zodiac - Robert Graysmith (Titan, 2007)

Without Consent (A Novel) - Jim Clemente (Over Easy Media, 2014)

ACKNOWLEDGEMENTS

To thank so many people who have played an influential part in my life would be an impossible task. From the secondary school teacher who on my last day in schooling, told me I would make nothing of my life and would end up in the gutter (she was a poor judge of character), through to the wonderful Police and pet dogs who have filled my life with unrequited love and devotion; Angel, George and more recently of course, the awesome and loyal Sherlock. My great-grandfather Will Scott, stands out above most, without him I wouldn't have become who I am today. Unbeknown to me until recently, Will was potentially one of the first criminal profilers in Victorian England. His written and investigative genes have certainly been passed down to me. Thank you doesn't seem sufficient appreciation to some closer members of my family who have been there to listen and support me. Often my greatest critics, these people, you know who you are, have stood by me even during my darkest periods (2006 - 2011) when I was ready to give up on everything, including my own life. Thankfully (for me anyway) I have no recollection of that period due to the prescribed medication I was taking.

I'd like to mention ex-colleagues in a number of Police forces, officers in the Ministry of Defence Police, Northamptonshire and West Yorkshire Police Forces who knew me and undoubtedly recognised I was different in my policing mindset. Thank you for the often hair raising experiences we somehow got through together. To, Jon Sharp, as good and loyal a friend as anyone could want over three decades (where did that time go mate?). A font of sound advice and a great listener. Sir David Joseph O'Dowd, CBE, OStJ, QPM the former Chief Constable of Northamptonshire Police, who was supportive of not only my crime writing but of my criminal profiling work also. Likewise, to John Reddington, ex-Chief Constable of the Ministry of Defence Police, who also backed my profiling and writing work. To the late Robert Ressler of the Federal Bureau of Investigation (Behavioural Science Unit) a greater mentor and tutor one could not have wished for. When he passed away, the world lost its greatest law enforcement officer of all time. A gentleman, kind, honest and never one to judge, he made himself available for phone chats and gave good advice whenever he could. To me, at least, he will forever be the master and 'the authority' on criminal profiling. Another absolute authority whose guidance I trusted implicitly was the late FBI profiler and sexual offence expert - Roy Hazelwood. We shared many beliefs including the fact that paedophilia is a life choice and cannot be treated as an illness. Roy's work in the sexual offender area was groundbreaking and has stood the test of time.

Thanks also go to Special Agent Cindy Lent, who was my first contact from Quantico, it was her belief in the subject that drove me to pursue profiling to its absolute maximum. I found each of the FBI people to be exceptional and knowledgeable, the best proponents of the skill to have a genuine connection with. I cannot list these eminent authorities without giving the highly respected John. E. Douglas a mention. I met John briefly, he is a true leader and an unquestionable expert in the field.

My sincere appreciation goes to Sir Stanley Burnton, and Sir John Mitting, both eminent barristers at law, and now retired High Court Judges, whom I worked with closely during their early years at the Royal Courts of Justice. Each of them offered a wealth of support in my true crime writing and would listen to my experiences of serial offenders and criminal profiling. Both were worthy of the esteemed positions they held and continue to do so since their retirement from the courts. To a new friend, Jayne Harris I'd like to say thank you for your support and intriguing work in the paranormal. Jayne's research into the crime popularly referred to as 'Bella and The Wych Elm' is exemplary.

To Robert D. Keppel, who, although I have never met him, is a man with whom I share a birthday. Now retired, he was an eminent law enforcement officer and former detective as well as a former associate professor at the University of New Haven and Sam Houston State University. Keppel was inspirational alongside forensic psychologist, Richard Walter, in the creation of HITS, the Homicide Investigation Tracking System following criminal investigations. His written works covering profiling and serial killers, and in particular his work on Ted Bundy, who he investigated and communicated closely with were truly educational in my own, and the profiling development of others. Sincere appreciation goes to fellow author and criminologist Peter Vronsky, as knowledgeable a man on the subject of murder and serial murder as I have ever met. Also to the late Jonathan Goodman, the greatest true crime author ever in my opinion. It was Jon who guided my early writings and who I regarded as a good and close friend. To the wonderful Professor Mike Berry, whose psychological profiling prowess I thoroughly respect, he's a great character too. My respect also goes to David Wilson, Tobin is not Bible John though. My utmost respect goes to the outstanding Professor of psychology Katherine Ramsland, whose writings and opinions on the subject I read with great enthusiasm.

I want to mention a fellow author and ex-Police officer now crime historian Chris Clark, whose knowledge of murder in the UK never ceases to amaze me, his books are great too. My appreciation goes out to Graham Bartlett, Andy Hill, Sven W. Pehla, Rebecca Stevens, Roger A. Price for supporting me throughout this work. Thank you also to the wonderful author Martina Cole whose work has been an inspiration for my own writing, and fellow author Guy Fraser Sampson for his great support.

Thanks also go to an exceptional publisher, Matthew Smith at Urbane Publications for believing in me, to Fiona Kimbell (Arlington Talent) my television agent, to David Howard and Rik Hall of Monster Films for their faith in me. A huge thank you to everyone who has backed me throughout this journey, I really do appreciate it, and to those who didn't, and tossed me to the wolves, you know who you are, I'm still here!

Finally, although he was one of my main abusers throughout my life, without him I wouldn't have been created and enjoyed so many amazingly positive life experiences as an adult, I feel it relevant to mention my late father, John Scott Harrison.

Paul Harrison has spent much of his professional life working within the UK's criminal justice system, primarily as a police officer, but also working with the Judiciary at the Royal Courts of Justice in London. He later worked voluntarily with victim focused agencies supporting abused children and males. As a police officer he had a diverse and interesting career, serving as a dog handler, intelligence officer, as a detective and later, as a profiler.

Working closely with the now defunct FBI Behavioural Science Unit in Quantico, he gained a unique and remarkable insight into the minds of some of the world's most violent criminals, including serious sexual offenders, serial killers and murderers. As a crime writer he has had conversations with many of the UK's most infamous felons and killers. His conversation portfolio reads like a Who's Who of murderers.

Paul has researched, studied and analysed serial killers for over three decades and is now widely regarded as one of the world's top experts on the phenomenon. As an author, he's penned thirty-three traditionally published books (mainly true crime) and has just completed his first novel – Chasing Monsters, also published by Urbane.

In his spare time, he enjoys watching his beloved Leeds United, walking his German Shepherd (Sherlock), and spending quality time with his family. A seasoned event speaker, Paul is popular across the entire crime genre (fiction and non-fiction) and discusses his police career and criminal conversations with killers to sell-out audiences. He's currently in discussions with several TV production companies across the globe for future Crime-related television series.

The first book in the DI Will Scott series.

In a sleepy northern seaside resort, The Eastborough Police Force is shocked into action when a heavily mutilated body is found in a quiet suburb. Murder rarely happens in these parts. Within a short space of time, the body count begins to rise rapidly, as a serial killer runs amok.

DI Will Scott is tasked with finding the killer. In doing so he walks paths he never expected to traverse and uncovers a web of deceit that leads to a world where no one can be trusted.

The killer relentlessly continues to strike terror across the community. Then without warning, the killing ground changes. Where will the killer strike next …?

CHASING MONSTERS is available now from Amazon and all good bookshops.

"Paul Harrison - the Zodiac expert I wish I had working the case with me."
Dave Toschi, lead investigator, the Zodiac killer case
HUNTING THE ZODIAC
PAUL HARRISON
THE ULTIMATE INVESTIGATION INTO THE ZODIAC KILLER

'Paul Harrison - the Zodiac expert I wish I had working the case with me.'
Dave Toschi, Lead Investigator, Zodiac Killer case

Former UK police profiler Paul Harrison has spent over two decades researching and interviewing many of the key people involved in one of the world's most intriguing murder mysteries: The Zodiac! An expert in serial killer interviews, he has travelled the globe interviewing many of the world's worst, most vicious murderers in an attempt to understand their psyche and what drives them kill.

Hunting the Zodiac is his journey and investigation into the crimes, potentially, outside the official police inquiries, the most comprehensive yet. He struck up a connection with SFPD Detective Inspector David Toschi, who led the police Zodiac investigation for nine years, at its height which opened up new avenues of investigation for this book. Using his police profiling skills, Paul dissects this case to its skeleton, taking the reader through the police investigation, providing bespoke profiles each suspect, crime scene and every facet of this mystery in a cold and objective manner.

Harrison clears away the debris of the myths created by misreporting to give us, for the first time, a clear look at the case and provides his professional opinion of the identity of The Zodiac. This is the ultimate book on The Zodiac.

HUNTING THE ZODIAC publishes May 2019. Order now on Amazon and at all good bookshops.

URBANE

Urbane Publications is dedicated to
developing author voices, and publishing
books that challenge, thrill and fascinate.

From page-turning thrillers to ground-breaking non-fiction,
as well as business books, our goal is to publish what YOU
want to read.

Find out more at
urbanepublications.com